Adrienne Rich

THE POET AND HER CRITICS

Adrienne Rich

THE POET AND HER CRITICS

CRAIG WERNER

AMERICAN
LIBRARY
ASSOCIATION
CHICAGO
AND LONDON
1988

THE POET AND HIS CRITICS

A series of volumes on the meaning of the
critical writings on selected modern British
and American poets.

Edited by CHARLES SANDERS, University of Illinois at Urbana-Champaign

Robert Frost by Donald J. Greiner
William Carlos Williams by Paul L. Mariani
Dylan Thomas by R. B. Kershner, Jr.
Langston Hughes by Richard K. Barksdale
Wallace Stevens by Abbie F. Willard
T. S. Eliot by Robert H. Canary
Robert Lowell by Norma Procopiow
Theodore Roethke by Randall Stiffler

Excerpt from *Ghazals of Ghalib* edited by Aijaz Ahmad. Copyright © 1971 by Columbia University Press. Used by permission.

Excerpt from "The Waste Land" in *Collected Poems 1909-1962* by T. S. Eliot, copyright 1936 by Harcourt Brace Jovanovich, Inc.; copyright © 1963, 1964 by T. S. Eliot. Reprinted by permission of Harcourt Brace Jovanovich, Inc., and Faber and Faber Limited.

Excerpt from "Little Gidding" in *Four Quartets*, copyright 1943 by T. S. Eliot; renewed 1971 by Esme Valerie Eliot. Reprinted by permission of Harcourt Brace Jovanovich, Inc., and Faber and Faber Limited.

Excerpt from *The Great American Poetry Bake-Off*, 2nd Series, by Robert Peters. Published by Scarecrow Press Inc. 1982. Used by permission.

Diagram and quotation from p. 200 of Elaine Showalter, "Feminist Criticism in the Wilderness," *Critical Inquiry* 8 (1981): 179-206. © 1981 by the University of Chicago Press. All rights reserved.

Excerpt of "Queen Anne's Lace" from *William Carlos Williams: Collected Poems 1909-1939*, Volume I. Copyright 1938 by New Directions Publishing Corporation. Reprinted by permission of New Directions and Carcanet Press.

Verses from *The Fact of a Doorframe; A Wild Patience Has Taken Me This Far; Your Native Land, Your Life; The Diamond Cutters; The Dream of a Common Language;* and *The Will to Change* by Adrienne Rich. Reprinted by permission of W.W. Norton and Company, Inc.

LIBRARY OF CONGRESS CATALOGING-IN-PUBLICATION DATA
Werner, Craig Hansen, 1952-
    Adrienne Rich: the poet and her critics / Craig Werner.
    p. cm. — (The Poet and his critics)
    Bibliography: p.
    Includes Index.
    ISBN 0-8389-0487-4
    1. Rich, Adrienne Cecile—Criticism and interpretation.
2. Feminism and literature. I. Title. II. Series.
PS3535.I233Z93 1988
811'.54—dc19
                                                      87-31005
                                                         CIP

Printed in the United States of America.

Contents

Preface

In a response to a critical essay on her work, Adrienne Rich poses the fundamental question: "How does the feminist critic approach the work of a writer who is still alive, able to feel the air on her skin, who continues to argue, experiment, learn, create?" Having spent the last four years living with Rich's poetry and process, my only answer is "partially." When I began to write this study, I was upset by what I then saw as the reactionary solipsism of *A Wild Patience Has Taken Me This Far*. As I write today, that angle of vision seems nearly incomprehensible. The reasons are complex, some having to do with Rich's subsequent process, some having to do with my own. Rich has published a great deal since *A Wild Patience Has Taken Me This Far: The Fact of a Doorframe*; the chapbook *Sources*; *Your Native Land, Your Life*; *Blood, Bread, and Poetry*; the tenth anniversary edition of *Of Woman Born*. Each volume reflects a new stage of Rich's self-understanding and, particularly in light of Rich's aesthetic of process, requires a thorough rethinking of any critical commentary. This rethinking is rendered both much easier and much more difficult by the appearance of a substantial amount of critical commentary—much of very high quality—concerning Rich's work. Since the final revision of this study, new books by Claire Keyes (*Adrienne Rich: The Aesthetics of Power*) and Paula Bennett (*My Life a Loaded Gun: Female Creativity and Feminist Poetics*) and essays such as Betsy Erkilla's "Dickinson and Rich: Toward a Theory of Female Poetic Influence" (*American Literature* 56, 541-59) have led me to reconsider certain conclusions presented in the current study. Nonetheless, as Rich has often observed, no work can be complete. At some point, it is simply necessary to send one's words into the world and hope they will be understood as part of an inevitably continuing process. It is in this spirit—in the hope that my readers will make use of what is useful and go beyond what is limited—that I offer this book.

I would like to make a brief comment on the structure of my critical response. As I considered my audience, I was confronted with a somewhat uncomfortable sense of conflicting demands. On the one hand, I am writing a reference book for an audience of nonspecialists unfamiliar with Rich's work and its significance in a number of complex cultural, political, and theoretical debates. With this audience in mind, I have attempted to introduce Rich's basic concerns by placing them in the context of an ongoing debate. The numerous references to other critics and the subheadings (which help locate discussions of specific issues or individual poems) are intended to make this study more useful as a reference work. My own observations, while framed from the perspective of other writers, are engaged in an ongoing dialog with their views. Because my book takes a systematic view of the criticism and reaches its own conclusions, this work will invite readers to explore more knowingly the questions which provide the shifting center of the debate on Rich's achievement. In addition, I am writing for a second audience, a feminist audience already familiar with the basic issues concerning Rich's work and sensitive to her underlying commitment to political and aesthetic (Rich would deny any sharp difference) transformation. With this audience in mind, I have attempted to provide a sympathetic (white, male, heterosexual) response to the challenge she presents.

Sources for the quotations included in the text may be located by referring to the list at the end of each chapter. When referring to Rich's essays, I have cited the pages from the easily accessible collections *Of Lies, Secrets, and Silence* and *Blood, Bread, and Poetry*. Also in the interests of accessibility, citations of reviews or essays reprinted in Jane Roberta Cooper's collection *Reading Adrienne Rich* or Albert and Barbara Charlesworth Gelpi's critical edition, *Adrienne Rich's Poetry* refer to those volumes.

I would like to thank all those who have provided personal and professional support throughout the writing of this book. Without the encouragement and continuing editorial sensitivity of Charles Sanders, this book would not have been conceived, much less completed. The Graduate College of the University of Mississippi, the Graduate College of the University of Wisconsin, the National Endowment for the Humanities, and the Institute for Research in the Humanities at the University of Wisconsin have all provided support at various stages of the project. I have benefited immensely from the excellent published commentary of the feminist critical communities. Nellie McKay, Malin Walther, Judylyn Ryan, Robert Philipson, Sandy Adell, Faith Smith, Maggie Brandenberg, Franklin Wilson, Clovis White, Henry Boyi, Naana Horne, John Gruesser, and Eli Goldblatt are only a few of the individuals who make the Department of Afro-American Studies at the University of Wisconsin an ideal setting for serious, committed research. Although the listing is inevitably partial, I would also like to acknowledge the various contributions of Barbara Ewell, Geoff King, Kathy Cummings, Tess Scogan, Steve Schultz, Barbara Talmadge, Steve and Olivia Baker, Ben Fisher, Richard Howorth (whose Square Books in Oxford, Mississippi, establishes a standard by which all other book stores should be judged), my extended family—particularly my mother, Donna (who did not live to see the completion of the work), my father, Ray, and, most specially, my wife, Leslee Nelson, and our daughter Riah Wakenda Werner, who I hope will grow into a world where many aspects of Rich's vision have become realities. Finally, I want to express my deepest thanks to Missy Kubitschek, whose patience at crucial points in my process probably made it possible for me to respond to Rich. This book is dedicated to her.

CHAPTER 1

Poetry and Process: The Shape
of Adrienne Rich's Career

Adrienne Rich's poetry changes lives, its own and ours. From the modernist formalism of *A Change of World* (1952) through the cultural deconstructions of *The Will to Change* (1971) to the lesbian-feminist reconstructions of *Your Native Land, Your Life* (1986), a powerful commitment to the re-vision of lived experience and aesthetic expression characterizes Rich's work. Intensely personal and increasingly political, Rich's poetry challenges the premises of patriarchal discourse whether manifested in academic criticism, political rhetoric, or her own residual solipsism. Addressing herself primarily but not exclusively to women, Rich insists that poetry be of use in the actual lives of actual human beings. In her essay "Blood, Bread, and Poetry" (1983), Rich defines art as "a long conversation with the elders and with the future" (Rich, *Blood*, p. 187) and asserts her belief in process and community as the keys to such utility. Honoring a group of elders which includes her grandmothers, her father, Emily Dickinson, James Baldwin, and H. D., Rich consistently attempts to shape a common language capable of articulating alternatives to the conditions of life in a hostile culture.

Rich has been acutely aware of her work as a multileveled process since the mid-1950s. Early in her career, she assented, at least consciously, to the late modernist assumptions of W. H. Auden's introduction to *A Change of World*: "So long as the way in which we regard the world and feel about our existence remains in all essentials the same as that of our predecessors we must follow in their tradition; it would be just as dishonest for us to pretend that their style is inadequate to our needs as it would have been for them to be content with the style of the Victorians" (in Cooper, p. 210).

These assumptions seem inappropriate only in retrospect. As a young poet with a "universal vision" of poetry as the "expression of a higher world view," Rich articulated a distinctly Audenesque aesthetic in "At a Bach Concert" (c. 1950), which proclaims "A too-compassionate art is half an art." Like much of her early work, this poem clearly deserves Auden's praise of her "capacity for detachment from the self and its emotions" (in Cooper, p. 211). As she came to feel that her regard for the world differed substantially from that of the male poets who presided over her poetic apprenticeship—Yeats, Thomas, Mac-Neice, Stevens, Auden himself—Rich explicitly repudiated the detach-ed ironies and polished performances which had come to dominate academic modernism.

When she began to date her poems in the mid-1950s, she understood the act as both personal and political: "By 1956, I had begun dating each of my poems by year. I did this because I was finished with the idea of a poem as a single, encapsulated event, a work of art complete in itself; I knew my life was changing, my work was changing, and I needed to indicate to readers my sense of being engaged in a long, con-tinuing process. It seems to me now that this was an oblique political statement—a rejection of the dominant critical idea that the poem's text should be read as separate from the poet's everyday life in the world. It was a declaration that placed poetry in a historical continuity, not above or outside history" (Rich, *Blood*, p. 180). When Rich introduced her *Poems: Selected and New* (1974) "not as a summing-up or even a retrospective, but as the graph of a process still going on" (Rich, 1975, p. xv), she sounded a note which echoes down through "Contra-dictions: Tracking Poems," the final section of *Your Native Land, Your Life.*

Rich's Prose

In conversation with Wendy Martin, Rich described her writing as "the process of going from the conflicts and strife of the unconscious into the sayable, into the actable" (Martin, 1984, p. 169). This process is at once personal and political. Early in her career, Rich focused primarily on her struggle to bring personal conflicts to consciousness. Gradually, her emphasis shifted to the ways in which the political con-text discourages both articulation and action. Recently she has con-centrated on synthesizing her lesbian-feminist political insights and her complex personal experience. An increasingly vital part of her process since about 1970, Rich's prose charts her developing understanding of these shifts, which both reflect and create changes in her life. In *Of Woman Born: Motherhood as Experience and Institution* (1976), Rich describes her movement to a process-oriented aesthetic as an attempt to maintain creative integrity while raising the three sons born (all between 1955 and 1959) during her marriage to Harvard economist

Alfred Conrad. Only after the end of the marriage in 1970 did she discuss the tension between "the girl. . . who defined herself in writing poems" and the "girl who was to define herself by her relationships with men" (Rich, *Lies*, p. 40) in specifically political terms. Drawing on Rich's reading of feminist writers such as Mary Daly and Susan Griffin, "When We Dead Awaken: Writing as Re-Vision" (1971) and *Of Woman Born* extend the political focus, emphasizing the historical origins and contemporary operations of patriarchal culture. "Disloyal to Civilization: Feminism, Racism, Gynephobia" (1978) and "Compulsory Heterosexuality and the Lesbian Existence" (1980), essays which contributed to Rich's growing prominence among feminists, explore the impact of patriarchy on individual experience.

Even as her lesbian-feminist awareness increased, Rich continued to test her perceptions against the ambiguous personal experiences which had motivated her political development. As she wrote in "Women and Honor: Some Notes on Lying" (1975): "Much of what is narrowly termed 'politics' seems to rest on a longing for certainty at the cost of honesty" (Rich, *Lies*, p. 193). Revising ideological positions which she had arrived at only after an extended process, Rich's recent autobiographical writing is, however paradoxically, an inevitable outgrowth of her growing political certainty. Although she explored her personal experience of motherhood in *Of Woman Born*, Rich had rarely discussed her childhood or marriage before her essay "Split at the Root" (1982), published in *Nice Jewish Girls: A Lesbian Anthology*. Using her lesbian identity as a base for new explorations, Rich reconsiders her childhood and marital experiences, paying special attention to her Jewish heritage. This reconsideration proved acutely painful because it forced her to engage her father's extreme alienation, her husband's suicide, and what she sees as several failures of personal courage. Although Rich's reconciliation with her Jewish identity seems somewhat problematic—she is not a Jew under traditional Jewish law—it nonetheless provides a strategy for coming to terms with her father on a much deeper level than had been reflected in her previous writings. Focusing on these "personal" experiences dictated re-vision, though by no means repudiation, of Rich's feminist politics. Aware that she is describing her own tendencies, Rich criticizes the cultural narrowness of the feminist movement which "claimed universality, though it had not yet acknowledged its own racial, class and ethnic perspectives, or its fears of the differences between women" (Rich, 1982, p. 68). A major statement on Rich's political, personal, and aesthetic processes, "Blood, Bread, and Poetry: The Location of the Poet" (1983) seeks to overcome these limitations and fears. From her current perspective, accepting the diverse experience of "others" is a precondition for accepting the complexity of the self. Ultimately, Rich presents personal integrity and political extension as complementary aspects of a single process: "I write for the still-fragmented parts in me, trying to bring them together. Whoever can read and use any of this, I write for them as well" (Rich, 1983, p. 540).

This process demands an uncompromising integrity. At no time can personal fears or political beliefs serve as justification for distortions or simplifications. Although particular poems or statements may seem intemperate or simplistic, such moments play an important role in Rich's overall process. She repeatedly acknowledges the tentative nature of all positions: "No writer has spoken her last word until she is dead, and. . . the 'last word' will, in fact, be the entirety of her life-work read *in its political and historical context*. I underscore these words because they are at the heart of feminist criticism, and of all criticism that is engaged, that is not written with the pretense of detachment, that does not isolate the text from the world" (quoted in Martin, 1984, p. 213). As this statement indicates, Rich sees each stage of her process in relation to both preceding and subsequent stages.

It seems pointless, for example, to suggest that Rich should have come to terms with her Jewish heritage, with its strongly patriarchal traditions, before acknowledging her lesbianism. It seems equally pointless to suggest that she should have embraced her lesbianism while struggling to raise a family, fulfill the role of "Harvard wife," and continue to write. Rich's importance stems in large part from her willingness to provide a public model of a process which acknowledges its limitations and encourages constant revision. As Rich asserts in "Split at the Root," such openness is of particular importance in a world which provides few opportunities for unambiguous action: "We can't wait for the undamaged to make our connections for us; we can't wait to speak until we are wholly clear and righteous. There is no purity, and, in our lifetimes, no end to the process" (Rich, *Blood*, p. 123).

Poetry as Process

Rich's prose outlines her conscious understanding of her process; her poetry provides the map of her passage from the "unconscious into the sayable, into the actable" (Martin, 1984, p.169). As most critics sympathetic to Rich's feminist aesthetic recognize, her public visibility is itself a significant element of this passage. Observing that few women poets have had "careers in the same sense that men always have, which involves solving problems and moving on to other problems," Alicia Ostriker notes the recurrence of the word "change" in

Rich's titles, concluding with an unqualified expression of support: "It is a joy, reading through a woman's work, to watch her grow too large for herself, shed her skin, and emerge new" (p. 102). From this perspective, Rich can be seen as part of a "mainstream" tradition of twentieth-century male poetry: that of Yeats, Eliot, Williams, and Auden, each of whom has been praised for his ability to re-create his poetic voice in response to new philosophical and/or political influences. When viewed by critics—most of them affiliated with the academic institutions which have canonized the Euro-American male tradition while generally overlooking H. D. and Langston Hughes, each of whom had a career of extraordinary complexity—who share Auden's preference for "detachment," however, Rich's process frequently elicits resistance. Reflecting the traditional academic preference for "masterpieces" and his own preference for self-reflexive texts, Cary Nelson criticizes Rich precisely because of the uncompromising commitment to re-vision which Ostriker praises: "The personal pressure she feels—to 'be/ more merciless to herself than history'—makes it difficult to read much of her poetry except for what it tells us, in retrospect, about her previous work, and what it shows her aching to become. Without at least some sense of achievement in individual poems, that radical version of poetry as a continuing process can also blunt the impact of her work, since we are implicitly urged to delay coming to terms with any given poem" (p. 150). Implying that "coming to terms" with poetry involves reaching a conclusion immune from future re-vision and that recognition of individual poems as part of an open-ended process in some way precludes "achievement," Nelson declares that the cost of Rich's commitment to process has been "a loss of finished poems and the loss of readers willing to live with her work" (p. 150). Nelson's comment concerning the loss of readers may be accurate within an academic context, although the increasing number of critical articles on Rich and the inclusion of her work in most anthologies suggests that even within academia the actual loss is minimal. Outside that context, Nelson's claim carries no validity. Rich's public readings continue to attract enthusiastic crowds and, as Ostriker comments, many feminists respond to her work as a "mirror in which multitudes are seen as one" (p. 103).

This clash of academic and feminist perspectives constitutes the defining tension in the reception of Rich's work. Given her belief in the importance of an actual audience, much of which comes into contact with her work in the classroom context, the implications of contrasting critical stances deserve close scrutiny. Even critics and teachers ostensibly sympathetic to her premises may generate readings that diminish the utility of individual poems, books, or phases of her career if they fail to engage her entire process. Before the way in which such failures affect the reception of poems from various stages of her process is demonstrated, it is necessary to establish a tentative outline of the shape of Rich's career as it appears from the perspective of the mid-1980s.

Given the political and aesthetic controversies surrounding Rich's work, surprisingly little disagreement exists concerning the major divisions of her career. As of the publication of *The Fact of a Doorframe* (1984), her second volume of selected poems, Rich had "emerged new" twice in her career. Her recent collection, *Your Native Land, Your Life,* strongly implies a third "shedding of the skin" in progress. To be sure, critics describe these changes using various terminology. Rich's career has been seen as a passage through "phases of self-reconstruction, political engagement, and feminism" (Ostriker, p. 103); a psychological journey centered on her developing understanding of her animus (A. Gelpi, in Gelpi, pp. 138-39); a fall from controlled ambivalence into intense but indulgent fragmentation (Boyers, in Gelpi, p. 157); a movement "from patriarchy to the feminine principle" (Martin, in Gelpi, p. 175); a gradual recognition of "subjectivity" as the crucial link between private and public experiences (Juhasz, p. 197); a passage through the stages of women's isolation from "victimization" to "validation" (Pope, p. 9). Anne Newman, emphasizing the development of a communal "we" in place of the individualistic "I," would probably argue for a sub-division of the third phase (p. 194); Peter Romonow seems content with a two-part division between Rich's early "formalism" and her later "conversational" poetry (p. 2365). Despite such minor disagreements on the precise demarcation of periods (which contrast sharply with the acerbic arguments concerning the value of the work created during those periods), few critics would be likely to argue seriously against a division of Rich's career into three basic phases, with *Snapshots of a Daughter-in-Law* (1963) and *Diving Into the Wreck* (1973) as crucial transitional VOLUMES.

A CHANGE OF WORLD, THE DIAMOND CUTTERS, SNAPSHOTS OF A DAUGHTER-IN-LAW

Rich's first two volumes, *A Change of World* and *The Diamond Cutters* (1955), attracted the attention of established poets, including Auden, Randall Jarrell, and Donald Hall. Their unanimous praise of Rich's formal control and "objective" perspective established what remains the dominant, and essentially accurate, critical image of her early period. Articulated in comparatively unstructured fragmented forms, *Snap-*

shots of a Daughter-in-Law marked a significant transition, turning attention directly to the feminist themes which would develop throughout Rich's career. Auden praised A Change of World, which he selected for the Yale Series of Younger Poets, in somewhat patronizing tones: "The poems a reader will encounter in this book are neatly and modestly dressed, speak quietly but do not mumble, respect their elders but are not cowed by them, and do not tell fibs" (in Cooper, p. 211). Only slightly less patronizing, Jarrell described The Diamond Cutters with the stereotypically feminine adjectives "sweet" and "enchanting." In retrospect Snapshots of a Daughter-in-Law, which won Poetry magazine's Hokin Prize, appears to be precisely the "breakthrough" volume envisioned by Hall when he challenged Rich to reach for the "greater profundity and greater strength" (in Cooper, p.213) he sensed in The Diamond Cutters. Although Philip Booth recognized Snapshots of a Daughter-in-Law as a "risk" reflecting her effort "to get life said" (in Cooper, p. 215), most contemporary reviewers found it disappointing.

Speaking with Robin Morgan, a younger poet greatly influenced by her work, Rich described her feelings concerning the reception of Snapshots of a Daughter-in-Law: "This book was ignored, was written off as being too bitter and personal. . . . I was also very conscious of male critics, then, and it was like flunking a course. It was as though they were telling me, 'You did well in book two, but you flunked book three'" (Morgan, p. 107). Although she has commented on her inability to use the first person pronoun in the intensely personal title poem, the volume nonetheless sounds a much more individual voice than her early work. In addition to her earliest dated work, the volume includes the first poems in which she juxtaposes fragments written at different times, a structure she would employ in some of her strongest later work. Stressing Rich's growing concern with her situation as a woman defined by her relationship to men, Snapshots of a Daughter-in-Law anticipates the intense struggle for personal integrity and political understanding characterizing the second major phase of her work.

NECESSITIES OF LIFE, LEAFLETS, THE WILL TO CHANGE

Necessities of Life (1966), Leaflets (1969), and The Will to Change chart Rich's accelerating passage into the public sphere, a passage that forced critics to develop new approaches to her work. In the mid-1960s her reviewers, most of them males with academic credentials, still viewed her work from the perspective established by Auden. A decade later, even her least empathetic readers had been forced to recognize her political commitment and to respond accordingly. Robert Lowell's 1966 review of National Book Award nominee *Necessities of Life*, despite its favorable tone, echoed Auden in the phrase "modesty without mumbling." However applicable it seemed at the time, Lowell's perception of Rich as a deferential aesthetic presence would shortly seem anachronistic. Still, Lowell recognized that Rich was engaged in a complex process which had arrived at a "poised and intact completion" (p. 5). In contrast, John Ashbery's review of the same volume condescended to Rich as a "traditional poet. . . a kind of Emily Dickinson of the suburbs" (in Cooper, p. 217). The combination of images suggests an extremely circumscribed reading of both Rich and Dickinson. Ashbery, then emerging as exemplar of a process differing radically from Rich's, declared her work unlikely to challenge readers familiar with William Burroughs and Allen Ginsberg.

Both Lowell and Ashbery interpreted Rich primarily in relation to their own poetic tradition, the tradition which had in fact directed her early work. Anticipated by her poetic dialogs with a Dickinson more subversive than suburban, Rich's political/aesthetic challenge to that tradition assumed a foreground position in *Leaflets* and *The Will to Change*, forcing reviewers to reconsider their basic assumptions concerning her relationship to the tradition. Denis Donoghue noted the "apocalyptic" formal and thematic elements of *Leaflets* (in Cooper, p. 220) while Mona Van Duyn's *Poetry* review of the same volume was the first discussion of Rich's work specifically in the context of women's poetry. To an even greater extent, *The Will to Change* provided a psychological/aesthetic/political test for reviewers. Comparing the diversity and intensity of responses suggests the inadequacy of any claims to "detached" critical judgment. For example, Robert Boyers condemned *The Will to Change* as the "nauseous propaganda of the advance-guard cultural radicals" (in Gelpi, p. 156) while David Kalstone defended it as "a force deeply subversive of radical politics" (in Cooper, p. 225). Written at the height of the political energy and turmoil associated with the Civil Rights Movement and the Vietnam War protests, such responses hardly seem surprising. Rich's fascination with controversial subjects, ranging from Godard's cinema to the trial of Bobby Seale, guaranteed that her work would excite passions incompatible with the dispassionate modernism Auden has praised in her earlier work. Every aspect of *The Will to Change*, which was awarded the Shelley Memorial Award of the Poetry Society of America, manifested Rich's desire to expand her confrontation with the issues raised in *Necessities of Life* and *Leaflets* into a wider public sphere.

DIVING INTO THE WRECK, THE DREAM OF A COMMON LANGUAGE, A WILD PATIENCE HAS TAKEN ME THIS FAR, YOUR NATIVE LAND, YOUR LIFE

Diving Into the Wreck, Rich's second major transitional work, did as much as any single volume by a twentieth-century American poet to transform this desire into reality. Articulating her political vision in uncompromising feminist terms, the book attracted an extraordinarily heated critical response and established Rich as a major voice in the women's movement. Typifying the enthusiastic reviewers, Margaret Atwood praised Rich for writing a book which "subsumes manifestos" and "makes proclamations" without becoming either manifesto or proclamation (in Cooper, p. 238). Where Atwood responded to the intensely personal dimension of *Diving Into the Wreck*, however, Rosemary Tonks, upset by Rich's "simpler idiom" condemned the volume as "abstraction, or politics," asserting a position which would recur frequently in academic criticism of Rich's later work (in Cooper, p. 233). Even while repudiating Rich's decisions, however, Tonks, like most of the unsympathetic reviewers, realized that she could not simply dismiss the book without reference to the feminist issues Rich raised.

The Dream of a Common Language (1978) and *A Wild Patience Has Taken Me This Far* (1981) forced further adjustments in the discussion of Rich's work in both academic and feminist forums. Where her poems of the early 1970s advanced an "androgynous" or "humanist" vision of feminism, these later volumes reflected Rich's public advocacy of a lesbian separatist position. Developing the critique of patriarchy that had remained implicit during her second phase, Rich attempted to shape a language capable of articulating the unique experiences of women. Predictably, the immediate responses to this work consistently reflected reviewers' assumptions concerning the validity of her political positions and/or aesthetic choices. Academic reviewers such as Helen Vendler frequently found Rich's feminism overly didactic while feminist critics such as Olga Broumas concentrated on applying her insights directly to problems affecting the lesbian community. Neither surprising nor undesirable, the disagreements indicate both Rich's impact on public debate—even the hostile reviewers discuss the issues she raises—and the potential for polarization in her radical commitment to lesbian-feminism.

What many critics failed to understand was that, like all Rich's stances, the separatism of *The Dream of a Common Language* and *A Wild Patience Has Taken Me This Far* remained subject to revision. *Your Native Land, Your Life*, which includes both the important chapbook "Sources" (1983) and the significant section of new poems included in

The Fact of a Doorframe, suggested that Rich had in fact subjected her separatism to extensive reconsideration. Together, Rich's poems of the mid-1980s may well signal a third major transition in her career. Extending the reengagement with personal history reflected in her recent prose, *Your Native Land, Your Life* no more repudiates Rich's lesbian-feminism than her lesbian-feminism repudiated the political commitment of the 1960s. Rather, it reasserts her unwavering belief in poetry as a process continually demanding revision if it is to be of use in the continuing "conversation with the elders and with the future" (Rich, *Blood,* p. 187).

Rich's Public Presence

Several decisions affecting the critical and financial position of her poetry indicate Rich's willingness to accept the implications of her process, specifically of her lesbian—feminist commitment. Throughout her career, Rich has received numerous grants and awards, including the National Institute of Arts and Letters award for poetry (1961), two Guggenheim Fellowships (1952-53, 1961-62), a Bollingen Foundation grant (1962) and an Amy Lowell traveling fellowship (1962-63). In addition, she has served as a faculty member at several institutions, including Swarthmore College, Columbia University, Brandeis University, Douglass College, and the City College of New York, where she taught in the SEEK and Open Admissions programs. The latter position was particularly significant because Rich's fellow faculty members included Afro-American poets Gwendolyn Brooks (briefly), Audre Lorde, and Alice Walker. When *Diving Into the Wreck* won the National Book Award in 1974, Rich rejected the prize as an individual but, at the same time, accepted it—as a statement written with Walker and Lorde asserted—"in the name of all women whose voices have gone and still go unheard in a patriarchal world" (in Gelpi, p. 204). At about the same time, she began publishing her poetry in feminist reviews rather than the prestigious (and more lucrative) mainstream publications in which, she wrote, "women's words, even when they are not edited, can get flattened and detonated in a context which is predominately masculine and misogynist" (Rich, *Lies,* p. 107). Dismissing the attempt to reach the relatively large but frequently detached audiences of magazines such as *American Poetry Review, Antaeus,* the *New York Review of Books,* the *Saturday Review,* and *Partisan Review* (where poems collected in *Diving Into the Wreck* were first published), Rich chose to contribute her work to feminist publications such as *Amazon Quarterly* (in which she first publicly identified herself as a lesbian), *Heresies, 13th Moon,* and

Sinister Wisdom, a lesbian journal which she co-edited with Michelle Cliff from 1981 to 1983.

As Rich revised her approach to lesbian-feminism during the mid-1980s, she moved somewhat nearer to the cultural mainstream, a decision consistent with the synthetic concerns of her recent work. In addition to accepting a position on the faculty of Stanford University, she again placed poems in mainstream publications such as the *Boston Review* and *Parnassus*. These adjustments, it should be reiterated, do not imply a repudiation of her lesbian-feminism. Her Stanford appointment is in both English and Feminist Studies; the issue of *Parnassus* in which her work appeared was devoted exclusively to women poets; and she has continued to place her work in feminist journals such as *Sojourner* and with feminist presses such as the Heyeck Press, which published "Sources". Upon receiving the first Ruth Lilly Poetry Prize in 1986, Rich explicitly reiterated her political position by indicating that part of the award would be "tithed to places where it could aid more than óne person and make survival and writing more possible, particularly in the feminist and lesbian community."

Central Themes

Paralleling the general agreement on the direction of Rich's career, a similar consensus exists concerning her central thematic concerns: the critique of patriarchy, the creation of a woman-centered alternative, and the need for a synthesis of personal and political experience. Her critique of patriarchy, discernible in her work before she began to employ the term, focuses both on oppressive institutions and on their repressive impact on individual consciousness. Connecting problems of racism, environmental destruction, and economic exploitation with those of sexual oppression, Rich condemns the patriarchal tendency toward "solipsism, a preoccupation with our own feelings which prevents us from ever connecting with the experience of others" (Rich, *Lies*, p. 306). Following *Diving Into the Wreck*, Rich's second major theme—the attempt to envision an alternative culture, both practically and metaphorically woman-centered—assumes a more central position in her thought. Repudiating the Cartesian-Newtonian premises (i.e., mechanistic atomism and psychological subjectivity) of contemporary Euro-American patriarchy, Rich envisions a sense of personal integrity based on the acceptance of shared experience. Ideally, this integrity will nurture a community capable of challenging the linguistic, institutional, and mythological premises of the patriarchy.

Rich's third central theme—the attempt to unify personal and political experience—grows directly out of her attempt to realize this ideal.

Acutely aware of the continuing presence of solipsistic elements in her own process, Rich acknowledges that most actual alternative communities suffer from a profound fragmentation of consciousnes frequently manifested in the split between personal and political impulses. This awareness in turn influences Rich's orientation toward the feminist communities both within and beyond the academic/literary world. Maintaining her distance from the highly theoretical "French" feminist discourse which employs a technical philosophical vocabulary accessible primarily to academics conversant with the Cartesian tradition, Rich (who is certainly aware of the theoretical developments) adopts an anti-elitist "American" stance. Even when she engages in what amount to deconstructions of patriarchal discourse (see Chapter 4), she attempts to communicate in a "common language." Although Rich's approach at times recalls the willed naivety of other highly intellectual American anti-intellectuals, such as Whitman and Faulkner, she has contributed substantially to the understanding of the relationship between the political formulations of feminist thinkers and the experiences of women from diverse socioeconomic backgrounds. Whether or not they endorse Rich's positions, feminist writers such as Barbara Rigney (*Lilith's Daughters*), Dale Spender (*Women of Ideas and What Men Have Done to Them*), Josephine Donovan (*Feminist Theory*), Barbara Smith (*Toward a Black Feminist Criticism*), Hester Eisenstein (*Contemporary Feminist Thought*), and Gerda Lerner (*The Origins of Patriarchy*) routinely use her work as a significant point of reference.

Somewhat ironically, Rich's "anti-French" stance mirrors that of French "anti-theorist" Michel Foucault, who insists that theoretical discourse remain accountable to "particular, local, regional knowledge, a differential knowledge incapable of unanimity. . . which owes its force only to the harshness with which it is opposed by everything surrounding it" (p. 82). For both Rich and Foucault, this "genealogical" approach implies repudiation of "globalising discourses with their hierarchy and all their privileges of a theoretical *avant-garde*." As Timothy J. Reiss brilliantly demonstrates in *The Discourse of Modernism*, the dominant discourses are inextricably based on precisely the Cartesian-Newtonian premises which Rich sees as the foundations of patriarchy. In place of these discourses, Foucault envisions "anti-sciences" based on a "union of erudite knowledge and local memories which allows us to establish a historical knowledge of struggles and to make use of this knowledge tactically today" (p. 83). The center of Rich's treatment of her major themes, then, lies in her attempt to forge a language more capable than Foucault's of encouraging *actual* tactical use of this complexly interrelated knowledge by women with immediate access only to the "local knowledge." Realization of this goal precludes the use of any form which implies the superiority of theory or encourages the creation of a new privileged avant-garde. As the inter-relationship of her major thematic, stylistic, and tactical concerns sug-gests, Rich attempts to include all aspects of her experience in her vision of an actual alternative to patriarchy. Her attempt to unify the multiple levels of experience—personal and political; academic and popular; aesthetic, emotional and intellectual—dictates her continuing emphasis on process. Perhaps the process itself is her most basic thematic concern.

Process and Individual Poems

In contrast to the consensus on the development and thematic con-cerns of Rich's work are the sharp disagreements concerning its aesthetic value and political validity. Frequently, critics differing with the ideological or aesthetic premises of a particular period simplify Rich by failing to address the relationship of an individual work to her complex process. Critics who evaluate her work primarily in terms of prevailing academic ideologies tend to prefer the work of her middle period and to dismiss poems directed to nonacademic audiences of women. Conversely, though ultimately less subversive of Rich's inten-tions, some feminist critics undervalue the stages of Rich's process that do not explicitly endorse a feminist vision or, at worst, their own par-ticular type of feminist vision. Reading Rich requires constant aware-ness that each poem and book of poems is recreated by each new book or poem, which in turn assumes its meaning only when considered in relation to the preceding stages of the process. Whether or not it is articulated from an academic perspective, criticism which removes Rich's poetry from her process can lead to as serious a misapprehen-sion of her achievement as the imposition of a hostile critical ideology. The following analysis of critical responses to poems from different periods of Rich's career—"Aunt Jennifer's Tigers" (1951), "Necessities of Life" (1962), and "Rape" (1972)—demonstrates the value of understand-ing each poem, in Suzanne Juhasz's phrase, as "a part of the world and an act towards a new one" (p. 200).

"AUNT JENNIFER'S TIGERS"

In "When We Dead Awaken," Rich wrote that "Aunt Jennifer's Tigers" typifies her early use of formalism as a means of distancing herself from the tensions of her experience (Rich, *Lies*, p. 40). Interesting as evidence concerning Rich's sense of her own process, the statement has contributed to the serious undervaluation of a poem which, while not confessional or ideological, introduces Rich's challenge to the patriarchal understanding of women's creative powers. A description of a woman creating a piece of needlework, "Aunt Jennifer's Tigers" is a deceptively complex poem which provides a surprisingly complex comment on psychology and aesthetics. Numerous anthologies present the poem as an example of Rich's early period, usually contrasting it explicitly with her later feminist work in "open forms." Ironically, the critics most likely to undervalue or misapprehend Rich's challenge are those most sympathetic with her overall process. In her book *An American Triptych*, Wendy Martin, who elsewhere speculates that Rich's artifice may mask "a quiet, persistent building of her own vision" (*American Writers*, p. 552), echoes Rich by describing the poem as a "carefully distanced portrait" (p. 180). Similarly, Albert Gelpi remarks a "partial evasion of the conflicts" behind the craft of her early work (in Gelpi, p. 131). Judith McDaniel's monograph *Reconstituting the World: The Poetry and Vision of Adrienne Rich* associates its rhymed form directly with Rich's attempt to "accommodate the power of a masculine school of critical thought" (in Cooper, p. 4). Although each is a sensitive reader and critic, each fails, at least partially, to place the distance and restraint in the context of Rich's overall process.

Anticipating many later poems which combine aspects of traditional prosody with open forms, "Aunt Jennifer's Tigers" demonstrates Rich's ability to use her control of sound, rhythm, and metrical emphasis to explore an issue of great importance in the development of her personal and political vision: the creativity of women not recognized as artists by the dominant culture. Seen as a subversive counterbalance to the acceptance of the dominant aesthetic articulated in "At a Bach Concert," "Aunt Jennifer's Tigers" assumes major importance in Rich's development. In addition, it introduces several stylistic signatures, especially involving the use of particular sounds as thematic fulcrums, that continue to characterize Rich's poetic voice long after she abandons "archaic restraint."

"Aunt Jennifer's Tigers" explores the tension between the protagonist's creativity and her social circumstances, imaged primarily in "The massive weight of Uncle's wedding band." The institutional definition exerts a stultifying influence over Jennifer's sense of self; she is "terrified," "mastered." Nonetheless, her tapestry provides an emblem of the way in which "folk arts" protect and assert a more positive self-image. This implicit presentation of an alternative women's sensibility frequently escapes the notice of critics preferring explicit

statements of feminist commitment. Transforming the materials of traditional prosody into a verbal analog of Jennifer's tapestry, Rich not
only discusses but embodies a process she would openly celebrate in
"From an Old House in America" (1974) and "Transcendental Etude"
(1977). To overlook this achievement is to risk surrendering a potentially valuable demonstration of the early stages of a process leading to
an explicitly feminist awareness. So long as women continue to be
educated in patriarchal institutions, demonstrations of alternative
forms of "mastery" maintain a very real tactical utility.

Rich quickly demonstrates just such mastery, establishing the basic
thematic tension in "Aunt Jennifer's Tigers" through the traditional use
of accent clusters formed by the substitution of spondees or trochees
for iambs; the addition of stressed syllables at the beginning of lines;
and enjambment. In addition to stressing the tension between the
protagonist's individual name and her institutional definition (Aunt
Jennifer), the accent clusters define both the oppressive atmosphere of
her marriage ("bánd/ sits heávĭly̆"; "lie/ stíll ringed") and the world of
her creative transcendence ("bríght tópăz"; "dó nót feár"; "shé máde";
"gó oń prańcing"). Reinforcing this imagistic tension with variations in
cadence, Rich establishes a rapid tempo for the tigers in stanza one
before disrupting the rhythm upon the introduction of the wedding
band in stanza two. Line one moves forward with a dactylic/trochaic
meter before its resolution by the final accented syllable into the
underlying iambic pentameter: "Jéńnifer's tígĕrs prańce ăcróss ă
scréen." In contrast, the first line of stanza two, disrupted by the three
syllable "fluttering" followed by the weak accent on "through," divests
Jennifer's action of both vitality and power: "Aunt Jeńnifer's fingĕrs
flúttĕring through hĕr woól." Where the first stanza builds to the assertive iambic pentameter of line four—"Théy pace iń sleék chiválric
certăinty"—stanza two ends with the tense erratic meter reinforcing the
sense that Jennifer has been mastered: "Sits heávĭly̆ ŭpón Aunt Jeńnifer's hand."

The real evidence of Rich's technical mastery, however, involves the
poem's thematically resonant music. In stanza one, she weaves a verbal tapestry which, like Jennifer's cloth tapestry renders the "men
beneath the tree" harmless. The bright p ("prance," "topaz," "pace") and
z ("topaz," "denizens") sounds complemented by the long vowels
necessary to the quick cadence ("tigers," "bright," "screen," "green,"
"sleek," "tree") establish the music of the stanza. Incorporating the
"men" into Jennifer's pattern of female expression, Rich counteracts the
potentially disruptive sound of the word "men" with echoes which connect it with the previously established music of the tapestry
("denizens," "prance," "green," "screen"). Anticipating the threat to this

imaginative world, however, the *f* in Jennifer's name, while loosely
connected with the *z*'s, recurs only in "fear." In stanza two, this
undercurrent develops into uncertainty ("fingers," "fluttering"), providing the verbal and thematic transition to the *v* sounds introduced by
the seemingly harmless "chivalric" in the final line of the first stanza.
Strongly associated with Jennifer's faltering before masculine power
("ivory," "massive," "heavily"), the *v* sound, along with *h* ("hand,"
"heavily," "hard"), *d* ("needle," "hard," "wedding," "band") and flat
vowel sounds ("pull," "massive," "Uncle," "upon"), forms the center of a
second sound texture emphasizing Jennifer's entrapment in marriage.

  The final stanza resolves this verbal and thematic tension in a manner
which suggests that, even in her "student work," Rich was aware of the
need for a women's aesthetic capable of transforming a hostile external
context into an aspect of a wider vision. Reiterating the *f*, *h*, and *d*
sounds from stanza two, the first two lines of stanza three suggest the
ultimate destruction of Jennifer's creativity ("terrified," "dead," "hands,"
"ordeals"). The lines also bring to the foreground the *m* sound of "men"
and "massive" in what momentarily seems the clinching word,
"mastered." The final lines, however, demonstrate the aesthetic genius
that enables Rich and Jennifer to incorporate the experience of male
mastery into a tapestry testifying to the transformative power of
women's creativity. "The tigers in the panel that she made" emerge
unexpectedly, but not without careful preparation, out of the sounds
associated with male dominance. "Tigers" transforms the *g* of "ringed"
and the *er* of "mastered"; "made" emerges from "mastered," "dead," and
"ordeal," all words associated with masculine power and female suffering. In addition to reasserting the long vowel base of stanza one,
"made" prepares the resolving rhyme sequence ("made," "proud,"
"unafraid"). This rhyme scheme emphasizes the creative confidence
which provides Jennifer with a potential (though as the slant rhyme of
"proud" suggest, still tentative) means of coping with her marital context. Together, the process of art (made) and the content of art (the
tigers) provide a frame within which Rich reasserts the *p* sounds which
recall the first stanza's transcendent vision and underscore the rhyth-
mically confident concluding couplet: "The tigers in the panel that she
made/ Will go on prancing, proud and unafraid."

  It would seem clear, then, that Rich has not, as McDaniel claims
"nearly crafted herself out of feeling." Rather, like Yeats, Edna St. Vin-
cent Millay, Robert Frost, and Gwendolyn Brooks, she taps the power
of traditional prosody to confront her feelings on a deeper level than
she was willing to risk consciously at the time. This is not to deny the
presence of an ambivalence in the resolution of "Aunt Jennifer's Tige rs"
that would present serious problems from a feminist perspective *if* it

were the end point of a process. The power of the proud chivalric tigers seems derived in part from their possession of traditionally masculine attributes; the image of the tapestry as a vindication of Jennifer recalls the view of art as "a vehicle for personal immortality," a view Rich would later dismiss as part of the "detached" academic aesthetic used to deny women's experiences. The actual form of Jennifer's art, however, suggests that traditional images may be charged with subversive significance within the women's tradition.

Despite her lack of conscious artistic vocation, Jennifer assumes a place in a collective tradition of immortal but anonymous women artists who, partially as a means of maintaining sanity, transformed the apparently unpromising leftovers of daily experience into beautiful and useful aesthetic forms such as quilts. As McDaniel observes, Rich's use of the quilt image in later poems, such as "Sibling Mysteries" (1976) and "Natural Resources" (1977), reflects her commitment to recognizing the validity of the aesthetic expression of women living in hostile contexts (in Cooper, p. 26). Clearly, it would be a mistake to dismiss or undervalue their carefully crafted quilts because they were praised or used by men. Just as their work, which was only rarely conceived in explicitly political terms, commands respect as a vital base for the development of a more assertive women's aesthetic, so "Aunt Jennifer's Tigers" deserves appreciation as a beautiful and useful part of Rich's process, the oldest square salvaged from the scraps of everyday life for use in her quilt.

"NECESSITIES OF LIFE"

In "Necessities of Life," one of her first poems employing the first person pronoun to challenge formalist aesthetics, Rich's awareness of this process emerges as a central focus. Tracing several stages in the development of a persona who gradually withdraws from familiar contexts into a potentially regenerative isolation, the poem provides a sequence of voices appropriate to each stage of the persona's (and Rich's) process. Critics who extract the poem from that process risk misunderstanding its central theme and underestimating its exceptionally complex prosody. In his insightful book *Five Temperaments*, David Kalstone interprets the poem as part of Rich's attempt "to experience a various self," accurately noting the emotional advance over her anguished recognition of internal variety in *Snapshots of a Daughter-in-Law* (p. 151). Interpreting the volume *Necessities of Life* as an attempt to bring together "the energies of the solitary ego and the energies of the dialogue," Kalstone sees the title poem as a metaphorical enactment of "the rebirth of a tough little self" belonging to a young woman who, while ready to listen to the "old wives'" tales, "is clearly eager and gathering strength to tell her own" (p. 154). This reading is not inaccurate so much as it is incomplete and slightly misleading. One of Rich's most sensitive academic critics, Kalstone admits that he finds aspects of *Necessities of Life* difficult to comprehend. First, he describes as "odd. . . the way the book moves from an emerging self to poems where Rich does, repeatedly, a vanishing act" (p. 152). In addition, he finds it "strange" that "the assertive self of some of these poems does not penetrate the poems of love and marriage" (p. 154). The roots of both difficulties lie in Kalstone's failure to recognize fully the significance of either rebirth or anticipation in relation to Rich's process. By the mid-1970s, when Kalstone wrote, that process had begun to center clearly on communication between women. Seen in relation to Rich's increasingly explicit indictment of patriarchal conceptions of "love and marriage," the rebirth motif appears less monolithic or individualistic than Kalstone implies. At once reflecting and anticipating Rich's development, "Necessities of Life" portrays at least three distinct "vanishing acts," each followed by a tentative rebirth. Even at the end of the poem, the "assertive self" has not yet emerged into the world to reengage forces which had driven her into hibernation. Seen in relation to the later stages of Rich's process, the anticipatory quality of the poem's conclusion suggests that no real rebirth can take place before the tales of the young woman and the old wives merge to create a communal rather than an egocentric conception of the self.

The opening lines caution against the assumption that "Necessities of Life" will portray a completed process: "Piece by piece I seem/ to re-enter the world." These lines imply that her previous position within the world has fragmented Rich's persona and, as the line break on "seem" emphasizes, rendered her perception tentative. (Although I identify the "I" of "Necessities of Life" with Rich, it should be emphasized that she is not yet writing in the openly autobiographical mode found in some of her later work.) The poem is divided into four sections signaled by time shifts ("Now," "Till," "Soon"). After recapitulating two stages of past experience, Rich describes her present endeavor, and anticipates her future direction. Her hibernation, like that of Ralph Ellison's Invisible Man, both expresses and responds to the definitions imposed on her by the "surface" world. To express the development of selves out of materials provided by past experiences, Rich creates a new kind of verbal music in "Necessities of Life." Constantly metamorphosizing, this music both echoes the technical accomplishment of her early work in strict forms and anticipates the "open," but by no means unstructured, forms of her later work.

Recollecting a period during which she unconsciously accepted external definitions, the first section of "Necessities of Life" presents the persona as a "small, fixed dot" in an impressionist painting, someone else's
picture of reality. The somewhat obvious end rhymes linking the first
lines of the first three stanzas ("seem," "scene," "see") emphasize her
acceptance of and contribution to an archaic aesthetic. The traditional
music, however, is disrupted when the "dot"—the only evidence of a
complete "I" in the section—proves incapable of fitting smoothly into
the pattern. The self disrupts the scene she seems to see. Her sharp-
ness ("thumbtack") and stubborn intellectual assertiveness ("hard little
head protruding") clash thematically and musically with the pastoral
picture, "the pointillist's buzz and bloom." Finally, however, the pain
inherent in her status as decorative object dictates an end to this stage
of the process. Even as she provides rhymes superficially compatible
with the pastoral aesthetic, Rich describes her first vanishing act:
"After a time the dot/ begins to ooze. Certain heats/ melt it." The
music of the impressionist "buzz and bloom" dissolves into "ooze." The
t sound associated with her fixed identity as a woman-thing ("dot,"
"certain," "it") metamorphoses into a "heat" that both torments and
frees ("melts") the old self. The use of sound as a thematic fulcrum
recalls "Aunt Jennifer's Tigers." Again, only now more consciously,
Rich implies that experience within a constricting context provides the
raw materials that can be used to articulate new possibilities.

As the following section warns, however, alienation from one fixed
identity does not automatically generate a viable alternative. Melting
out of her old fixed form, the persona first experiences a rush of
unfamiliar sensation. Emphasized by the repetition of internal *er*
sounds ("hurriedly," "blurring," "burnt," "burning"), her confusion
manifests her earlier problem in a new form. Without her old sense of
self, however inadequate it may have been, she flickers into whatever
shape the flux of experience provides, assuming the personalities of
Jonah, Wittgenstein, Mary Wollstonecraft. Similarly, the music of this
section reflects Rich's initial uncertainty regarding the sound of her
"post-formalist" voice. Following the transitional rhyme of "green"
with the pastoral "scene" of the first section, Rich abandons the full
end-rhymes common in her first three books. Although five consecu-
tive lines end with words involving n sounds ("ranges," "green," "and,"
"Jonah," "Wittgenstein"), the tension between the vowels and/or concluding consonants emphasizes the persona's inability to resolve the
fragments of her perception. Although these words suggest a potential
connection between archaic ("Jonah") and contemporary ("Wittgenstein") identities, Rich employs a more subtle rhyme pattern to underscore the importance of Mary Wollstonecraft. Emphasizing the line

"Mary Wollstonecraft, the soul" with a stanza break, Rich creates a texture of *w* and *o* sounds ("swam," "swallowed," "Jonah," "soul," "whole") connecting the involuntary immersion in experience with the potential for unification. In addition, two significant rhymes involve the feminist philosopher's name: a full internal rhyme of "Woll" and "soul" implies spiritual healing while the bilingual rhyme (off-rhyme of sound, full-rhyme of meaning) of "stone" and "stein" intimates a solidity of identity within the flux. Despite this suggestive texture, however, neither the persona nor Wollstonecraft actually possesses the soul, which belongs to "Louis Jouvet, dead/ in a blown-up photograph."

The second movement of "Necessities of Life," like the first, concludes with the destruction of a fixed image. If the melting of the impressionist painting recalls Rich's rejection of the Audenesque formalism of "Aunt Jennifer's Tigers," the "blowing up" of the photograph suggests her dissatisfaction with "Snapshots of a Daughter-in-Law," which Rich later criticized as "too literary, too dependent on allusion." Rich does not reject the use of literary or cultural figures in the process of self-transformation. Rather, she implies that even a Wollstonecraft can exert an inordinate ("blown up") degree of influence. Wollstonecraft's insights contributed to the power of "Snapshots of a Daughter-in-Law," which praises her struggle with "what she partly understood." But, as the second vanishing act of "Necessities of Life" implies, these insights remained relatively abstract at this stage of Rich's process. Nonetheless Rich's growing comprehension of that process clearly benefited from her conscious immersion in the cultural context which includes Jonah, Wittgenstein, Wollstonecraft, and Jouvet. Although it led to explosion and hibernation rather than rebirth, the immersion played a vital role in Rich's process by reducing the temptation to accept external definitions of the self, however relevant or appealing they might seem.

"Wolfed almost to shreds" by her previous experience, the persona withdraws from the world into a metaphorical "cellar" where she learns "to make myself/ unappetizing." Introducing the central issue of the third movement, this phrase identifies an underlying tension between internal process and external threat. If the persona is to create her own self, she must first make herself unappetizing to avoid being wolfed down, as in the previous section where "whole biographies swam up and/ swallowed me." The off-rhyme of "myself" and "cellar" provides a transition between the tense music of the second section and the seemingly sparse "prosaic" lines associated with her hibernation. Once the persona states her intention to "let nothing use me," Rich abandons the appetizing embellishment of end rhyme entirely. Acknowledging the demand of the title—this section is the only one that includes the key words "necessities" and "life"—both poet and persona attempt to determine the minimal requirements for survival. "Kneading bricks in Egypt," Rich envisions slavery as a paradoxical source of freedom, a forced confrontation with the process of making ("kneading") her "needs" clear. No longer attempting to accommodate her identity to an external form (painting, book, photograph), the persona immerses herself in the process of brick-making, finding pleasure in the knowledge that despite her alienation, "What life was there, was mine." Her labor transforms the previous attempts to claim possession of her identity ("their") into a source of personal richness ("mine").

Following this epiphany, a soft music begins to whisper through the section. Buried within the unrhymed lines, subtle sound connections ("life," "mine," "warm," "sun's," "name") testify to the potential for rebirth inherent in the persona's acceptance of her personal experience, even though it has been primarily an experience of bondage. Reflecting Rich's developing insistence that art be of use, brick-making serves as emblem of the aesthetic shaping "Necessities of Life." Recognizing the futility of abstract rebellion, Rich immerses herself in the process of creating individual pieces for use in the construction of new premises. The final phrase of the section—"to name/ over the bare necessities"—encapsulates the major themes of the entire poem: the need for a process identifying the essential elements of the self; and the desire to articulate more than (to name *over*) the minimal requirements for survival in order to facilitate the rebirth of a unified self.

A feeling of suspension, of tentativeness, permeates the final section of "Necessities of Life." As Rich envisions the future stages of her process, houses and old women wait. The persona thinks she *may* become "middling perfect." The syntax of the final sentence suggests numerous ambiguous and shifting connections between the persona, her environment, other women:

> I have invitations:
> a curl of mist steams upward
>
> from a field, visible as my breath,
> houses along a road stand waiting
>
> like old women knitting, breathless
> to tell their tales.

Several images echo earlier sections of the poem: the steam suggests that the self melted down in the first section may have been transformed into a mist during the hibernation of the third section; the houses may have been built with the persona's bricks. The sound texture both reinforces these connections and suggests new ones: the sound of "steams" recurs not only in the "mist" but also in "stand," "field," and "women." Similarly, the syntax of the persona's description of her future introduces new possibilities: "I'll/ dare inhabit the world/ trenchant in motion as an eel, solid/ as a cabbage-head." Their relationship established by the syntax which would enable "trenchant" to modify either "I" or "world," the persona and her environment participate in new types of possibility. Both world and persona can be simultaneously at rest and in motion; their trenchancy can be physical or mental. The cabbage-head suggests stupidity and nurturance. Rich suggests. She does not resolve.

Internalizing the process described in the poem, this refusal to fix forms or meanings underscores the tentative nature of both the persona's awareness and Rich's expression. Rich highlights the implications of her developing stance in the phrase "I have invitations." Most critics understand these invitations as invitations received, rather than sent, by the persona. In addition to dismissing what seems an obvious syntactical ambiguity, such readings misapprehend Rich's vision of poetry as a conversation with the actual world. The persona's response to invitations from the surface world hinges on the response to the invitations Rich sends her readers. This association of the process within the poem with the process of communication between poem and world, like the persona's identification with the old women, anticipates Rich's future movement toward a woman-centered aesthetic. The strong *t* sounds in "knitting," "tell," and "tales" provide the least ambiguous musical-thematic statement of the section, suggesting a conscious endorsement of the forms of women's expression imaged in "Aunt Jennifer's Tigers." The tension between "breath" and "breathless" acknowledges that the women who contribute to this expressive tradition, however eager to tell their tales, only rarely are able to speak without hesitation. The space at the end of the final line, the shortest in the poem, provides a space in which their tales may be told and stresses that the process endorsed in "Necessities of Life" has not been completed. This in turn calls for an active response from readers, who, by accepting Rich's invitation and carrying out their own processes, help create conditions in which reentering the world will not necessarily reestablish fixed forms necessitating further meltdowns or explosions.

Read with an awareness of Rich's growing interest in woman-centered transformative processes, *Necessities of Life* poses fewer problems than Kalstone suggests. In fact, Kalstone's difficulties stem in large part from phrases he seems to have employed casually but which establish premises discouraging acceptance of the invitation Rich delivers. His choice of the phrase "tough little self" to describe the emerging persona reflects an individualistic perspective which overlooks the movement toward communal connection. The "little self" Kalstone describes does exist in the first section of the poem, where the image of the "hard little head" occurs. Passing through several transformations, however, the self alternately expands and contracts, taking in "whole biographies" and shrinking down to a "dry bulb" in a cellar. The rhythm of her process indicates that when/if the persona reenters the world, she will again expand.

Less circumscribed than Kalstone's phrase implies, "Necessities of Life" endorses a conception of selfhood based on connection with the environment (see the complex, and aesthetically charged, wordplay connecting "breath" and "field") and with other women. This expansive self, resisting simplifying definitions of all sorts, will inevitably continue to participate in the pattern of emergence and vanishing that Kalstone, who reads "Necessities of Life" as the tale of a single emergence, finds so odd. Similarly, Kalstone's phrase, "old wives' tales," which he uses to describe the persona's perception, is in fact entirely his own. Nothing in Rich's language suggests that the old women—who are *not* defined in relation to husbands—would express superstitions, certainly not in the sense implied by Kalstone's phrase. Reflecting his failure to understand the value Rich's "assertive self" places on communication with women, Kalstone's comment concerning the absence of that self from the poems of love and marriage effectively denies Rich's process by placing dialog with men at the center of *Necessities of Life*. If one rejects this phallocentric emphasis, however, the absence hardly seems surprising. In "Necessities of Life," Rich concentrates on the conditions that will make reentry into the world possible for women whose previous attempts to assert themselves in love and marriage failed. Although she considers her return, the persona remains in hibernation, imagining the first stage of her return as a dialog with women. The ideal dialog of male and female that Kalstone desires could not occur without a clear acceptance on both sides of the validity of the old women's experience. Certainly no such acceptance existed in the early 1960s. Not until at least a decade later could respect for "uneducated" women's stories be safely assumed even within feminist discourse. Within academic discourse, it cannot be assumed even yet.

"RAPE"

A profound unwillingness to respect the integrity of women's expression, even that of educated women, characterizes much academic discussion of Rich's politically explicit poetry. Although it is somewhat atypical in its reliance on traditional prosody, "Rape" typifies the assertive address to actual political problems which provides the foundation of Rich's work of the 1970s and 1980s. Failing to understand the significance of the actual audience in Rich's process, Cary Nelson and Helen Vendler advance separate readings of "Rape" which suggest the validity of Rich's comment on the aesthetic ideology of academic discourse: "The reading of poetry in an academic institution is supposed to lead you—in the 1980s as back there in the early 1950s—not toward a criticism of society but toward a professional career in which the anatomy of poems is studied dispassionately" (Rich, *Blood*, p. 173). While both Nelson and Vendler value some type of "passion" in poetry, neither shares Rich's commitment to poetry as a political act in the world or her concern with reaching an audience outside academia. As a result neither Vendler's essay "Ghostlier Demarcations, Keener Sounds" or Nelson's discussion of Rich in *Our Last and First Poets* recognizes anything of value in "Rape." Ironically, their responses illustrate one of the central themes of the poem: the refusal of individuals associated with the machinery of patriarchal culture to allow women to choose the terms in which their stories will be told.

Denying the ability of individuals to effect change, former Modern Language Association President Vendler condemns the poem as "an unthinking assault on plain reasonableness. . . annulling and untenable propaganda" (Vendler, 1980, p. 243). Nelson, who declares Vendler one of the two best critics of Rich's work, echoes her indictment, calling "Rape" "one-dimensionally didactic," rhetorically "lazy," and "mildly comic" (pp. 151-52). Even while paying lip service to the poem's politics, Nelson employs aesthetic criteria which deny the importance of the crucial feminist values of "utility" and "validity": "Rich's claim is a useful political challenge, and it may even be valid, but the poem's slick self-assurance is unlikely to convince us" (pp. 150-51). After identifying his own reading with that of a presumably universal "us," Nelson assures "us" that Rich "is not willing to risk the poem's politics" by expressing "the full range of feelings present in the writing situation" (p. 153). Clearly, any reader accepting Vendler's or Nelson's readings would find little in "Rape" save a litany of cliches that, as Vendler claims, should not "pass muster. . . when a volume is being gathered for publication" (Vendler, 1980, p. 243).

Three basic assumptions connect these repudiations of "Rape": first, that the poem's meaning is transparent; second, that its rhetorical strategy lacks subtlety; and third, that its message is obvious. Both critics accuse Rich of propagating feminist cliches unworthy of the serious attention of poet, critic, or any conceivable audience. Neither Vendler nor Nelson, however, appears to comprehend even the surface meaning of the poem. Certainly, neither understands its position in Rich's woman-centered process. Vendler discusses "Rape" as an "incrimination of all men in the encapsulation of brothers and fathers in the portrait of this rapist super-cop" (Vendler, 1980, p. 243). Further, she believes this portrait denies "the simple fact of possible decency" (Vendler, 1980, p. 243). Similarly, Nelson centers his discussion on the policeman who "instinctively identifies with rapist rather than with victim," and the "fascist bureaucracy" which forces the woman to confess "the crime of having been forced" (p. 151). Both see "Rape" as a poem concerned primarily with the policeman, as a self-righteous political attack on the male brutality that victimizes essentially powerless women.

This focus on the policeman reveals several problems with Nelson's and Vendler's readings. First, the assumption that Rich uses this figure to condemn all males distorts the opening lines: "There is a cop who is both prowler and father: / he comes from your block, grew up with your brothers." Despite Vendler's assertion that this identifies all brothers and fathers with the cop, the line simply indicates that the cop comes out of the same context as the males with whom the victim grew up. It is, Rich stresses, a serious mistake for any woman to believe she knows even familiar males well enough to be certain they are incapable of violating women. Similarly, the line "he has access to machinery that could kill you" is a plea for increased awareness of indirect forms of violation rather than a simplistic identification of policeman and rapist. Neither Vendler nor Nelson acknowledges Rich's exploration of the relationship between the "machinery" and the "certain ideals" dominating the policeman's psychology.

Drawing attention to the distance between the policeman's assumption that he understands the victim's reactions and her actual disorientation (her mind is "whirling like crazy"), Rich introduces a central, and by no means obvious, theme concerning the relationship between actual experience and ideological interpretations of that experience. Ultimately, Rich does not present stereotypes so much as she comments on the impact of stereotypes on experience. By reducing the victim to a stereotype in his report, the cop, who knows what she "imagined" and "secretly wanted," imposes an equally stereotyped identity on himself, all without committing any physically violent act. Rich does not claim imperial knowledge of the male. Rather, she emphasizes that, given the numerous stereotyped perceptions present in the situation, neither man nor woman can truly know self or other.

In order to understand the complexity of "Rape," it is necessary to abandon Nelson's and Vendler's belief that the cop, the male presence, occupies the center of the poem. Far from being a poem "about" male physical violence, "Rape" is primarily concerned with women's psychological response to that violence. The emphasis seems unambiguous in the concluding lines: "and if, in the sickening light of the precinct,/ your details sound like a portrait of your confessor,/ will you swallow, will you deny them, will you lie your way home?" Nelson interprets these lines as a "demagogic" counterpart of the cop's machinery, evidence of Rich's desire to coerce acceptance of the stereotyped portrait of the cop. Throughout the poem, however, Rich consistently emphasizes the uncertainty of any woman's knowledge of the cop. She repeats the phrase "you hardly know him" three times and concludes the poem in the subjunctive. Vendler's claim that "Rape" ends with an identification of the cop with the rapist is simply inaccurate. The only indisputable fact is that all perceptions conditioned by the "sickening light of the precinct" must be carefully examined in relation to the details of the victim's experience. Rather than insisting on an ideological position, which would in any case be more complex than that recognized by Nelson and Vendler, Rich urges women not to lie about what they have felt, not to validate the cop's report in order to regain their position in a world they hardly know.

Rich's concern with women's tendencies to accept male interpretations of their experience leads to the use of rhetorical strategies which frequently elude her academic critics. Reflecting his reading of the poem as a "rhetorical transcription of existing feminist analysis of police tactics in interviewing rape victims," Nelson contends that the "second-person voice is a way of distancing the poet from her subject" (p. 153). Further, he claims that the stanzaic pattern—six stanzas of five lines each—is "too regular and secure for an unsettling theme" (p. 151). Both positions reflect Nelson's failure to consider the poem in relation to Rich's overall process. In fact, the pronoun choice contributes to, rather than detracts from, the involvement of speaker and character, an involvement underscored by the stanzaic form. In her essay "When We Dead Awaken," Rich explicitly discusses her awareness of the significance of pronoun choice. Similarly, her comments on John Berryman and Richard Hugo, two poets who use the second person pronoun to explore divided consciousness, indicate an interest in such rhetorical strategies. In addition, Rich certainly understood when she wrote "Rape" that, as daughter, wife, and mother, she had repeatedly felt tempted to "lie her way home." Given this sense of context, it seems extremely unlikely that Rich intended the second person pronoun to establish superiority, rhetorical or experiential, over the victim.

The "you" in "Rape" can be much more coherently understood as a projection of the speaking voice. The absence of the first person pronoun reflects the extreme fragmentation of self inherent in the experience of rape rather than an attempted evasion. Torn between the violence of the rape and the cop's offer of a self-knowledge that would allow her to return home, the persona splits into fragments. In addition to communicating the actual emotional disorientation, Rich suggests that retreating to an earlier state of consciousness would destroy the part of the self capable of perceiving the inadequacy of the cop's approach. Far from expressing a "patronizing sense of class difference," Rich's rhetorical strategy acknowledges that her search for political insight cannot be divorced from her experience of personal disorientation. If any "detached" presence exists in the poem—there is certainly no "dispassionate" one—it is evidenced almost entirely in Rich's carefully controlled language which mediates between the parts of the fragmented self.

Nelson singles out the third stanza in "Rape" as evidence of the poem's rhetorical inadequacy, specifically dismissing the phrase "your mind whirling like crazy" as a trite cliche, a patronizing attempt to "use the language a less educated person might use" (p. 153). In addition to assuming that the victim is less educated than the poet—an assumption that unconsciously perpetuates misconceptions that poor women are the only rape victims and that educated women will in some way maintain their ability to articulate clearly after they have been raped—Nelson fails to hear the stanza's music, which draws much of its power precisely from the phrase he ridicules. The m and long i of "mind" establish a sound cluster associating the rape with male sexual violence ("time," "comes," "him," "maniac's," "sperm," "crime," "thighs"). Conversely, the cr and z of "crazy" associate the "crime" (a crucial transitional word belonging to both clusters) with the emotional confusion of the confession ("comes," "greasing," "guilty," "confess," "crime"). The second cluster emphasizes the dissociation of experience (the feeling of pollution, of greasiness) and interpretation (the necessity of confession) which makes the victim feel crazy. The internal r of "whirling"—repeated in "turn," "sperm," and "forced"—reiterates the alienation from experience which makes simplistic resolution impossible. Reinforced by the off-rhymes of the stanza's end words ("him-crime," "thighs-crime," "confess-forced"), these sound patterns suggest a much more profound engagement of Rich's controlling consciousness with the victim's situation than Nelson recognizes.

Similarly, the relatively strict stanzaic pattern indicates not distance from, but empathy with the victim. As the observing element of the fragmented consciousness perceives, the cop draws his greatest pleasure from the hysteria in the victim's voice, which validates his stereotype of women as unable to maintain control under pressure. Seen as a response to this pleasure, Rich's choice of a "mechanical" form can be seen as repudiation of the stereotype, an insistence that the victim's agony not be used against her. Ironically, Nelson—echoing a number of critics who accuse Rich of having lost her formal control when she began to express her anger—suggests that Rich herself loses control when she uses the phrase "mind whirling like crazy," an image which suggests to him "passionate swoon" (p. 153). This ostensibly objective critical comment offers clear evidence of the danger involved with even appearing to "give in" to emotional intensity.

As members of victimized groups have long recognized, failure to ccntrol rage reinforces stereotypes and carries with it the risk of total destruction. Rich, who in the years immediately before the composition of "Rape" had been associating with and teaching texts by Afro-American writers at CCNY, was certainly aware of the warnings against uncontrolled release of rage in works such as Richard Wright's *Native Son*, Countee Cullen's "Heritage," and numerous sonnets by her fellow faculty member Gwendolyn Brooks. Her own use of a tightly controlled prosody in "Rape" parallels the Afro-American use of tightly controlled metrical and stanzaic forms as organic expressions of the experience of anger. Etheridge Knight's 1968 poem "For Malcolm, a Year After" is a powerful expression of the "control-survival" strategy which makes the form of "Rape" profoundly appropriate to its unsettling theme:

> Adhere to foot and strict iamb;
> Control the burst of angry words
> Or they might boil and break the dam.
> Or they might boil and overflow
> And drench me, drown me, drive me mad.

The Wild Zone of Feminist Aesthetics

Vendler's and Nelson's attacks are most disturbing for what they suggest concerning the cultural ideology underlying much academic criticism. From a theoretical feminist perspective, it might seem desirable simply to ignore inappropriate criticism and concentrate on a fuller apprehension of Rich's process. Practically, however, academic discourse influences the actual impact of that process. In addition to conditioning the aesthetic responses of Rich's "educated" audience, academic mediators frequently discourage circulation of precisely those works which might communicate most directly with a nonacademic audience. Especially in light of Rich's increasing awareness of the actual "situation of the poet," it seems important to consider the full range of factors influencing the reception of her work. Rich has on several occasions demonstrated her personal concern with the power of critical discourse which affects the choice of poems for inclusion in anthologies, journalistic recognition of "important" writers, the shaping of canons and the contents of reading lists in courses intended for non-specialists.

The underlying dynamic of the clash between feminist aesthetics and academic criticism can be visualized in terms of the dominant group versus muted group dynamic described by Edwin and Shirley Ardener in their anthology *Perceiving Women* and adapted directly to the concerns of feminist literary critics by Elaine Showalter in her excellent essay "Feminist Criticism in the Wilderness." Showalter presents a model of the relationship between the experience and expression of dominant and "marginal" groups. The experience of the dominant group is represented by a solid circle and the experience of any group not recognized by the dominant group as a part of the dominant group by a dotted circle (p. 30):

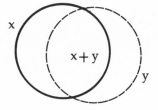

Showalter's gloss of the diagram emphasizes its relevance to women:

> Much of muted circle Y falls within the boundaries of dominant circle X; there is also a crescent of Y which is outside the dominant boundary and therefore. . ."wild." We can think of the wild zone of women's culture spatially, experientially, or metaphysically. Spatially it stands for an area which is literally no-man's land, a place forbidden to men, which corresponds to the zone in X which is off-limits to women. Experientially it stands for the aspects of the female life-style which are outside of and unlike those of men; again, there is a corresponding zone of male experience alien to women. But if we think of the wild zone metaphysically, or in terms of consciousness, it has no corresponding male space since all of male consciousness is within the circle of the dominant structure

and thus accessible to or structured by language. In this sense, the 'wild' is always imaginary; from the male point of view, it may simply be the projection of the unconscious. In terms of cultural anthropology, women know what the male crescent is like, even if they have never seen it, because it becomes the subject of legend (like the wilderness). But men do not know what is in the wild [p. 30].

This analysis closely parallels the observations concerning women's language advanced by Sheila Rowbotham, whom Rich has acknowledged as an important intellectual influence:

The underground language of people who have no power to define and determine themselves in the world develops its own density and precision. . . . But it restricts them by affirming their own dependence upon the words of the powerful. It reflects their inability to break out of the imposed reality through to a reality they can define and control for themselves. It keeps them locked against themselves. On the other hand the language of theory —removed language—only expresses a reality experienced by the oppressors. It speaks only for their world, from their point of view [p. 32].

Paralleling Foucault's genealogical perspective, these feminist models suggest several observations concerning the nature of academic discourse. First, academic positions which do not take into account the unique aspects of women's experience inevitably generate theories, propagated by legend and encoded in the dominant language, which "justify" continuing social oppression. This in turn discourages or precludes women from expressing experiences associated with the wild zone. Second, because they identify "reality" with the content of their own circle, academic critics frequently present their legends and theories as "universal" or "objective" and dismiss expressions of the wild zone as "limited," "subjective," or "incomplete." Third, this discourages even dominant group members from exploring the wild, external or internal. By repressing experiences which they associate with the wild zone, dominant groups close their theoretical systems to new energy, condemning both dominant and muted groups to simplistic apprehensions of reality. Inevitably, any academic theory generated primarily in response to the experience of those with access to institutional power reduces wild zone experiences to superficially comforting stereotypes, dependent functions of dominant group needs. Unless it demonstrates a willingness to repudiate the hegemony of dominant group experiences, academic criticism will simply perpetuate the kinds of oppressive discourse imaged in the cop at his typewriter in "Rape." In this situation, a potentially explosive tension between academic and feminist criticism seems inevitable.

"RAPE" IN CONTEXT

Seen in relation to this model, Nelson's and Vendler's readings of "Rape" contribute to the disturbing denial of women's wild zone experiences. While Vendler grudgingly grants the poem a "truth of feeling," she denies it all "truth of art" and refuses even to consider its "truth of experience," dismissing its content—the simplified content visible from the dominant group perspective—as "fictitious" (Vendler, 1980, p. 243). In light of the complex critical intelligence she demonstrates when discussing the work Rich wrote from positions closer to the dominant group circle, Vendler would probably not deny that police coercion of rape victims actually occurs or that women are made to feel guilty when forced to express their wild zone experiences in the language of the bureaucracy. It seems more likely that she considers recognition of the actual complexity of dominant group experience—which includes kindly policemen and supportive fathers and brothers—an essential part of any valid critique of patriarchal violence. Such insistence that muted group members acknowledge the complexity of the dominant group, however, effectively ignores the difficulty of any articulation at all. At some stages of some processes, complexity, as Vendler implicitly defines it, may be the single most effective piece of machinery enforcing silence. At any rate, Vendler clearly believes aesthetic statements should express a complex sensibility and finds little of value in "over-simplified" statements of truth designed to encourage changes in, rather than contemplation of, the context. Ultimately, for Vendler, there can be no poetic truth that does not acknowledge the complexity—as the term is understood in academic discourse—of the moment of consciousness.

Concluding her discussion of *Diving Into the Wreck* with the "hope that the curve into more complex expression visible in [Rich's] earlier books will recur" (Vendler, 1980, p. 262), Vendler invites Rich to return home to the safety of a discourse which praises her attempts to discover a new language, so long as that language can be incorporated into its own. From Rich's feminist perspective, of course, such an invitation could be accepted only in a cultural context purged of patriarchal violence, whether physical or psychological. Any woman accepting the terms of patriarchal discourse, in precinct station or scholarly journal, risks internalizing the policeman's "knowledge" of her imagination, her secret desires. Entering a wild zone rarely acknowledged in academic discourse, "Rape" assumes importance not as an aesthetic artifact but as an act toward a world in which women will no longer be forced to deny the integrity which provides the only acceptable base for the type of complex expression Vendler desires.

Nelson's assertion that "the argument [of "Rape"] is not new, nor was it new in 1972 when the poem was written" (p. 152) reflects an aspect of academic discourse substantially more disturbing than Vendler's insistence on a particular mode of complexity. Where Vendler prefers that wild-zone experiences be expressed in the dominant language, Nelson implies that once such experiences have been articulated (again, in the dominant language), the process has come to an end. Nelson's belief that there was nothing new about Rich's discussion of rape seems more a mark of his unwillingness to acknowledge the reality of the problem than an accurate observation concerning the poem's original, or for that matter, contemporary audience. Although the New York Radical Feminist Conference on Rape had taken place in 1971, rape emerged as a highly visible public issue only with the publication of Susan Brownmiller's *Against Our Will: Men, Women, and Rape* in 1975. Even then her work, like Rich's poem, was frequently dismissed as a shrill attack on men. [Certainly the "feminist analysis" of police complicity with and indifference toward crimes of sexual violence was not then and is not now generally known or accepted. Passing over the fact that sexual violence continues to exist as a major fact of life for women, many of whom remain unaware of any academic discourse concerning the institutional structures conditioning their experience, Nelson predicates his analysis on the premise that poetry is of value primarily inasmuch as it provides new insights for a cultural elite. His personal familiarity with the feminist analysis of rape provides sufficient grounds in his view for assuming the "objective" position that allows him to refer to the figure of the policeman as "mildly comic" (p. 151). Having "taken down" the "worst moments" of women and "filed them" in his awareness, Nelson is ready to move on to new issues.

From Rich's feminist perspective, such perspectives remain academic in every sense of the word so long as they consider issues without reference to the actual lives of individuals struggling with the multiple forms of patriarchal violence. Seen in relation to Rich's overall process, the "dispassionate" academic knowledge that sees no need for engagement with actuality is not really *known*. Any complexity or insight reflecting only the experience of the dominant group is at best incomplete. Almost inevitably simplistic, such complexity at worst supports the machinery that encourages rape and consigns its victims to the silence of the wild zone. However simplistic she may appear from an academic perspective, Rich seeks an alternative complexity. The remainder of this study explores the nature of the complex process which involves her understanding of the dominant patriarchal culture, her woman-centered exploration of the wild zone, and her attempt to create a radical poetic voice capable of transforming silence into conversation.

References

Ardener, Shirley
1975. (editor) *Perceiving Women*. London: J. M. Dent.
Ashbery, John
1966. "Tradition and Talent," *New York Herald Tribune Book Week* Sept. 4, p. 2. Rpt. in Cooper, pp. 217-18.
Atwood, Margaret
1973. "Review of *Diving Into the Wreck*," *New York Times Book Review* Dec. 30, pp. 1-2. Rpt. in Cooper, pp. 238-41.
Auden, W. H.
1951. "Foreword" in *A Change of World* by Adrienne Rich. New Haven: Yale Univ. Pr., pp. 7-11. Rpt. in Cooper, pp. 209-11; Gelpi, pp. 125-27.
Booth, Philip
1963. "Rethinking the World," *Christian Science Monitor* Jan. 3, p. 15. Rpt. in Cooper, pp. 215-16.
Boyers, Robert
1973. "On Adrienne Rich: Intelligence and Will," *Salmagundi* Spring-Summer, pp. 132-48. Rpt. in Gelpi, pp. 148-160.
Brownmiller, Susan
1975. *Against Our Will: Men, Women, and Rape*. New York: Simon and Schuster.
Cooper, Jane Roberta
1984. (editor) *Reading Adrienne Rich*. Ann Arbor: Univ. of Michigan Pr.
Donoghue, Denis
1970. "Oasis Poetry," *New York Review of Books* May 7, pp. 35-38. Rpt. in Cooper, pp. 219-20.
Donovan, Josephine
1985. *Feminist Theory: The Intellectual Traditions of American Feminism*. New York: Ungar.

Eisenstein, Hester
1983. *Contemporary Feminist Thought*. Boston: G. K. Hall.
Foucault, Michel
1980. *Power/Knowledge: Selected Interviews and Other Writings, 1972-1977*, ed. and trans. Colin Gordon. New York: Pantheon.
Gelpi, Albert
1973. "Adrienne Rich: The Poetics of Change," in *American Poetry Since 1960* ed. Robert Shaw. Cheadle, Cheshire: Carcanet Pr., pp. 123-43. Rpt. in Gelpi, pp. 130-48.
Gelpi, Barbara Charlesworth, and Albert Gelpi
1975. (editors) *Adrienne Rich's Poetry*. New York: Norton.
Hall, Donald
1956. "A Diet of Dissatisfaction," *Poetry* Feb., pp. 299-302. Rpt. in Cooper, pp. 212-14.
Jarrell, Randall
1956. "New Books in Review," *Yale Review* Sept., pp. 100-03. Rpt. in Gelpi, pp. 127-29.
Juhasz, Suzanne
1976. *Naked and Fiery Forms: Modern American Poetry by Women*. New York: Harper and Row.
Kalstone, David
1971. Review of *The Will to Change*, *New York Times Book Review* May 21, pp. 31-32. Rpt. in Cooper, 221-25.
Knight, Etheridge
1968. *Poems from Prison*. Detroit: Broadside, p. 27.
Lerner, Gerda
1986. *The Creation of Patriarchy*. New York: Oxford Univ. Pr.
Lowell, Robert
1966. "Modesty without Mumbling," *New York Times Book Review* July 17, p. 5.
Martin, Wendy
1975. "From Patriarchy to the Female Principle: A Chronological Reading of Adrienne Rich's Poems." In Gelpi, pp. 175-89.
1979. "Adrienne Rich." In *American Writers: A Collection of Literary Biographies*, supplement I, part 2, ed. Leonard Unger. New York: Scribner, pp. 550-78.
1984. *An American Triptych: Anne Bradstreet, Emily Dickinson, Adrienne Rich*. Chapel Hill: Univ. of North Carolina Pr.
Morgan, Robin
1975. "Adrienne Rich and Robin Morgan Talk about Poetry and Women's Culture," in *New Women's Survival Sourcebook* ed. Kirsten Grimstad and Susan Rennie. New York: Knopf, pp. 106-11.

Nelson, Cary
1981. *Our Last First Poets: Vision and History in Contemporary American Poetry.* Urbana: Univ. of Illinois Pr.
Newman, Anne
1980. "Adrienne Rich." In *Dictionary of Literary Biography: American Poets since World War II*, part 2, ed. Donald J. Greiner. Detroit: Bruccoli Clark, pp. 184-96.
Ostriker, Alicia
1979. "Her Cargo: Adrienne Rich and the *Common Language*," *American Poetry Review* July/Aug., pp. 6-10. Rpt. in her *Writing Like a Woman* (1983). Ann Arbor: Univ. of Michigan Pr., pp. 102-25.
Pope, Deborah
1984. *A Separate Vision: Isolation in Contemporary Women's Poetry.* Baton Rouge: Louisiana State Univ. Pr.
Reiss, Timothy J.
1982. *The Discourse of Modernism.* Ithaca: Cornell Univ. Press.
Rich, Adrienne
1969. "Living with Henry: Review of *His Toy, His Dream, His Rest* by John Berryman," *Harvard Advocate* Spring, pp. 10-11.
1972. "When We Dead Awaken: Writing as Re-Vision," *College English* Oct., pp. 18-30. Rpt. in her *On Lies, Secrets, and Silence* (1979), pp. 33-49. Rpt. in Gelpi, pp. 90-98.
1975. *Poems: Selected and New, 1950-1974.* New York: Norton.
1976. *Of Woman Born: Motherhood as Experience and Institution.* New York: Norton.
1977. *Women and Honor: Some Notes on Lying.* Pittsburgh: Motheroot Publications. Rpt. in her *On Lies, Secrets, and Silence* (1979), pp. 185-94.
1979. *On Lies, Secrets, and Silence: Selected Prose 1966-1978.* New York: Norton.
1980. "Compulsory Heterosexuality and Lesbian Existence," *Signs* Summer, pp. 631-60. Rpt. in her *Blood, Bread, and Poetry*, pp. 23-75.
1982. "Split at the Root," in *Nice Jewish Girls: A Lesbian Anthology*, ed. Evelyn Torton Beck. Watertown, Mass.: Persephone Pr. pp. 67-84. Rpt. in her *Blood, Bread, and Poetry*, pp. 100-23.
1983. "Blood, Bread, and Poetry: The Location of the Poet," *Massachusetts Review* Autumn, pp. 521-40. Rpt. in her *Blood, Bread, and Poetry*, pp. 167-87.
1986. *Blood, Bread, and Poetry: Selected Prose 1979-1985.* New York: Norton.
Rigney, Barbara Hill
1982. *Lilith's Daughters: Women and Religion in Contemporary Fiction.* Madison: Univ. of Wisconsin Pr.

Romanow, Peter
1982. "Adrienne Rich," in *Critical Survey of Poetry: English Language Series* ed. Frank N. Magill. Englewood Cliffs, N. J.: Salem Pr., pp. 2363-2371.
Rowbotham, Sheila
1973. *Woman's Consciousness, Man's World*. New York: Penguin.
Showalter, Elaine
1981. "Feminist Criticism in the Wilderness," *Critical Inquiry* Winter. Rpt. in *The New Feminist Criticism* ed. Showalter. New York: Pantheon, pp. 243-70.
Smith, Barbara
1977. *Toward a Black Feminist Criticism*. Trumansburg, N. Y.: Crossing Pr.
Spender, Dale
1983. *Women of Ideas and What Men Have Done to Them: From Aphra Behn to Adrienne Rich*. Boston: Ark.
Tonks, Rosemary
1973. "Cutting the Marble," *New York Review of Books* Oct. 4, pp. 8-10. Rpt. in Cooper, pp. 232-37.
Van Duyn, Mona
1970. "Seven Women," *Poetry* March, pp. 430-39.
Vendler, Helen
1973. "Ghostlier Demarcations, Keener Sounds," *Parnassus* Fall-Winter, pp. 5-10, 15-16, 18-24. Rpt. in her *Part of Nature, Part of Us* (1980). Cambridge, Mass.: Harvard Univ. Pr., pp. 237-62.

CHAPTER 2

Patriarchy and Solipsism:
Repression, Rebellion, Re-vision

No aspect of Adrienne Rich's thought is more problematic than her response to patriarchy. An important concern in her poetry even before she began using the term in the late 1960s, patriarchy paradoxically recedes as a central theme almost simultaneously with the emergence of the critical image of Rich as an obsessive man-hater. As her understanding of patriarchy clarified, Rich in fact came to feel that concentrating on patriarchy—even to repudiate it—indirectly reinforced patriarchal power. As a result, she gradually shifted her focus to the extended (though not "larger" or "more important") struggle against what I shall term _cultural solipsism_. Consistent with patriarchy but with additional manifestations, cultural solipsism is the tendency to treat only the self or a group, sharing specific characteristics with the self (gender, race, religion, class, nationality, etc.), as real and to establish fixed roles for those defined as "other." Consigning the expression of these others to the "wild zone," the cultural solipsist, unable to acknowledge those aspects of the self associated with the other, inevitably subverts his/her relationship to community, nature, and the unconscious mind. Rather than pulpiteering on patriarchy as such, therefore, Rich analyzes its limitations in order to develop alternatives to the cultural solipsism which supports the patriarchal system and at times infiltrates her own thought.

Patriarchal Attacks on Rich

Despite this thematic complexity, many critics implicitly identify Rich with the very attitudes she identifies and rejects. Presenting her as an irrational feminist railing against all things male, hostile critics in effect accuse Rich of an inverted form of cultural solipsism. Reiterating the classic patriarchal stereotype of the hysterical woman incapable of dealing with complex public issues, they redefine her alternative vision

as a dependent function in a patriarchal equation. This reductive attitude, presented in intentionally simplified form, assumes classic shape
in parodies of Rich by Robert Peters and David R. Slavitt. Peters,
whose two *Great American Poetry Bake-off* volumes frequently clarify
serious issues through the use of satire, reduces Rich (renamed
Adrienne Poor) to a stereotypical feminist who refuses to answer a
question about poetry and baseball because "so far as I can tell a male
asks it" (p. 109). More intricate and amusing, but ultimately similar in
its satiric point, Slavitt's "The Griefs of Women" presents Rich as a poet
who subordinates all concerns to her hatred of men. Following a series
of subdued domestic and natural images reminiscent of many Rich
poems, the parody broadly concludes: "Men are bums./ We're really
better than they are" (p. 388). Reflecting a similar failure to apprehend
the complexity of Rich's attitude toward patriarchy, Arthur Oberg
assumes that, because she repudiates traditional patterns of
heterosexual love, Rich has "cease[d] to feel the need to write the word
or concept 'love' at all" (p. 177). Each of these attacks simplifies or
simply ignores important elements of Rich's position. Many of her
most direct confrontations with patriarchy are cast precisely in the
form of dialogs with men ("Trying to Talk with a Man," section fourteen of "From an Old House in America"); she is acutely aware that
men and women share numerous psychic and emotional problems
("For L.G.: Unseen for Twenty Years," "Sources"). The fact that
"Twenty-One Love Poems" was published two years prior to Oberg's
commentary renders his claim that Rich has no interest in love little
more than an absurdity.

Not all of the patriarchal dismissals of Rich are so direct or simplistic
in their approach. Many critics simply omit all mention of her work in
books ostensibly concerned with the overall contours of contemporary
American poetry (Pinsky, Lieberman) or discuss only her early poems
(van Hallberg). Even Charles Altieri, who has become one of Rich's
most insightful academic defenders, ignored her in his first book on
contemporary poetry, *Enlarging the Temple*. The effect of such silence,
especially when viewed in a large number of studies (individual critics
of course may have legitimate justifications for the omission), is to suggest that Rich's refusal to endorse the terms of patriarchal discourse
renders her work unworthy of "serious" attention. Gradually, however, some critics, even while advancing the stereotyped image of Rich
and refusing to engage her work directly, have begun to feel some
uneasiness with the implications of their response. Charles Molesworth, who does not consider her in the main argument of *A Fiery
Embrace*, discusses the implications of his decision in his "Reflections in
Place of a Conclusion." Focusing on "August," one of Rich's most

direct engagements with patriarchal solipsism, Molesworth observes: "The male critic could take refuge behind the observation that the poem isn't aesthetically integrated, that what begins as some sort of natural description turns into an ideological argument; that the poem doesn't play fair, not with the 'other side of the story' or with its own premises" (p. 199). Although he understands the limitations of these criteria and is willing to grant the poem a certain power, Molesworth ultimately perpetuates the patriarchal simplification of Rich when he calls the poem's conclusion "a straightforward statement of a feminist claim, namely, that the paternalism European history and culture are founded on is the result of a nightmarishly self-destructive murderousness on the part of the male half of the species" (p. 200). Molesworth's defensive assumption that Rich feels a generalized hatred of men overlooks the fact that the line on which he bases his reading—"all the fathers are crying: *My son is mine!*"—is explicitly presented as the poet's nightmare, not as historical reality.

Nevertheless, Molesworth recognizes the aesthetic challenge posed by Rich, Amiri Baraka, and Gary Snyder:

> the question of form, even in esoteric poems like the *Cantos* and *The Waste Land*, was eventually answered, answered in part by a community of readers, not extensive in numbers perhaps, but extensive in time, as the commentary eventually grew toward clarification. But what of these two poems by Rich and Snyder, and other quite different poems, like those of Imamu Baraka that espouse racist hatred and vengeance? Such poems have a communal audience and may be widely read, but I think they are seldom *discussed*. Snyder, Rich, and Baraka seldom receive thoughtful reviews (I am speaking of the latest work of these poets), and the easy explanation for this is that reviewers know such poetry cannot be responded to in the usual critical terms without the reviewer being reduced to irrelevancy. The glib response is that such poets are merely "preaching to the converted." But once poetry no longer appeals to a "higher court" or pure aesthetic standards, then won't it necessarily have to rely for its truth—or its truths—on the pressing issues of the day, with all the attendant dangers of ideological confusion, emotional overcompensation, and historical guilt? [pp. 200-01]

There is much of value in Molesworth's observations and he carefully avoids "glib responses" and "easy explanations." The question of voice, as I will argue in chapter 4, is in fact central to an assessment of Rich's work; the critical commentary on her work does proceed on different premises than that on Eliot or Pound. It seems unlikely that Moles-

worth would simply endorse a pronouncement such as that issued by
James Atlas, who believes that Rich's decision "to address a particular
constituency. . . means sacrificing larger literary claims" (p. 10). Still,
Molesworth perpetuates several reductive assumptions. Claiming to
find a readily apparent ideological "message," he assumes that Rich has
sacrificed the type of "literary claim" based on "pure aesthetic standards." As Rich and feminist theoreticians such as Lucie Iragury have
demonstrated, however, these "pure" standards appear distinctly
tainted when subjected to external (not necessarily or desirably objective) consideration. The discourse which defines and supports these
standards can be seen as an expression of a patriarchal ideology as
firmly grounded in the pressing issues of the day as the supposedly
transitory feminist "truths."

More disturbing than his unintentional invocation of the hysterical
feminist stereotype, however, is Molesworth's orientation toward the
developing discourse on Rich's poetry. Although he understands that
clarification of the great modernist poems proceeded slowly, he implies
that the failure of the "communal feminist response" to immediately
clarify Rich's aesthetic proves that she works in the "service of an ideology" in some way incompatible with "serious discussion" (pp. 200-01).
Indirectly justifying critical silence, this places the burden of generating
serious discussion—defined in relation to the "pure aesthetic standards" of patriarchy—entirely on the feminist community. Despite his
awareness of the crucial questions, Molesworth neither confronts the
implications of Rich's relationship with that community nor pursues
the serious discussion he finds lacking. Of course, he is under no obligation to initiate this discussion. Nonetheless, especially when juxtaposed with his reading of "August," the decision underlines the
tendency of even highly aware critics to substitute reductive assumptions concerning feminist ideology for actual engagement with Rich's
process. This lack of engagement can be seen with particular clarity in
Molesworth's ignorance of (or at least failure to discuss) the actual
feminist response to Rich. All too often such silence reflects the critic's
unfounded belief in a monolithic feminist orthodoxy.

In a discussion of "The Comparable Worth Muddle," for example,
Bruce Majors labels Rich a "socialist" and suggests that she "is coming
dangerously close to posing the heretical question of whether feminist
goals would not best be attained by private and voluntary means (and
suggesting the even more heretical notion that perhaps men's and
women's different natures are responsible for their different levels and
kinds of success in the economic sphere" (p. 53). Given the widespread
awareness of coercive government as a patriarchal institution and
Rich's continuing exploration of gender-based differences, Majors'

statement is little more than a cartoon version of feminism. Far from uncritically accepting Rich's positions, feminist critics have in fact begun exactly the kind of rigorous discussion Molesworth sees as a crucial part of the aesthetic process. The publication in the feminist journal *Signs* of a complex debate concerning Rich's attack on patriarchy in "Compulsory Heterosexuality and Lesbian Existence" typifies a developing, and frequently skeptical, discourse that I shall discuss in Chapter 3 (Ferguson, Zita, Addelson).

Feminist Critiques of Patriarchy

Critical fixation on patriarchy, however reductive, does direct attention to an important *part* of Rich's work. Ironically, the fixation in itself provides evidence for one of her major points concerning patriarchal consciousness. As Wendy Martin comments: "Rich's poetry attacks patriarchal consciousness for narrowing perception to the part rather than the whole" (p. 231). Noting that this narrowing supports "dominance at the expense of the multiplicity of experience," Martin catalogs its impact in far-reaching terms: "By substituting abstraction for actual experience, it is possible to pollute the earth because the connection between human existence and other forms of life is lost. Rape is condoned or tolerated because empathy for the victims is reduced or nonexistent. War is perceived in terms of victory or loss and not in terms of human devastation and suffering or the loss of precious resources" (p. 231). Anticipating defensive responses, Martin concludes that "Rich rejects not men, but destructive masculinity," and places the critique of patriarchy in the context of Rich's movement toward an alternative vision. Nonetheless, such "ideological" catalogs contribute to the polarization of critical discourse and reinforce the defensiveness implicit in the patriarchal emphasis on Rich as "man-hater." The prevalence of assertions concerning Rich's ideological position in both attacks on and defenses of her work clearly testifies to the importance of examining her critique of "destructive masculinity" in detail. As I shall argue below, this critique challenges all fixations of consciousness, all modes of thought and ideology which circumscribe process. Rich does not simply substitute structurally identical counterfixations for patriarchal solipsism; rather, she encourages a thorough re-vision of the relationship between self and other on both personal and political levels.

Before she arrived at even the tentative ideological positions of the mid-1970s, Rich was forced to overcome both internal and external resistance. Feminist theologian Mary Daly, whose work Rich enthusiastically endorses, identifies the sources of such resistance in four basic psychological/rhetorical mechanisms used to deny or redirect individual awareness of patriarchal oppression. In *Beyond God the Father*, Daly observes that a given perception may be countered with trivialization ("the problem isn't important"); particularization ("the problem results from special circumstances and has no general significance"); spiritualization ("the problem is unimportant in relation to transcendent values"); or universalization ("the problem is one faced by all humans in some form") (p. 5). Throughout the 1960s, Rich became increasingly aware of the impact of such mechanisms on her own process. Recognizing an underlying consistency behind an array of seemingly diverse problems, she arrived, in *Of Woman Born* (1976), at a provisional definition of patriarchy as "a familial-social, ideological, political system in which men—by force, direct pressure, or through ritual, tradition, law, and language, customs, etiquette, education, and the division of labor, determine what part women shall or shall not play, and in which the female is everywhere subsumed under the male. It does not necessarily imply that no woman has power, or that all women in a certain culture may not have certain powers" (p. 57).

Providing a convenient point of reference, this definition (which remains subject to continuing revision) must be understood in relation to Rich's developing concern with its philosophical underpinnings and literary implications. Building on the work of feminist thinkers (Daly, Susan Griffin) and paralleling that of "New Age" analysts (Ken Wilbur, Fritjof Capra), Rich portrays patriarchy as the institutional concomitant of the Newtonian-Cartesian world view. Sometimes labeled the "rational/analytic" world view (Reiss), this complex of ideas—which I shall refer to as the "Cartesian paradigm"—views physical phenomena in terms of atomistic entities, and human experience in terms of subjective consciousness. Like many contemporary critics of the Cartesian paradigm, Rich argues that it implies and creates indifference toward or exploitation of nature, women, and the unconscious or emotional aspects of experience.

At least as early as *Necessities of Life*, Rich recognized the impact of this paradigm on the development of the American literary-cultural tradition. Her analysis parallels those of numerous literary critics who have identified a constituting immaturity in American male behavior and expression, an immaturity grounded in a fear of blacks, women, nature, and/or the unconscious (Lawrence, Fiedler, Kolodny). Rich's critique of cultural solipsism clearly implies that such fears are basic to patriarchy and reinforce the Cartesian tendency toward abstraction and reductionism.

"STORM WARNINGS"

The remainder of this chapter will focus on several crucial elements in Rich's confrontation with cultural solipsism, primarily but not exclusively in its patriarchal manifestations. In essence, Rich focuses on the interrelated struggles to reach a wider understanding of "experience" than that offered by the Cartesian paradigm; to understand the ways in which her experience has been conditioned by patriarchal forces; and to counteract its impact, particularly inasmuch as it predisposes her to treat others in a solipsistic manner. In exploring Rich's treatment of these issues in her poetry, I shall concentrate on her growing awareness of the need for immersion in experience ("Storm Warnings," "The Wave," "The Demon Lover"); the development of a unified awareness of the nature of patriarchy out of the fragmented perceptions montaged in the germinal poem "Snapshots of a Daughter-in-Law"; and her concern with the implications of this more integrated perspective ("The Burning of Paper Instead of Children," "From an Old House in America").

Between "Storm Warnings" (c. 1950) and "The Wave" (1973), Rich's basic orientation toward experience underwent a profound change. The initial poem in *A Change of World*, "Storm Warnings" advocates self-protective withdrawal, reflecting an uneasy acceptance of the Cartesian paradigm. Aware of the patriarchal forces shaping the earlier poem, "The Wave" transforms a similar set of images into a distinctly post-Cartesian meditation on immersion and relationship. Alienated from her surroundings and without human contact, the persona of "Storm Warnings" exemplifies the situation of the Cartesian "subject." Although she senses the futility of her stance, she can conceive of no alternative. Repressing the intuitive knowledge she senses to surpass that of the measuring instruments, the persona relies on rational thought but cannot overcome her feeling of helplessness before both "Weather abroad/ And weather in the heart." Despite her attempt (which James Breslin sees as analogous to Rich's defensive "yearning for the well-made autotelic poem") to seal out the storm, the persona recognizes that she will be unable to protect herself with "shattered fragments of an instrument." Still, unable to conceive an alternative, she attempts to attain "mastery of elements" through subjective reinterpretation of her circumstances. Acknowledging that this attempt entails both isolation and fragmentation, she sees no alternative to withdrawal: "We can only close the shutters." Nonetheless, Rich seems aware that her survival depends on the continuing relationship with the outside world, which she attempts to sever. Although "the

whine of weather through the unsealed aperture" disturbs the persona's subjective retreat, it also provides the air necessary to keep her
candle burning in the darkened room.

Rich's persona senses the insufficiency of the "objective" scientific
truth of the Newtonian "clocks and weatherglasses." She does not,
however, recognize that her conception of protective "subjectivity"
remains grounded in the dichotomies and atomism which characterize
both the Cartesian and the Newtonian perspectives. Exemplifying
Rich's early ambivalence, "Storm Warnings" suggests no alternative to
the persona's defensive attempt at "foreseeing and averting change,"
even as it intimates the situation cannot continue indefinitely.

"THE WAVE"

An expression of Rich's growing interest in post-Cartesian thought,
"The Wave" celebrates the collapse of the earlier withdrawal:

And I think of those lives we tried to live
in our globed helmets, self-enclosed
bodies self-illumined gliding
safe from turbulence
and how, miraculously, we failed

These lines bring to a climax a crucial stage in Rich's development:
her repudiation of the dangerous "mind that isolates itself from human
relationships and [the] physical world" (Slowik, p. 145). In addition to
this basic shift in attitude, "The Wave" rejects numerous specific motifs
from "Storm Warnings": the emphasis on thought (the globed helmet);
the solipsism (self-enclosure, self-illumination, closed shutters); above
all, the desire for a static safety based on the denial of relationship with
the turbulent troubled regions. Re-envisioning this desire as a shared
impulse of all those isolated in Cartesian subjectivity, Rich creates a
paradoxically triumphant "we." This new "we" contrasts sharply with
the "we" of "Storm Warnings," which underscores the isolated persona's internal fragmentation. From its opening lines, "The Wave"
images the deepest ground of being in terms of relationship. In Rich's
feminist (perhaps Heisenbergian) poetic universe, "the black spaces,"
"the whitest churn," and "the blankness underlying" interact in both
formation and perception of the wave. This emotional/intellectual
acceptance of relationship frees the persona to immerse herself in the
waves of experience. No longer passive and withdrawn, she connects
(laces) and cures (lances) the diseased fragments of her former sensi-

bility. Combining Rich's post-Cartesian and anti-patriarchal positions —the title alludes to Virginia Woolf's novel *The Waves*—the new consciousness links images traditionally viewed as either masculine ("the blue knife of radiant consciousness") or feminine ("the deepest grotto"). Imagistically and thematically, this synthesis, which respects the integrity of each perception, revolves around the connecting image of "vision": "the blue knife of radiant consciousness/ bent by the waves of vision as it pierces/ to the deepest grotto." By bending the knife, the wave modifies, without destroying, the qualities (phallic and transcendent) which in another context would identify it as an instrument of destructive masculinity. At once external (the waves in the field of vision, the medium) and internal (the waves of consciousness, the act of observation), the wave illustrates the Heisenbergian principle that the act of perception inevitably alters the phenomenon perceived. To isolate either the internal or the external aspect—to define the field as "objective" and the vision as "subjective" for example—would seriously distort their significance. This seems a particularly important point since even sensitive critics occasionally underestimate the extent of Rich's challenge to patriarchal thought (and her own previous positions). Deborah Pope, for example, argues that "Rich will eventually pursue this distinction between ways of knowing as a basic differentiation between masculine and feminine forms of perception, roughly dividing between objective and subjective sensibilities" (p. 132). "The Waves," however, indicates that on a more profound level, Rich traces the specious masculine concept of objectivity to an equally specious concept of subjectivity.

"THE DEMON LOVER"

The process leading to the immersion signaled by the title of *Diving Into the Wreck* involved periodic attacks of dis-ease and fragmentation. One of Rich's strongest transitional poems, "The Demon Lover" (1966), describes the "seasickness" experienced by a woman redefining her relationship to the patriarchal system. Echoing Byron, Poe, and countless other romantic writers, the title introduces a disorienting and multivalent ambiguity which challenges the persona's basic mode of thought. Does the title refer to the persona or to another figure? Is the other figure male (the coexistent friend of stanza seven) or female (the daughter/muse of stanza two)? Is the persona's desire to leave the patriarchy demonic? Her desire to remain within it?

While any specific reading of the ambiguity is to some degree arbitrary, its emotional impact on the persona as she experiences her internal and external contradictions is unquestionable. Beginning with "Fatigue, regrets," she experiences an overpowering sense of weariness as she remembers old stories and dreams of war: both images of the social forces conditioning her experience. Doubtful that either language or touch truly matters, the persona feels the urge to withdraw into an inanimate silence reminiscent of that in "Storm Warnings": "Things take us hard, no questions." The suggestion of rape imagery, along with the eight questions posed in the poem, however, suggests Rich's dissatisfaction with the withdrawal strategy. Similarly, immediately after presenting a Cartesian vision in which the persona's "heart utters its great beats/ in solitude," she imagines a "new era" which leads to the first explicitly demonic image: a young girl replaces the weary woman who had imagined the new era simply as an extension of her familiar isolation.

The remainder of the poem explores the energies released by the appearance of this ambiguous figure. Sexual tensions radiate in the third stanza, which concerns the persona's failure to touch or speak with an unidentified (by sex or name) companion during the Northeastern blackout, a momentary abatement of technological/patriarchal power. In the eighth stanza, while "hands and minds/ erotically waver," the persona questions the "dear child" concerning the importance of sex. Seen in relation to Rich's later process, the erotic energy of the poem seems implicitly lesbian. When the persona says "I'd like to be gay," it is difficult not to read the phrase as a veiled assertion of Rich's repressed sexual orientation. Nonetheless, of the other poems in *Leaflets*, only "Three Women" indicates any explicit interest in lesbianism; it too can be read without strain as a meditation on mythological rather than personal concerns.

As a preliminary venture into the waters in which Rich would later immerse herself, "The Demon Lover" can only hint at the sexual implications of the "seasick way/ this almost/ never touching." The words of the "gay song" remain unspoken by either the persona or the demonic young girl: "How could a gay song go?/ Why that's your secret, and it shall be mine." The erotic wavering of the hands intimates a profoundly disturbing truth—"*In triste veritas?*"—but breaks off suddenly, leaving the persona to her patriarchal demons. Believing that "Only where there is language is there world," she returns to the world where voices "press" her down, where language, despite its necessity, seems futile. Given this futility, which parallels that in "Storm Warnings," she can only lie nervelessly and unquestioningly endure a sequence of metaphorical rapes; she is "wrestled . . . with language," "take[n] hard" by "things."

Her return to the patriarchal context, however, is not entirely a withdrawal from experience. Even as she "falters," accepting her isolation, the persona nurtures the image of the demon lover, the part of herself where sex and language remain vital: "your tongue knows what it knows." She commits herself to articulating the secret knowledge she shares with the apparition: "I want your secrets—I *will* have them out." Yet even this determination underscores the poem's ambiguity. Given the inadequacy of the "necessary" language, the persona's desire to articulate the secrets, especially when imaged in terms of domination (the italicized word *will* suggests a traditional patriarchal attitude), recasts her as rapist rather than victim. Confronted with the presence of this patriarchal tendency in her emerging lesbian sensibility, the persona can neither actively advance nor passively withdraw. The splits between self and other, language and experience, public persona and repressed desire, all reflect the persona's Cartesian sensibility. Even though she attempts to resist her weariness by increasing her understanding of her experience, her mode of thought enforces an isolated subjectivity. The final image tentatively resolves the contradiction in an image of "passive advance." Recognizing the inevitability of immersion, the persona as yet feels little actual relationship to the post-Cartesian world of "The Wave": "Seasick, I drop into the sea."

"SNAPSHOTS OF A DAUGHTER-IN-LAW":
THE REALITY OF ALIENATION

Rich's passage from withdrawal to immersion can be traced back to "Snapshots of a Daughter-in-Law," which more than any other early poem suggests an etiology of the seasickness. Although Rich has criticized the poem for relying too much on allusion and for evading the first person pronoun, it nonetheless seems certain to stand as a major work. Widely recognized as her "transitional" or "breakthrough" poem (Pope, Ostriker), "Snapshots of a Daughter-in-Law" introduces her central themes regarding patriarchy: the emptiness of women's experience in patriarchally defined roles; the role of repression in enforcing patriarchal values; the relationship between this repression and oppressive institutions relying directly or indirectly on force, particularly the threat of rape; and the need for an active response to both repression and oppression based on a post-Cartesian sense of interrelationship. Structured to recall the "fragments and rough drafts" it associates with women's creativity in a hostile context, "Snapshots of a Daughter-in-Law" provides a touchstone for analyzing the development of these themes into more integrated forms over the course of Rich's career. As she overcomes the fragmentation, her focus shifts from the repressed "victim" to the assertive rebel. Increasingly, Rich addresses problems that seemed too threatening to consider as long as she maintained her position within the patriarchal system: the impact of patriarchy on men, the solipsistic elements of feminist thought, and the extreme difficulty of articulating an alternative vision in a patriarchal language.

Rich portrays the simple but painfully difficult admission of the emptiness of traditional roles as the necessary precondition for feminist processes. "Snapshots of a Daughter-in-Law" opens with the image of an aging Southern belle, her mind "moldering like wedding-cake,/ heavy with useless experience, rich/ with suspicion, rumor, fantasy." The line break on "rich" certainly identifies the belle with the Maryland-born poet, but it also intimates an imaginative potential denied by the phallic "knife-edge/ of mere fact." Encouraging the belle to dismiss her experience as illusion, the patriarchy actively discourages artistic transformation. The alienation from experience originates in the collapse of romantic ideals—the moldering wedding cake—and leads inexorably to the withdrawal pictured in "Storm Warnings." Section eight of "Snapshots of a Daughter- in-Law" recasts the shuttered window as an image of imaginative potential reduced to isolated fantasy: "Still, eyes inaccurately dream/ behind closed windows blankening with steam." Withdrawal into a trivialized Cartesian subjectivity devoid of real thought (which lies outside the traditional realm of women) simply reinforces the original emptiness. At worst, it severs contact even with the traditionally feminine realm of feeling. Trapped in the "mere fact" of her domestic duties, the woman struggling with the angelic/demonic voices in section two establishes contact with her emotional responses only by transforming kitchen work into a masochistic ritual. She takes her inability to feel pain —even when she lets "the tapstream scald her arm/ a match burn to her thumbnail"—as proof that the voices she hears are angelic. Like the description of the belle in the "prime of [her] life," these ironically charged lines underscore the extreme alienation of women from their intellectual and emotional experience.

As Claire Keyes observes, Rich seems hesitant throughout *Snapshots of a Daughter-in-Law* to accept fully the angels' Blakean proverbs: "*Have no patience.*" "*Be insatiable.*" "*Save yourself; others you cannot save.*" These proverbs, demonic from the patriarchal and daemonic from the feminist perspective, would in fact dictate something like the repudiation of "*all* patriarchal traditions" which Keyes seeks (in Cooper, p. 42). At this stage of her process, Rich, like the housewife, cannot unambiguously declare herself a demon lover and fully develop her creative potential. Yet Keyes' judgment that "Rich longs for the full expression of a female consciousness, yet manages to sabotage it at the same time" seems unduly harsh (in Cooper, p. 48). Judged as part of a process moving toward full expression, "Snapshots of a Daughter-in-Law" marks an advance over the ironic treatment of the collapse of romantic (and especially matrimonial) ideals, which had emerged as an important, if only partially articulated, concern in her previous work.

Stylistically and thematically reminiscent of Robert Frost ("Home Burial"), Edwin Arlington Robinson ("Firelight"), and William Faulkner (Addie's monolog in *As I Lay Dying*), two monologs from *The Diamond Cutters* portray the individual experience of marriage as torment rather than relationship. "Autumn Equinox" (c. 1954) focuses on a woman, like Rich a vaguely dissatisfied academic spouse, who suffers a sickness originating in her belief "that life is different than it is." Hating her husband's engravings for "priggishly enclosing in a room/ The marvels of the world," she feels herself similarly reduced to a static image. Anticipating the first section of "Snapshots of a Daughter-in-Law," Rich associates this denial with the persona's wedding:

> In the picture
> We are the semblance of a bride and groom
> Static as figures on a mantelpiece,
> As if that moment out of time existed
> Then and forever in a dome of glass.

Similarly, "The Perennial Answer" (c. 1954) depicts a woman's withdrawal into subjective isolation, a metaphorical "dome of glass," following a failed attempt to experience relationship. Reflecting on her life as she lies dying, the persona senses that the violence of her husband and the puritanical repudiation of a would-be lover have driven her into isolation; her "mouth unkissed" anticipates the "memory of refused adultery" in section eight of "Snapshots of a Daughter-in-Law." Raped by her husband as punishment for a "sin she did not commit," she experiences herself as static image rather than living being: "I was a woodcut on the page." Yet, like the persona "pictured" in "Autumn Equinox," her awareness of the source of her alienation remains fragmentary.

Rich employs the Frost-Robinson monolog form, which, unlike Browning's dramatic monologs does not imply the presence of a listener, in order to emphasize the absence of communication in both marriages. "Living in Sin," formally recalling third person limited poems such as Frost's "The Subverted Flower," makes it clear that accepting illicit sexual experience without altering the underlying sexual roles does nothing to avoid the problems faced by women in a patriarchal context. Willingly seduced by romantic images of "A plate of pears,/ a piano with a Persian shawl," the central figure finds herself actually living in a world of "mere facts" which leaves her susceptible, like the woman in section two of "Snapshots of a Daughter-in-Law" to the jeering of "minor demons"; the piano needs tuning, her lover yawns in boredom. Although the woman claims to be "back in love again" each evening, she recognizes it is "not so wholly" as before, that what she had envisioned as romantic sacrament seems destined to become a source of fragmentation. Rich clearly implies that soon she will no longer be able to feel the pain if the coffee pot she lets boil over should scald her arm.

Most of the poems concerning male-female relationships in *Snapshots of a Daughter-in-Law* ("Novella," "The Loser," "Passing On") portray a passive acceptance of alienation. The only substantial exception besides the title poem is "A Marriage in the 'Sixties" (1961), which acknowledges alienation but also recognizes the need for a larger perspective. Most of Rich's early marriage poems are monologs or carefully distanced third person reports; "Novella," for example, recalls Henry James both rhetorically and in its concluding image of stars "separate as minds." In contrast, "A Marriage in the 'Sixties" directly addresses the persona's husband, as "Dear fellow particle," her "twin." Wandering "the raging desert of our thought," the marriage partners seek solace in one another. Even their shared struggle for communication, however, collapses into an isolation as emotionally devastating as that of "The Perennial Answer":

> Two strangers, thrust for life upon a rock
> may have at last the perfect hour of talk
> that language aches for; still—
> two minds, two messages.

Rather than simply presenting the alienation as an idiosyncrasy of a specific situation, Rich begins to pursue its relationship to the larger context.

Political and scientific imagery, juxtaposed with specific details of the marriage, brings to the foreground connections dimly sensed but ultimately distanced by the persona of "Storm Warnings." Although the persona of "A Marriage in the 'Sixties" maintains a distinctly Cartesian posture when addressing her husband as a "particle," she senses the shift to the Heisenbergian paradigm (which, at least in popular versions, emphasizes relativity and the interrelationship of observer and event) when she observes "the second's getting shorter," and "pieces of the universe are missing." Unarguable evidence of a dislocation in the familiar political world of the 1950s, Castro appears in the

New York Times. The fact that he seems a "walk-on out of *Carmen*" simply emphasizes the importance of the observer's perspective, reiterating the poem's Heisenbergian implications. These changes clearly affect the marital experience; the husband's benevolent patriarchal brow—"part Roman emperor"—creases with concern. Unable to integrate her fragmentary understanding of the relationship between personal experience and the larger context, the persona nonetheless articulates the futility of withdrawal: "Some mote of history has flown into your eye"; "the world breathes under our bed." This irresistible invasion of subjective space dooms any attempt to shut out the external weather.

"SNAPSHOTS OF A DAUGHTER-IN-LAW":
NIGHTMARES OF MASCULINITY

As "Snapshots of a Daughter-in-Law" clearly recognizes, many women either fail to perceive or refuse to acknowledge the futility of withdrawal. Rich traces this hesitancy, clearly similar to her own, to a widespread tendency to conceive experience in terms of patriarchal images, thereby assuring a tension between experience and the interpretation of experience. Echoing Diderot, Yeats, and the Cavalier poets, "Snapshots of a Daughter-in-Law" catalogs the idealized romantic images of self and marriage provided for women by patriarchal art. Rich emphasizes the dissociation experienced by women who attempt to live the image: "When to her lute Corinna sings/ neither words nor music are her own." Nonetheless, both positive and negative images, infused with glamor by the patriarchal psyche, seduce numerous women: the woman who shaves her legs "until they gleam/ like petrified mammoth-tusk"; the belle who copies her dresses from an earlier era, redolent of Chopin; Corinna, who invests her total energy in a physical appearance "adjusted in reflections of an eye."

These snapshots of women—or perhaps of an Everywoman of infinitely greater complexity than the patriarchal definition of "daughter-in-law" implies—reflect a communal acceptance of destructive romantic images which render women "part legend, part convention." Identifying "Woman" with "Nature"—the "still commodious steamer-trunk of *tempora* and *mores*"—these legends and conventions declare "love" to be "the only natural action" for women. Any woman, like Mary Wollstonecraft in section seven, who resists the "partly understood" ideal faces reclassification as "harpy, shrew, and whore." Both the negative and the ostensibly positive images alienate women from one another and channel potentially liberating energy into conventional "feminine" bickering. The two "handsome women" in section three, "like Furies cornered from their prey" argue endlessly "*ad feminam*." Implicating herself in this self-imposed fragmentation, Rich recasts Baudelaire's taunt to the "hypocrite reader" as a challenge to women to repudiate the shared self-contempt that leads them to fight to protect their victimization: "all the old knives/ that have rusted in my back, I drive in yours,/ *ma semblable, ma soeur!*"

While Rich recognizes the power of conventional images in "Snapshots of a Daughter-in-Law," her perception that they serve the interests of patriarchal power grows increasingly clear during the 1960s. Typifying her early ambivalence, "Juvenilia" (1960) portrays the pressure placed on a talented girl by an artistic and intellectual tradition identified with her father. Even as the clearly autobiographical persona copies her compositions in order to earn her father's praise, "Huge leaves" from his library set "Unspeakable fairy tales" raging in her head. Exacerbated by her father's explicit support and by the presence of Ibsen's masculine feminism in the library, the ambiguity of Rich's situation leaves her with a profound, if unfocused, sense of disease. Although *A Doll's House* and "When We Dead Awaken" offer important insights into the deeper implications of her position in patriarchal culture, the girl's obsession with her father's approval perpetuates the very tension Ibsen identifies. The specific images may be transformed but the sexual hierarchy remains unchanged.

Only in *Diving Into the Wreck* did Rich directly confront the connection between the patriarchal images and women's experience of the "tragedy of sex." Tracing their origins to dislocations of masculine consciousness similar to those described by Fiedler, Kolodny, and Griffin, "Waking in the Dark" (1971) questions the "law of nature" used in "Snapshots of a Daughter-in-Law" to justify the static images of women. Rich catalogs patriarchal responses to women's blood, whether menstrual or that shed as a result of violence:

> You worship the blood
> you call it hysterical bleeding
> you want to drink it like milk
> you dip your finger into it and write
> you faint at the smell of it
> you dream of dumping me into the sea.

The final figure provides a transition between the seasick descent of "The Demon Lover" and the willing immersion of "The Wave." Cast out by patriarchy, women must either actively rebel or surrender their experience entirely. However painful, this realization provides a path past the "old shelters and huts . . . scenes of masturbation and dirty jokes." Understanding that patriarchal creativity contains contradictory and ultimately self-destructive elements, Rich identifies the dichotomy between *man* and nature—imposed on men by their own Cartesian sensibility—as the corollary of the oppression of women by men. Men dream of writing in women's blood in part because their own vitality has been sold "to the machines." Moving through the "unconscious forest," Rich seeks a post-Cartesian standpoint from which to examine "the wildwood/ where the split began." Not merely a source of oppression, patriarchal imagery also helps identify structural weaknesses in the foundation of patriarchal power.

"Incipience" (1971), "August" (1972), and "The Ninth Symphony of Beethoven Understood at Last as a Sexual Message" (1972) pursue the implications of Rich's perception that the oppressive images of women originate in the patriarchal fear of nature and the unconscious mind. In section two of "Incipience," a woman neurosurgeon dissects the (presumably split) brain of a man dreaming of women who metamorphose into strange mythological creatures. Similarly, Rich repudiates the "simple" nightmares of the male sleeper in "August" in order to confront her own unconscious fears of the "village lit with blood/ where all the fathers are crying: *My son is mine!*" Reaching its extreme in "The Ninth Symphony of Beethoven Understood at Last as a Sexual Message," Rich's repudiation of patriarchal images assumes a truly nightmarish intensity. Even the most apparently beautiful patriarchal art implies a "terror of impotence," the "beating of a bloody fist upon/ a splintered table."

All *patriarchal* images seem to Rich, at this stage of her process, expressions of isolation, of flight from connection. Rich's simplification of the patriarchal tradition in response to the unleashing of unconscious fears ironically parallels the patriarchal simplification of women. The difference lies in the significance of the stereotyping in Rich's process. Like many of the Afro-American writers who influenced her aesthetic and political development, Rich argues that at some points it might be necessary to repudiate the "masters" of the Euro-American tradition without qualification. Her position parallels James Baldwin's argument that such repudiation is necessary for the development of an individual/communal integrity which would allow the writer to "welcome them back, but on one's own terms, and absolutely, on one's own land" (p. 87).

Before extending the tentative welcome discernible in *Your Native Land, Your Life*, Rich explored the full extent of the patriarchal presence on women's terrain, balancing macro- and microcosmic perspectives in poems such as "Hunger" (1974-75), "Heroines" (1980), and "The Images"

(1976-78). Section two of "Hunger" echoes Daly's analysis of the patriarchal denial of women's experience: "They can rule the world while they persuade us/ our pain belongs in some order." Repudiating the trivialization and universalization of suffering, Rich identifies the order that "kills us or leaves us half-alive" with "that male god" and "that male state." Emphasizing the global dimensions of patriarchal power, Rich portrays its impact on the contemporary United States, the wartime Europe of Kathe Kollwitz, and the Africa she associates with Afro-American poet Audre Lorde, to whom the poem is dedicated. Developing the same point in temporal rather than spatial terms, "Heroines" traces the impact of patriarchy on the "exceptional" and "devout" women whose experience was denied by laws circumscribing their economic, personal, and political expression. Together, "Hunger" and "Heroines" create an image of women forced to survive in a macrocosm shaped almost entirely by patriarchal power.

Approaching similar concerns from a microcosmic perspective, "The Images" connects the analysis Rich had developed during the 1970s with the focus on personal experience which had set the process in motion two decades previously. Telling her woman lover "touch knows you before language/ names in the brain," Rich asserts the primacy of relationship and experience over separation and definition. This assertion of anti-Cartesian premises is accompanied by a recognition of the impact of patriarchy on women's relationships. In the "queasy electric signs of midtown" or the "worm-worn Pietas," Rich perceives symbolic images of "lynching" which women cannot ignore without risking martyrdom. Experiencing freedom of speech as violent pornography and the legal system as threat rather than protection, Rich declares: "there are no boundaries/ no-man's-land does not exist." More measured than "The Ninth Symphony of Beethoven Understood at Last as a Sexual Message," "The Images" nonetheless reasserts Rich's distrust of all patriarchal expression, whether manifested as language, music, or "any form created."

Ultimately more insidious than the cinema screens and "newsrags blowing the streets," the aesthetic tradition alienates women from their experience as effectively as does the popular culture. Rich describes high art as a means of "reorganizing victimization . . . translating/ violence into patterns so powerful and pure/ we continually fail to ask are they true for us." Recalling the image of immersion, Rich imagines "waves irrhythmically washing," creating a post-patriarchal space where she can lie "clean of the guilt of words," "free of speech."

"SNAPSHOTS OF A DAUGHTER-IN-LAW": REPRESSION AS COLLABORATION WITH PATRIARCHY

The "war of images" that Rich declares near the conclusion of the poem aims both to subvert patriarchal authority and to unite women in an acceptance of their experience. As Rich realized long before "The Images," the success of this struggle depends largely on the development of conceptions of both freedom and speech applicable to the needs of the women who remain in the patriarchal camp, many of their own "free will." The unwillingness of many women to admit the inadequacy of patriarchal definitions appears as a growing concern of Rich's as early as "Snapshots of a Daughter-in-Law." Acknowledging the collaboration of women with patriarchy, Rich provides a sequence of images emphasizing their failure of vision. The woman who scalds her arms in section two suffers from "grit blowing into her eyes": the eyes of the legendary/conventional woman of section eight "inaccurately dream/ behind closed windows." Accepting the status of "precocious child" or "precious chronic invalid," the woman who retreats to the specious safety of patriarchal kindness surrenders her creative self in trade.

The question first posed in "Snapshots of a Daughter-in-Law" —"would we, darlings, resign it if we could?"—recurs in many of Rich's poems concerning women's response to their position in patriarchy. Like Aunt Jennifer, the persona of "Peeling Onions" (1961) seems entirely reconciled to repression. Dimly remembering a time when she felt her "eyes like wounds/ raw in my head," she allows her pain to remain unarticulated, "stifled in my lungs like smog." Trapped in domestic emptiness, she is nearly lifeless, hovering over the memory of "old tears in the chopping-bowl." Later poems, such as "Re-forming the Crystal" (1973), shift the center of attention to the ways in which this repression comes to seem natural. As the persona struggles against patriarchal images that define her purely in relation to husband, father, and male lovers, she perceives the connection between her own situation and her mother's previous repressions: "The woman/ I needed to call my mother/ was silenced before I was born." Similarly, "Mother-in-Law" (1980) identifies the core of the dilemma in the tradition of repression which isolates women from one another and forces each individual woman to begin the process anew. While the mother-in-law senses "some secret/ we both know and have never spoken," she continues to accept "placebos/ or Valium" as a substitute for the acceptance of experience which provides the base for honest communication. Without a tradition of positive alternatives, the speakers of both poems feel the need to create their own alternative visions or else abandon their own daughters to the cycle of alienation and repression.

Rich acknowledges that the creation of an alternative will require more than simple recognition of the problem. Even the perceptive women she celebrates in "Heroines" are frequently forced to keep their "interpretations/ locked in your heart." Representing one major direction in feminist criticism of Rich, Deborah Pope sees the movement from "an isolation of women enforced by men toward the energy and prophecy of an isolation chosen by women . . . a fiercely willed rejection of the ruined and ruining heritage" as the single most important element of Rich's process (p. 149). As Rich recognizes in *On Lies, Secrets, and Silence*, this transformation necessitates an extensive reconsideration of both silence and speech. The brilliant essay "Women and Honor: Some Notes on Lying" suggests that the first stage of the transformation is refusing to turn all experience into words. To articulate experiences denied by patriarchy in the language of patriarchy inevitably acclimatizes the individual to lying, which in turn reinforces repression. Women who speak within the patriarchal context risk losing contact with their "wild zone" experiences. Rich argues that "To lie habitually . . . is to lose contact with the unconscious" (Rich, *Lies*, p. 187). Even if individual lies can be "justified" as expressions of love, tact, or kindness, their impact on the liar is devastating. Acclimatizing the liar to silence as an evasion of experience, lying subverts the silence which can protect the "chosen isolation" Pope sees as Rich's immediate goal. Rich writes: "In lying to others we end up lying to ourselves. We deny the importance of an event, or a person, and thus deprive ourselves of a part of our lives. Or we use one piece of the past or present to screen out another. Thus we lose faith even with our own lives" (Rich, *Lies*, p. 188). Without faith in her own experience, the liar retreats further into the patriarchal consciousness predicated on "the fear of losing control" (Rich, *Lies*, p. 187).

For most women, however, the desire for control is simply an illusion. In the American tradition, masculine alienation from the unconscious has repeatedly generated open rebellion against anything perceived as female control. Considering the failure of vision imaged in the snow scene of *Citizen Kane*, Rich's poem "Amnesia" (1974)—a term she defines as "the silence of the unconscious"—reflects the American imaginative patterns described by Fiedler, Lawrence, and Kolodny. Focusing on a male hero continually "lighting out for the territories," most "classic" American literature directs attention away from women. Fixed in the static images generated by the hero's unconscious fears, women become props in his heroic "plot." Rich writes:

> Becoming a man means leaving
> someone, or something—

still, why
must the snow-scene blot itself out
the flakes coming down so fast
so heavy, so unrevealing
over the something that gets left behind?

As long as they allow their vision to be directed by the patriarchal "eye" (whether cinematic or psychological), women help blot out their own reality. Rich admits her complicity in this repression in "A Woman Dead in Her Forties," an intensely personal poem including nearly a dozen images of lies, secrets, and silence. Thinking back to her own marriage, Rich admits that both she and her dead woman friend "lied about our lives." As a result, she is now "left laboring/ with the secrets and silence." Although the image intimates an eventual rebirth, Rich admits that what she thought of at the time as "mute loyalty" expressing love was actually an acceptance of patriarchy: "We stayed mute and disloyal/ because we were afraid."

Seeking the source of the fear that makes repression seem preferable to communication, Rich explores the context in which patriarchal images are presented to women. Repression, "Snapshots of a Daughter-in-Law" indicates, is rewarded superficially with patriarchal approval. The belle of section one identifies with the "delicious" Chopin prelude; the "ladies" of section nine are toasted by gallant men who forgive their "every lapse." These rewards, however, are typically withdrawn as time—described as "male"—erodes physical beauty, leaving only "the drained and flagging bosom of our middle years." To some extent the young women's ignorance (or willingness to repress their awareness) of this recurring pattern reflects the lack of mother\daughter communication. Both the ignorance and the silence, however, reflect what Rich sees as a more basic aspect of the patriarchal context.

"SNAPSHOTS OF A DAUGHTER-IN-LAW":
THE THEME OF RAPE

Although Rich remains hesitant in "Snapshots of a Daughter-in-Law," the poem suggests what will emerge as one of her most important themes concerning patriarchy: the ultimate power of patriarchal images over women's consciousness rests on the threat of rape. Alluding to Yeats' "Leda and the Swan," Rich presents the terrifying image of a male poet, whom she acknowledges as a major influence, celebrating rape as the source of creative and cultural energy. Rich's line "the beak that grips her, she becomes" emphasizes the woman's acceptance of patriarchal mythology, her identification with the rapist. In addition, the "becoming" image of the victim suggests an underlying connection between the ostensibly objective patriarchal aesthetics and the realities of patriarchal power. In section six, Rich again recasts a Yeatsian image, that of the mechanical birds of Byzantium, when she addresses a woman as "you bird, you tragical machine." Facing rape if she leaves her cage, the woman paradoxically suffers rape as long as she remains within the cage of patriarchal definition: "Pinned down/ by love, for you the only natural action."

Rich's reluctance to see rape in Yeats, in Beethoven, reflects a deeply ingrained fear, shared by many women, that no zone of safety, no "no-man's-land" exists within patriarchy. To recognize the full extent of rape, both actual and symbolic, is to risk losing access to the only experiences—particularly those of love and culture—which make life bearable for the woman struggling to increase her awareness. Faced with the terrifying prospect of being drowned in the tidal wave of violence released by the repressed patriarchal unconscious, many women prefer not to risk immersion at all. Nonetheless, once perceived, however unwillingly, the threat of rape inevitably remains an aspect of women's psychological and social reality. A line from "Snapshots of a Daughter-in-Law," which has been used as an epigraph by several feminist writers, articulates Rich's nightmarish sense of the tension between the urges to accept and to repress her knowledge of repression, acquiescence, and rape: "A thinking woman sleeps with monsters."

These monsters, blending external reality and internal fear, haunt Rich's poetry as early as "The Snow Queen" (1954). Exploring a version of "woman as legend" derived from a Hans Christian Andersen tale, the poem contains a great deal of repressed rape imagery. After the persona feels a "needle" digging into her in the first stanza, the poem culminates with the image of "a frozen spear that drives me through." Focusing on more concrete threats, "Charleston in the Eighteen-Sixties" (1966) links sexuality and violence in the opening image: "He seized me by the waist and kissed my throat." In the remainder of the poem, Rich explores the social implications of her theme by montaging the image of woman as "angel" with the carnage of the Civil War. Although the persona's despairing feeling that she has "No imagination to forestall woe" refers directly to the war, it is equally applicable to the sexual war described in "The Images." The power imbalance in this struggle, reinforced by women's acceptance of images portraying them as intrinsically powerless, creates a complex psychological dilemma. "Snapshots of a Daughter-in-Law" describes the situation in which even the aware woman may choose to repress her rebellious impulses: "our crime/ only to cast too bold a shadow/ or smash the mold straight off./ For that, solitary confinement,/ tear gas, attrition shelling." Since both alternatives contribute to the intensity of the thinking woman's nightmare, repression may seem preferable to physical destruction or externally enforced isolation. It is hardly surprising that, in a context dominated by the patriarchal imagination, Rich finds "Few applicants for that honor."

"SNAPSHOTS OF A DAUGHTER-IN-LAW": CONFRONTATION AND TRANSFORMATION

On the most important level, attracting the wrath of patriarchy *is* an honor. In "Snapshots of a Daughter-in-Law," signs of resistance and assertion survive, frequently on the margins of consciousness, in spite of patriarchal hostility. The belle's glowering daughter in section one and the woman listening to the angelic/demonic voices in section two anticipate the ambiguous promise of the young girl in "The Demon Lover." Rich suggests that an apparently selfish immersion in experience—"*Be insatiable,*" "*Save yourself,*" the angels say—may be the first step toward what Wollstonecraft imagined as the "stay which cannot be undermined." Further, Rich suggests that patriarchal images, by consigning women to a "separate sphere," may ironically encourage a post-Cartesian mode of thought enabling women to overcome their repression:

are you edged more keen
to prise the secrets of the vault? has Nature shown
her household books to you, daughter-in-law,
that her sons never saw?

What begins as hesitant questioning emerges in the poem's final section as promise of fulfillment. The messianic figure of the new woman, "beautiful as any boy," arrives in concord with, rather than separated from, nature. Echoing Simone de Beauvoir's image of the soul as helicopter-bird, Rich imagines a figure capable of transforming the technological power normally channeled by patriarchy into the domination of nature. Although "her fine blades [make] the air wince," she nevertheless combines intellect and experience: "Her mind full to the wind, I see her plunge/ breasted and glancing through the currents."

The promise remains unfulfilled in "Snapshots of a Daughter-in-Law": Rich locates the description in the future, admitting "she's long about her coming." As she notes in the essay "When We Dead Awaken," Rich did not accept the vision of woman as fully realized creative force without a long struggle. The first poem in which she claims full possession of traditionally masculine capacities, "Orion" (1965) marks a major advance in Rich's sense of her creative power. Her choice of a constellation as central focus suggests that both men and women have been rendered "half-legend" by patriarchal images. Even as she repudiates images which deny her "masculine" potentialities, Rich grounds her vision in an acceptance of female sexuality: "I throw back my head to take you in." This sexuality, inextricably involved with her intellectual capacities, has little in common with the aesthetically pleasing rape imaged by Yeats. Unlike the individual "coming" of the new woman in "Snapshots of a Daughter-in-Law," it involves a relationship, however tense and confrontatory, with another person. The sexual assertion in "Orion" enables Rich to recognize the underlying impotence of the "simplified west." Addressing Orion as a representative of the Euro-American patriarchal tradition, Rich dismisses the traditional emblem of potency: the "old-fashioned thing, a sword" that now "weighs you down." Extremely painful and disorienting, the recognition of her own power moves Rich beyond the patriarchal grasp. When a man attempts to reach behind her eyes, he no longer finds his own reflection. Rather, Rich confronts him with her "starlike eye," an emblem of the transcendent vision denied women in traditional patriarchal imagery. Shattering the old reflections, Rich assumes the conventionally masculine power of the "cold and egotistical spear." Even as she adopts the phallic image and accepts the necessity of focusing on her own experience, she redefines its meaning, taking care to throw the spear where "it can do least damage."

"Trying to Talk with a Man" (1971), again focusing on a confrontation between a man and an articulate woman, recasts the metaphysical issues of "Orion" in socially specific terms. In order to reach the desert where real communication seems at least possible, the two characters repudiate the sources of patriarchal imagery: "whole LP collections, films we starred in/. . . the language of love-letters, of suicide notes." Rich accentuates the connection between the images and the repression that previously kept the characters out of the desert: "everything we were saying until now/ was an effort to blot it out." Most importantly, when the man attempts to retreat into Cartesian isolation, the persona refuses to be swept along by his desperation which "feels like power." Rather, she challenges his description of "the danger/ as if it were not ourselves," a description which implies a split between subjective experience and cultural context. Confronted with so basic a misapprehension, Rich reasserts the need, as she phrases it in "Incipience," to move

"Outside the frame of his dream." In "The Spirit of
again repudiates the framing images, including th
one time necessary to her own development: "Or
drunken hunter." Cautioning against romantici
against repression and patriarchal imagery, Rich e:
claim of women to "our own world" is of little significance unless they
are willing to confront that world "if not as it might be/ then as it is:
male dominion, gangrape, lynching, pogrom."

The Impact of Patriarchy on Men

The last two images seem particularly significant in relation to the
recent development of Rich's thought concerning patriarchy. Without
compromising her insights concerning the oppression of women, Rich
now places patriarchy in the context of an encompassing cultural solipsism that affects blacks, Jews, the poor: ultimately, all individuals
unwilling to deny aspects of their experience and accept dominant
group definitions. Despite the persistent image of her as a man-hater,
Rich recognizes that patriarchy exerts a destructive impact on men as
well as on women. Locked in the same rigid definitions which circumscribe women's roles, men too become "half-legend, half-
convention." Repressing large parts of their awareness, men share
women's fear of leaving the superficially safe, if ultimately empty,
patriarchal roles. As D. H. Lawrence observes in his essay on James
Fenimore Cooper, the American male imagination effectively places
men in a double-bind. Their recurrent attempts to escape the stultifying structures they associate with women accomplish little. Since the
structures exist primarily in the male psyche, the attempts to flee their
external manifestations merely extend the territory in which those
structures exert their power (Lawrence, p. 59). Rich has long been
aware of this problem, which has significant implications for her own
attempt to redefine the poetic tradition in which she writes. "The
Knight" (1957) images the male as victim of self-imposed legends and
conventions which he nonetheless seems unwilling to abandon. Even
the "gaiety of his mail" implies his internal fragmentation; the bright-
ness reflects "a thousand splintered suns." Unwilling to acknowledge
the emptiness of his experience, the knight looks out through an eye
which reflects his sense of himself as a "lump of bitter jelly/ set in a
metal mask." The final stanza implies that in order to free himself from
the "walls of iron" the knight must enter into a process which, like that
suggested by "Snapshots of a Daughter-in-Law," begins with the recognition and repudiation of traditional images. If he fails to repudiate the

parkling illusion created by his armor, the patriarchal "emblems/ crushing his chest," he can expect only to die "on the green/ his rags and wounds still hidden." As a result of the conventional demand that men not express their emotions, the knight experiences alienation in terms of activity rather than passive withdrawal. Ironically, this presents a substantial threat to women—his pointed helmet and feeling of impotent power can explode in the form of rape—without providing him any real solace or lasting benefit.

As early as *Necessities of Life*, Rich explored the relationship of this masculine mythology to the specifically American manifestations of patriarchy. Recalling the emphasis on departure in "Amnesia," "The Parting: I" (1963) focuses on a man who feels free only when he stands on the headland. Condemned to an isolation she has not chosen for herself, the woman he leaves behind experiences their relationship as "a knife/ where two strands tangle to rust." A similar situation recurs in "Face to Face" (1965), which associates the isolated figure on the beach with the Mosaic prophet and the Newtonian scientist, both of whom circumscribe the world in an attempt to establish dominion. Alone before the immense ocean, this figure evokes both the Puritan and the pioneer heritage of American men when he asserts his individual power by drawing boundaries. Rich describes him as "circling [his] little all," claiming "to be Law and Prophets/ for all that lawlessness." Rich's treatment of the patriarchal figure in "Face to Face" recalls her tentative identification with Orion. While she shares his desire for prophetic isolation, she recognizes the limitations of a vision which sees that isolation as intrinsically hostile to relationship. Rich's revision of the boundary-maker in "Mother-Right" (1977), like her revision of Orion in "The Spirit of Place," emphasizes the insufficiency of the patriarchal prophet as a model for women seeking a post-Cartesian perspective. In "Mother-Right," the steps of the man "walking boundaries,/ measuring," delineate nothing save the extent of his illusion; mother and child plunge through the field beyond his self-imposed limits of vision, "making for the open." Although she understands the emotional impulse behind the American male's urge for escape, Rich redefines its meaning by accepting the continuing relationship between mother and child.

As she came to terms with the mythic and cultural underpinnings of the patriarchal images of masculinity, Rich began to examine the struggles of individual men in poems such as "Trying to Talk with a Man," "From a Survivor" (1972) and "For L.G.: Unseen for Twenty Years" (1974). In "From a Survivor," Rich laments a man's inability to make the transition to a post-patriarchal sensibility where his body is "no longer/ the body of a god/ or anything with power over [the woman's] life." The autobiographical source of the poem in the suicide of Rich's husband dictates its pessimistic vision. Like the prototypical knight, the man in "From a Survivor" dies "wastefully." Another poem with an autobiographical source, "For L.G.: Unseen for Twenty Years" considers a wider range of possibilities. Remembering her friendship with a homosexual man during "the early 'fifties/ of invincible ignorance," Rich emphasizes that patriarchal images of masculinity distorted both of their self-images. Alienated from his social context by his sexual preference, L.G. ironically shares numerous characteristics with the knight; Rich describes "a fragment of mind," and a face "taut as a mask of wires." Recognizing her own complicity in the formation of this mask, Rich remembers a conversation in which L.G. identifies masculinity with heterosexual potency. Her ambiguous denial—"*But you're a man . . . /the swiftness of your mind is masculine*"—reveals her implicit acceptance of the patriarchal definitions. It was precisely this belief in a masculine intelligence, inaccessible to women, that necessitated Rich's confrontation with Orion. Her later poems addressed to men recognize the earlier confrontation as necessary to the freedom of both men and women.

In retrospect, Rich understands that her response to L.G. reveals her continuing similarity to Aunt Jennifer; she describes her words as "some set-piece I'd learned to embroider/ in my woman's education/ while the needle scarred my hand." At this point in her process, Rich acknowledges that "Uncle," too, bears the scars inflicted by the phallic needle. She presents a litany of possible effects of the patriarchal images on L.G., most of them stressing the degradation of gay men in American culture. Even while acknowledging the destructive potential, however, Rich imagines a release for L.G. analogous to that for which she had struggled during the twenty years since their meeting. Significantly, her image of this release stresses its accessibility; it can be attained by any couple, homo- or heterosexual, capable of repudiating the patriarchal images which discourage "the strange coexistence/ of two of any gender." Still, the final image of Rich and L.G., leaving one another in search of "the love of men," cautions against any simplistic vision of escape. By defining their quest narrowly, both men and women risk, like the classic American heroes, re-creating the boundaries they seek to leave behind.

Although *The Dream of a Common Language* and *A Wild Patience Has Taken Me This Far* concentrate on a woman-centered alternative to patriarchy, Rich suggests parallel possibilities of masculine development. "Family Romance" (1974), a collective monolog subtitled "the brothers speak," revises the standard Freudian patriarchal image by focusing on a group of men who experience relationship more intensely than separation. Repudiating patriarchal definitions, they accept both the "feminine" and a revised sense of the "masculine" in themselves. Immersed in the "black forest" which Rich associates with the unconscious, the brothers communicate in a "wordless collusion" which enables them to "love each other with a passion understood/ like the great roots of the wood." Retaining a dim awareness of "another country" where they might have fought one another for the "father's blessing," the brothers accept their relationship to one another as a source of strength. Accepting their masculinity enables the brothers to acknowledge their link with the maternal figure who protects them while they sleep. Clearly an aspect of the brothers' collective psyche rather than an actual woman consigned to a passive nurturing role, this figure helps them overcome the internal and familial divisions intrinsic to patriarchy. Opening with the departure of the mother, "Family Romance" closes with her internalized return. Similarly, the first lines describe the father-king, who, like the knight, is "always absent at the wars." The return of the father, like that of the mother, takes place in the brothers' psyche. Paradoxically blessed by the absence of the paternal blessing, the brothers accept their masculine nature without defining it in opposition to women. This image of an integrated and supportive masculinity parallels that advocated by Robert Bly in his volume *The Man in the Black Coat Turns* and his essay "What Men Really Want." Bly's career, like those of Richard Hugo and Gary Snyder, suggests that some contemporary male writers are aware of the need for a masculine equivalent of Rich's process.

The Problem of Language

As her treatment of the impact of patriarchy on men suggests, Rich gradually comes to believe that no individual can afford to ignore either the personal or the political dimensions of cultural solipsism. From a post-Cartesian perspective, the very distinction between personal and political may be nothing more than an illusion. Overemphasizing personal problems risks underestimating the institutional forces enforcing repression; concentrating exclusively on political issues, as novelists such as Doris Lessing and Ralph Ellison have observed, risks leaving the psychological sources of solipsism untouched. During the late 1960s, Rich came to see the language encoding the patriarchal perspective as the crucial link between the personal and political dimensions of her experience. As a result, she turned her attention to the problem of articulating an alternative vision in a patriarchal language designed to obscure relationships and fix boundaries. "Focus" (1965) expresses the tension between "The mind's passion . . . for singling out" and Rich's belief that "Obscurity has another tale to tell."

"Our Whole Life" (1969), one of a number of poems on language and perception in *The Will to Change*, reflects Rich's deeply felt fear that no conceivable language could be adequate to experience, either personal or political. Seeing "Our whole life" as a texture of "permissible fibs," "a knot of lies," she envisions all expression as a politically corrupt translation: "dead letters/ rendered into the oppressor's language." At perhaps the most terrifying point in her intellectual/emotional process, Rich creates the image of a burning Algerian, the victim of cultural solipsism as manifested in global imperialism. Entirely unable to articulate his experience, he has "no words for this/ except himself." The "whole body" of the Algerian, like the "whole life" of the title, transcends definition; as an emblem of the need for a language adequate to that experience, the Algerian challenges readers to accept their relationship both to his experience as victim and to the culture which victimizes him.

"THE BURNING OF PAPER INSTEAD OF CHILDREN"

Rich's exploration of the connection between victimization and the "oppressor's language" culminates in "The Burning of Paper Instead of Children" (1968), one of her most powerful and complex poems. After quoting draft resister David Berrigan's admission that "I was in danger of verbalizing my moral impulses out of existence," Rich establishes fire as the central image of the poem. As it has for writers from St. Augustine and Dante through T. S. Eliot and Jean Rhys, Rich's fire signifies torment, purgation, and the renewal of creative energy. A male neighbor of Rich's, upset that their sons have burned a mathematics textbook, remembers Hitler and informs Rich that "there are few things that upset me so much as the idea of burning a book." Immediately, Rich's thoughts turn to libraries as emblems of both oppression (the *Encyclopaedia Britannica*) and inspiration (the *Trial of Jeanne d'Arc*). Her ambivalent response stems in part from the dislocation of her neighbor's concern. Bothered by an abstract *idea*, he shows little interest in the boys' hatred of the educational institution or their choice of a math book, itself a symbol of abstract systematization. While she refuses to romanticize the boys' action, Rich perceives a complexity invisible to her neighbor. The juxtaposition of his response with the Berrigan quote suggests he may be destroying his ability to respond to a whole life. Verbalization of moral principles without reference to their experiential context may itself become a distinctly immoral source of oppression. This suggests to Rich a sequence of profoundly disturbing questions revolving around the fact that books provide "knowledge of the oppressor." Reflecting the ambiguity of language that precludes easy answers, this phrase suggests both oppressive knowledge encoded in the dominant group language and insight into the nature of the oppressive system which can be used for purposes of resistance. After introducing these constituting tensions, Rich concludes section one with another sentence emphasizing the ambiguity of her perceptions. Even as it echoes the neighbor's moral principle, the sentence resists simplification: "I know it hurts to burn."

Momentarily releasing the tension at the start of section two, Rich envisions a "time of silence" in which sexuality generates a sense of relationship providing "relief/ from this tongue." The last phrase, however, directs Rich's thought back toward the oppressive culture. Even her sensual experience (the tongue as sexuality) cannot be separated from the rigid mode of expression (the tongue as "oppressor's language") which has destroyed more organic expressions such as the "signals of smoke." This reflection on the destruction of Native American expression renews Rich's awareness that even her critique of oppression is cast in the language of "fanatics and traders." Inevitably participating in the oppressor's discourse, the poem makes no attempt to conceal its own contradictions. Rather, Rich challenges the reader to acknowledge the complexity of his/her participation in the poetic process: "knowledge of the oppressor/ this is the oppressor's language/ yet I need it to talk to you."

Returning to this cluster of images in section four, Rich emphasizes the similar contradictions involved in making love. Especially when lovers speak with one another, sexuality involves both relieving and reliving alienation. Paradoxically, the sexual experience heightens the lovers' dissatisfaction with language, even in the form of literary attempts to articulate the contradictions: "there are books that describe all this/ and they are useless." When Rich quotes Artaud's dictum *"burn the texts,"* she refers primarily to inherited structures of thought, particularly the abstract moral principles which circumscribe individual perception and help ensure alienation.

In sections three and five of "The Burning of Paper Instead of Children," Rich emphasizes the distance between abstract analyses of suffering and the actual experience of the sufferers. Patriarchal language, Rich suggests, contributes directly to oppression by creating the impression that the "illiterate" sufferers are less than fully human. In response to this perception, Rich reconceives the relationship between "literacy" and moral perception. Following a "standard English" sentence concerning the "dignity and intelligence" needed to overcome the suffering caused by poverty, Rich catalogs several "illiterate" expressions of the suffering: "a child did not had dinner last night: a child steal because he did not have money to buy it: to hear a mother say she do not have money to buy food for her children and to see a child without cloth it will make tears in your eyes." Questioning the meaning of the abstract terms "dignity" and "intelligence," these sentences montage concrete images, socio-political commentary, and direct address to the reader. Clearly, the "broken" English communicates its moral impulse much more forcefully than either the articulate abstractions of the first sentence or Rich's neighbor in section one. Somewhat paradoxically, Rich concludes section three with a grammatically ambiguous statement of an abstract moral principle: "(the fracture of order/ the repair of speech/ to overcome this suffering)."

This call for transformation of the patriarchy involves both linguistic and institutional orders. Echoing Artaud's call for burning of the texts, Rich's principle contrasts sharply with her neighbor's identification of burning with Naziism in section one. Obviously, Rich does not endorse Hitler when she questions her neighbor's indignation. Resisting any "order" which claims the right to define individuals without comprehending their experience, she establishes a perspective clearly opposed to those of Hitler and her neighbor. Rich does not label her neighbor a Nazi. Rather, she focuses on her own analogous tendency to use language to escape from engagement. Synthesizing the major motifs of the previous sections, section five of "The Burning of Paper Instead of Children" presents a charged picture of the tension between Rich's solipsism and her urge to engage the suffering. Contemplating her experience as a poet, Rich comments ironically on her "successful" articulation of the suffering, suggesting an analogy between her position and that of Frederick Douglass, who "wrote an English purer than Milton's." The ability of the former slave and the twentieth-century feminist to "master" forms of expression deeply connected with racism and misogyny (as well as with spiritual grandeur and aesthetic power) represents only a limited triumph. Observing that "A language is a map of our failures," Rich illustrates the point by translating the suffering of section three—which drew part of its power from the black dialect Douglass chose not to use—into a correct but morally neutral English: "People suffer highly in poverty. There are methods but we do not use them."

Recasting the previous expressions of economic and sexual suffering, Rich recognizes that her own involvement with the oppressor's language is also a form of suffering: "Some of the suffering are: it is hard to tell the truth; this is America; I cannot touch you now." Inevitably influenced by the "moral" masks of America's cultural solipsism, Rich can only repudiate all abstract generalizations, differentiating carefully between her actual experience and her moral principles: "The burning of a book arouses no sensation in me. I know it hurts to burn." She thinks of the flames in Catonsville, Maryland, where draft records were burned as an act of resistance to the system which, despite its principled opposition to book-burning, is willing to burn human beings with napalm. Rich's final "sentence," technically a run-on, compresses her own articulate suffering with the fracture of order anticipated in section three: "The typewriter is overheated, my mouth is burning, I cannot touch you and this is the oppressor's language." To omit any element or to establish rational connections would belie the experience of contradiction. Rich realizes her own complicity with the patriarchal system, which tempts her either to translate her perceptions into the oppressive language which perpetuates the suffering or to perceive herself as a powerless victim. The latter temptation is in some ways the most insidious because it encourages both a "useless" sense of moral superiority and a passive response to suffering. Expressing both the elements of continuity and change in Rich's process, "The Burning of Paper Instead of Children," surprisingly similar to "Aunt Jennifer's Tigers," transforms fragments salvaged from the patriarchy into expressions of a sensibility potentially capable of moving beyond the patriarchal confines.

"FROM AN OLD HOUSE IN AMERICA"

"The Burning of Paper Instead of Children" marks a crucial transition in Rich's understanding of her process. The shift can be seen in the comparison of her two volumes of collected poems. Viewed retrospectively, the process "graphed" in *Poems: Selected and New* leads inevitably toward recognition of the inadequacy of Rich's previous engagements with the oppressor's language. The process graphed in *The Fact of a Doorframe* incorporates almost all of the poems included in the earlier volume but, by placing them in a new context, emphasizes their contribution to the development of an alternative "common language." Providing a crucial transition between these stages of Rich's process, "From an Old House in America" (1974), the final poem in *Poems: Selected and New*, reconsiders the major concerns of "Snapshots of a Daughter-in-Law"—alienation, repression, rape, the need for alternatives—from a position of greater political experience and personal awareness. This reconsideration supports Deborah Pope's and Erica Jong's arguments that the crucial transition in Rich's career involves her ability to perceive silence as a stage in a process of rebirth rather than as a cause for despair.

Rich's limited awareness of patriarchy invested the snapshots of the earlier poem with an alienating power that discouraged use of the first person pronoun. In "From an Old House in America," she claims her own vision while subjecting the old images to revision. In section seven, a brilliant consideration of the position of women in American patriarchy, Rich asserts her power:

> I never chose this place
> yet I am of it now
> In my decent collar, in the daguerrotype
> I pierce its legend with my look.

The passage asserts both Rich's identification with the half-legendary woman in the picture and her ability—expressed in the phallic image of "piercing"—to comprehend and transform the legend. In addition, the passage suggests that the woman in the daguerrotype shares the power which, if recognized, would enable her to resist the patriarchal pressures. Throughout the poem, Rich associates her transformative power with a developing, if still implicit, post-Cartesian sensibility. Attending to the "soft speech" of "plain and ordinary things," she perceives in seemingly disconnected experiences an interrelationship which subverts patriarchal definitions:

> I do not want to simplify
> Or: I would simplify
> by naming the complexity
> It was made over-simple all along
> the separation of powers
> the allotment of suffering.

Before turning to the generation of a language both simpler and more complex than that of the oppressors, Rich recapitulates her insights concerning patriarchal power. She does this in part to remind her readers of the reality of the forces she perceived as overwhelming during earlier stages of her process:

> If you do not believe
> that fear and hatred
> read the lesson again
> in the old dialect.

The lessons she includes in "From an Old House in America" are familiar to readers who have shared her process. Rich portrays the alienation of women whose lives are "mostly un-articulate." Like Aunt Jennifer, the immigrant woman of section nine sews a quilt "through iron nights"; like the woman in "Face to Face," she must come to terms with a husband with "fingers frozen around his Law." Identifying repression as a form of violence against the self, Rich describes a line of portraits on the wall of the old house. These frozen images portray suicidal women mechanically learning to imitate "the final autistic statement/ of the self-destroyer"; women giving birth while chained to corpses; women "Hanged as witches, sold as breeding wenches"; and women immolating themselves physically and spiritually while praying to the "father" for release from the burden of selfhood. Section seven, which begins with the line "I am an American woman," culminates in Rich's identification of alienation, experienced as individual isolation but actually a shared burden, as the crux of American women's historical experience: "Most of the time, in my sex, I was alone."

Where "Snapshots of a Daughter-in-Law" portrayed this isolation in a series of seemingly disconnected fragments, "From an Old House in America" synthesizes Rich's perceptions concerning its patriarchal sources. Exploring the "irreducible, incomplete" connections in the "savagely fathered and unmothered world," Rich asserts "It was lust that had defined us—/ their lust and fear of our deep places." Even as she identifies the core of the Cartesian/patriarchal American imagination in the "mother-hatred driving him/ into exile from the earth," Rich refuses to assume the role of man-hater. Rather, she determines to use her knowledge of patriarchal "lust and fear" as a "key" to a far-reaching transformation. Men as well as women are victimized by patriarchy in "From an Old House in America"; the male victims resemble the women in "Snapshots of a Daughter-in-Law" in that they remain unaware of the source of their malaise. Apparently addressing her dead husband in section five, Rich observes that even men capable of seeing past the obvious patriarchal distortions may not have the strength to reconstruct their own sense of identity:

> If they call me man-hater, you
> would have known it for a lie
> but the you I want to speak to
> has become your death.

Recalling the anguished atmosphere of "Trying to Talk with a Man," a deeply felt pain permeates both this section and section fourteen, which consists of a conversation with a man attempting simultaneously to salvage his sense of worth and to deny his relationship to the "collective guilt" of patriarchal history. The woman refuses to accept any rhetorical or theoretical pronouncements, insisting that worth and/or guilt can be measured only by direct perception: *"let me look in your eyes."* The image of the woman in the man's eyes metamorphoses from an emblem of oppression in "Snapshots of a Daughter-in-Law" into a challenge to the man to undertake the process of re-vision which the woman has already begun.

Rich knows this process will not be painless for either men or women. She fears that her own re-visions may reflect an image of herself still chained to the patriarchal corpse. Even as she declares women's independence near the end of "From an Old House in America," she reminds her readers of the danger of re-creating the patriarchal images grounded in Cartesian modes of thought:

> Isolation, the dream
> of the frontier woman
> levelling her rifle along
> the homestead fence
> still snares our pride.

Carefully avoiding this snare, Rich claims her independence—which inevitably involves her assumption of the "masculine" powers imaged in Orion's sword or the frontier woman's gun—without denying her developing sense of relationship. At the beginning of "From an Old House in America," a vacuum cleaner sucks up the fragments of the past which clutter Rich's environment. A relatively rare bit of humor in Rich's poetry, the use of the stereotypically feminine domestic machine recalls the transformation of technology imaged in the helicopter-woman of "Snapshots of a Daughter-in-Law." After Rich takes control of the literal and rhetorical premises, she addresses her dead husband with confidence in her independence: "If I dream of you these days/ I know my dreams are mine and not of you."

Rich's new-found confidence carries over into her interaction with women. Placing her hand on an "invisible palm-print/ on the door frame," she connects her own experience with that of the woman who had preceded her in the house. This gesture anticipates the aesthetic of "The Fact of a Doorframe" (1974), in which Rich endorses a poetry which is "violent, arcane, common,/ hewn of the commonest living substance/ into archway, portal, frame." Envisioning a communion based on common experience, Rich restates her vision of the woman artist/savior of "Snapshots of a Daughter-in-Law" in section fifteen of "From an Old House in America."

Weaving her revision around the image of the Erinyes who judge, comfort, and inscribe, Rich asserts that the "Mother of reparations" has now arrived. She challenges her audience to move forward, to accept the image of a woman no longer defined by patriarchy. Specifically, Rich challenges her readers to accept their experience without evasion. This entails confessing the damage done by patriarchy; recognizing the "Mother"; and accepting "the woman in the mirror," who, as Rich emphasizes in "The Mirror in Which Two Are Seen as One," is at once individual and collective. Rich issues this challenge in full awareness that "the line dividing/ lucidity from darkness/ is yet to be marked out." Certain only that "Any woman's death diminishes me," that relationship rather than isolation must shape any new delineations, Rich departs from the old house in search of new premises. Patriarchy continues to condition her process, but by 1974 she had arrived at a point where it no longer determined the direction of her journey.

References

Atlas, James
    1980. "New Voices in American Poetry," *New York Times Magazine* Feb. 3, 1980, pp. 6, 9-11, 17.
Baldwin, James
    1972. *No Name in the Street.* New York: Dial.
Breslin, James
    1984. *From Modern to Contemporary.* Chicago: Univ. of Chicago Pr.
Capra, Fritjof
    1982. *The Turning Point.* New York: Simon and Schuster.
Christ, Carol
    1980. *Diving Deep and Surfacing: Women Writers and Spiritual Quest.* Boston: Beacon.
Cooper, Jane Roberta
    1984. (editor) *Reading Adrienne Rich.* Ann Arbor: Univ. of Michigan Pr.
Daly, Mary
    1973. *Beyond God the Father: Toward a Philosophy of Women's Liberation.* Boston: Beacon.
de Beauvoir, Simone
    1952. *The Second Sex,* trans. H. M. Parshley. New York: Knopf.
Fiedler, Leslie
    1966. *Love and Death in the American Novel.* New York: Stein and Day.
Gelpi, Barbara Charlesworth, and Albert Gelpi
    1975. (editors) *Adrienne Rich's Poetry.* New York: Norton.

Griffin, Susan
1978. *Woman and Nature: The Roaring Inside Her*. New York: Harper and Row.
Iraguray, Lucie
1985. *Speculum of the Other Woman* trans. Gillian C. Gill. Ithaca: Cornell Univ. Pr.
Jong, Erica
1973. "Visionary Anger," *Ms.* July, pp. 31-33. Rpt. in Gelpi, pp. 171-74.
Keyes, Claire
1984. "'The Angels Chiding': *Snapshots of a Daughter-in- Law*." In Cooper, pp. 30-50.
Kolodny, Annette
1975. *The Lay of the Land: Metaphor and History in American Life and Letters*. Chapel Hill: Univ. of North Carolina Pr.
Lawrence, D. H.
1964. *Studies in Classic American Literature*. New York: Viking.
Lieberman, Laurence
1977. *Unassigned Frequencies*. Urbana: Univ. of Illinois Pr.
Majors, Bruce Powell
1984. "The Comparable Worth Muddle," *Journal of Contemporary Studies* Summer, p. 53.
Martin, Wendy
1984. *An American Triptych: Anne Bradstreet, Emily Dickinson, Adrienne Rich*. Chapel Hill: Univ. of North Carolina Pr.
Molesworth, Charles
1979. *The Fierce Embrace: A Study of Contemporary American Poetry*. Columbia: Univ. of Missouri Pr.
Oberg, Arthur
1978. *The Modern American Lyric*. New Brunswick, N.J.: Rutgers Univ. Pr.
Ostriker, Alicia
1986. *Stealing the Language: The Emergence of Women's Poetry in America*. Boston: Beacon.
Peters, Robert
1982. *The Great American Poetry Bake-off*, 2nd series. Metuchen, N.J.: Scarecrow.
Pope, Deborah
1984. *A Separate Vision: Isolation in Contemporary Women's Poetry*. Baton Rouge: Lousiana State Univ. Pr.
Rich, Adrienne
1976. *Of Woman Born: Motherhood as Existence and Institution*. New York: Norton.

1980. "Compulsory Heterosexuality and Lesbian Existence," *Signs* Summer, pp. 631-60. Rpt. in *Blood, Bread, and Poetry*, pp. 23-75.

Slowik, Mary

1984. "The Friction of the Mind: The Early Poetry of Adrienne Rich," *Massachusetts Review* Spring, pp. 142-60.

Von Hallberg, Robert

1985. *American Poetry and Culture, 1945-1980.* Cambridge, Mass.: Harvard Univ. Pr.

CHAPTER 3

The Lesbian Vision: "The Meaning of Our Love for Women Is What We Have Constantly to Expand"

When Rich wrote in 1980 of "woman-identification" as "a source of energy, a potential springhead of female power" (Rich, *Blood*, p. 63), her words reflected a clear consensus among feminist poets and theorists, a consensus shaped in part by the critique of patriarchy in *Of Woman Born* and *On Lies, Secrets, and Silence*. If the concept of "woman-identification" attracts substantial agreement, however, the essay in which the words appear continues to evoke a much more ambivalent response. "Compulsory Heterosexuality and Lesbian Existence," in which Rich repudiates the "androgynous" alternative to patriarchy suggested in "Diving Into the Wreck" (see Chapter 5), challenged all feminists—lesbian and straight, female and male—to purge themselves of the heterosexism which Rich identified as the foundation of patriarchal power. Touching on extremely volatile social and psychological issues, Rich insisted on the primary role of lesbianism in releasing the energy "curtailed and wasted under the institution of heterosexuality." The ensuing debate, still very much in progress, ultimately involved issues such as the nature of the "women's aesthetic" in poetry, the relationship between "marginal" perspectives and "mainstream" culture, and the potential lesbian contribution to the solution of problems such as racism, economic injustice, and the threat of nuclear war.

Underlying Rich's involvement in these debates is the desire expressed in the title of a 1977 essay which anticipates many positions developed more fully in "Compulsory Heterosexuality and Lesbian Existence": "The Meaning of Our Love for Women Is What We Have Constantly to Expand." As she has joined poets such as Audre Lorde, Judy Grahn, Alta and Olga Broumas in grappling with the complexities of lesbian existence, Rich has focused less frequently on the patriarchal solipsism which commanded her attention from "Snapshots of a Daughter-in-Law" through "From an Old House in America." During the early stages of her specifically lesbian development, Rich at times assumed positions which, when removed from her on-going process,

appear reactive and exclusive. When understood as aspects of the
(re)discovery of personal and communal integrity, however, even these
"solipsistic" stages contribute to the firmly grounded expansive posture
of her most recent poetry. Like all explorers of the "wild zone" of lesbian experience, Rich found it necessary to accept her love for
women—which entailed accepting her own creative energies—before
she could devote energy to its expansive implications.

The "Lesbian Continuum"

The point of departure for the debate over Rich's approach to definitional strategy is her expansive concept of the "lesbian continuum,"
which includes

> a range—through each woman's life and throughout history—of
> woman-identified experience; not simply the fact that a woman has
> had or consciously desired genital sexual experience with another
> woman. If we expand it to embrace many more forms of primary
> intensity between and among women, including the sharing of a
> rich inner life, the bonding against male tyranny, the giving and
> receiving of practical and political support . . . we begin to grasp
> breadths of female history and psychology that have lain out of
> reach as a consequence of limited, mostly clinical, definitions of
> "lesbianism" [Rich, *Blood*, pp. 51-52].

The emphasis on access to wider areas of "female history and
psychology" seems particularly important to an understanding of the
actual uses of this expansive definition. Rich's conception of the
lesbian continuum articulates a visionary approach to women's experience, one designed to reduce women's sense of isolation and expand
access to a "usable past." As I shall discuss below, the idea of the lesbian continuum has served just such a purpose, inspiring numerous
revisions of women's history and helping release the power of poets
such as Emily Dickinson and H.D. from patriarchal distortion. Even
scholars who hesitate to use the term "lesbian" (Ratner) or to identify
themselves with it (Christ) draw freely on the woman-centered visions
developed by lesbian critics such as Bulkin, Grahn, and Mary Carruthers. Although Rachel Blau DuPlessis does not identify her book
Writing Beyond the Ending specifically as a piece of lesbian criticism, she
accepts the validity of an expansive sense of a lesbian continuum:

> in part, Rich uses the term "lesbian feminist" as we have been using
> the terms "feminist" or "critical" throughout this study, to describe a

person who has made an analytic severing from certain patriarchal cultural practices, whose acts of oppositional deliberation have brought her to the "other-side of everything"—to the questioning of primary institutions of social, sexual, and cultural organization. Rich's stance is consistent with the perspective of all the writers [Olive Schreiner, Dorothy Richardson, Virginia Woolf, H.D., Gwendolyn Brooks, Alice Walker, Doris Lessing, Charlotte Perkins Gilman, Denise Levertov, etc.] who are the subject of this study [p. 134].

While the expansive definition of lesbianism helps reclaim repressed elements of women's culture and history, it does not address certain equally important needs. In a thoughtful response to "Compulsory Heterosexuality and Lesbian Existence," Ann Ferguson insists on the continuing importance of genital sexuality to an adequate definition of lesbianism:

> The ability to take one's own genital sexual needs seriously is a necessary component of an egalitarian love relation, whether it be with a man or a woman. Furthermore, I would argue that the possibility of a sexual relationship between women is an important challenge to patriarchy because it acts as an alternative to the patriarchal heterosexual couple, thus challenging the heterosexual ideology that women are dependent on men for romantic/sexual love and satisfaction. Therefore, any definitional strategy which seeks to drop the sexual component of "lesbian" in favor of an emotional commitment to, or preference for, women tends to lead feminists to downplay the historical importance of the movement for sexual liberation [p. 164].

In arriving at her definition, Ferguson enumerates three goals of definitional strategy: "First, valorizing the concept *lesbian*; second, giving a sociopolitical definition of the contemporary lesbian community; and finally, reconceptualizing history from a lesbian and feminist perspective" (p. 161). Acknowledging that the first goal may be impossible to attain under present conditions, Ferguson claims that Rich's definition "oversimplifies and romanticizes the notion of [women's] resistance to patriarchy without really defining the conditions that make for successful resistance" (p. 160). Reflecting her own emphasis on actual conditions of life at specific historical moments, Ferguson proposes the following alternative to Rich's definition: "*Lesbian* is a woman who has sexual and erotic-emotional ties primarily with women or who sees herself as centrally involved with a community of self-identified lesbians whose sexual and erotic-emotional ties are primarily with women; and who is herself a self-identified lesbian" (p. 166).

This definition leads to a much narrower sense of women's history than does the concept of the "lesbian continuum." Applied to poetry, it excludes Dickinson (certainly) and H.D. (probably) from the lesbian tradition, exclusions which would seriously trouble most critics of lesbian poetry. When applied to a wide range of historical materials, Jacquelyn Zita observes, Ferguson's definition appears to be "deceptively solipsistic": "One side of Ferguson's definition requires that a woman be aware of herself as a lesbian and be recognized by the lesbian community as such. This is automatically exclusive. Not only does it exclude many of our dead sisters, but it also ignores women who, for various reasons, refused to turn their private lesbian lives into a social issue" (p. 176). Nonetheless, Ferguson's definition seems superior to Rich's in relation to the goal—inevitably grounded in the specifics of a historical moment—of giving a sociopolitical definition of the contemporary lesbian community. As Zita observes, given its tenuous position in a hostile patriarchal context, the lesbian community must defend its integrity against all attempts at infiltration and co-optation: "Trust becomes a major concern in accepting a woman as a lesbian, especially when infiltration and exploitation of the lesbian community have been all too common occurrences. Lesbian community is a place where lesbians can relax; where the worry of offending straight women no longer exists; where homophobia is erased; where the women you meet share common interests, and experiences, and desires; where lesbian sensibility and erotic caring are givens" (p. 175).

On occasion, Rich shares this insistence on genital sexuality as a component of her lesbian vision. In part this reflects her awareness of what Mary Daly calls "universalization": the patriarchal strategy of dismissing challenges by generalizing their meaning, a process which drains their experiential energy. In an interview with Elly Bulkin, Rich commented:

> Two friends of mine, both artists, wrote me about reading the *Twenty-One Love Poems* with their male lovers, assuring me how "universal" the poems were. I found myself angered, and when I asked myself why, I realized that it was anger at having my work essentially assimilated and stripped of its meaning, "integrated" into heterosexual romance. That kind of "acceptance" of the book seems to me a refusal of its deepest implications. The longing to simplify, to defuse feminism by invoking "androgyny" or "humanism," to assimilate lesbian experience by saying that "relationship" is really

all the same, love is always difficult—I see that as a denial, a kind of resistance, a refusal to read and hear what I've actually written, to acknowledge what I am [Bulkin, 1981, pp. 270-71].

The specificity of Ferguson's definition helps guarantee the individual self-identified lesbian an integrated base, a "lesbian space" where she can exist, if only temporarily, outside the realm of patriarchal definitions. Such a space, as Rich tacitly acknowledges when she resists universalization of her work, plays a vital role in enabling her to constantly expand the meaning of her love for women. Only when women acknowledge the reality of their specific experiences, including the experience of "clinical lesbianism," will they be able to make effective use of the entire range of Rich's lesbian continuum. Ultimately, Rich seeks to eliminate the tension between the needs of the lesbian community as defined by Ferguson and increased access to the rich historical and aesthetic traditions of women who may or may not have shared these specific needs. At present, however, the tension exists. The only approach consistent with Rich's commitment to a socially useful aesthetic is to use the definition of lesbianism most adequate to the situation immediately at hand and to reject academic criteria of consistency which would circumscribe her process.

In the aesthetic sphere, the expansive definition of lesbianism possesses great power, in part because women's poetry has received relatively little attention from mainstream academics. Released to a degree from the constant pressure of what Kathryn Pyne Addelson, following W. E. B. DuBois, refers to as "double consciousness," feminist critics have begun to focus on the realization of Rich's "dream of a common language." Building on the central image of Judy Grahn's influential volume The Common Woman (1969), Rich asserts the normalcy of experiences defined as grotesque by the patriarchal mainstream and invokes a shared form of expression capable of "asking women's questions, demanding a world in which the integrity of all women—not a chosen few—shall be honored and validated in every aspect of culture" (Rich, Lies, p. 17). Rich's celebratory introduction to Grahn's collected poems emphasizes the expansive aspect of this anti-elitist language: "The point . . . is not the 'exclusion' of men; it is that primary presence of women to ourselves and each other first described in prose by Mary Daly, and which is the crucible of a new language" (Rich, Lies, p. 250; italics Rich's).

A brief survey of recent feminist criticism of women's poetry reveals the profound impact of Rich's re-visionary dream, a dream shared with Daly, Grahn, Audre Lorde, and many other contemporary women writers. Accurately identifying the dominant impulses in lesbian poetry, Bulkin describes the developing language as "anti-literary, anti-intellectual, anti-hierarchical." In her study *The Highest Apple: Sappho and the Lesbian Poetic Tradition*, Grahn emphasizes that "commonality means we belong to a number of over-lapping groups, not just one" (p. 77). Grahn endorses the expansive definition of lesbianism in relation to aesthetic concerns when she celebrates "a bond of community whose definitions can be indefinitely expanded as long as the principles of central integration, of factuality rather than idealism, and of the centrality of woman to herself are kept" (p. 131). Variations on these principles frequently recur as touchstones in feminist criticism not directed specifically to lesbian poetry. Alicia Ostriker, for example, celebrates Rich's ability to articulate the common language of a wide range of women: "If we look at the poetry American women have been writing for the last two decades and want to delineate their discoveries, it is Rich, over and over again, who says a thing most plainly, most memorably" (p. 105).

Commenting on the visionary nature of Rich's recent work, Ostriker reiterates the consensual understanding that the "'Common' language means a faith that attempts to communicate can succeed, that we can connect, not as privileged persons or under special circumstances, but in ordinary dailiness" (p. 104). Similarly, Suzanne Juhasz's discussion of Rich in *Naked and Fiery Forms: Modern American Poetry by Women* (which draws its title from Rich's poem "Blood-Sister") endorses the ideal of feminist poetry as a means of "[altering] the communication between poet and reader/listener itself in accordance with feminist values, promoting nonhierarchical interchange rather than a power trip" (p. 197). Both Barbara Charlesworth Gelpi's essay "A Common Language: The American Woman Poet" and Wendy Martin's *An American Triptych* derive their re-visions of the history of American women's poetry from the concept of, as Gelpi phrases it, "the common language . . . which [makes] it possible to transcend the divided victim's consciousness into that of a common experience as ordinary women" (p. 279). Marge Piercy and Nancy Milford provide personal testimony to Rich's impact on the development of their sense of the common language. To continue listing examples of Rich's impact on feminist criticism seems pointlesss. What seems clear is that the attempt to transform Rich's dream into reality occupies a central position on the feminist critical agenda.

Integrity and the Lesbian Civitas

Of particular interest in regard to the realization of a dream which by its very nature requires the collaborative energies of many women from diverse backgrounds are recent essays by Catharine Stimpson and Mary Carruthers which provide more specific discussions of the underlying values of "Lesbian poetry." Stressing the link between "cultural feminism" and Rich's lesbian/feminist sensibility, Stimpson emphasizes Rich's attempt "to reconcile the claims of autonomy (being free, having will) and the claims of connection (being together, having unity)" (p. 261). Among the principles Stimpson identifies as crucial to this reconciliation are "cultural feminism's preference for women's communities, its commitment to women's self-determination, and its loathing of patriarchal heterosexuality" (p. 257). Carruthers' brilliant essay "The Re-Vision of the Muse: Adrienne Rich, Audre Lorde, Judy Grahn, Olga Broumas" endorses the expansive definition of lesbianism—"nor are all Lesbian poets always lesbian"—as a crucial element of the lesbian vision of community.   Carefully distinguishing between the aesthetic and social dimensions of her discussion, Carruthers focuses specifically on the visionary dimension of lesbian poetry, which seeks to effect a social transformation which would render the distinction between aesthetic and social meaningless. Stressing the crucial function of a new "myth of women together and separate from men," Carruthers identifies an implicit movement from "revolution to eschatology" in Rich's recent work. Carruthers describes Rich's vision of

the Lesbian *civitas* . . . a society predicated on familiarity and likenesses, rather than oppositions. It is a world of daughters and mothers, of women in infinite variety discovering a language which celebrates their recovered energy and power.   What is most troublesome in this image to the general public, of course, is its use of the lesbian bond to signify that wholeness, health, and integrity which are minimized or negated by the death-devoted sickness of male-inspired civilization. Yet the logic of this image is right, even necessary, to the task which these poets have set themselves. Poetic tradition has not given women a language in which they can readily imagine their lives with integrity and completeness [p. 304].

The crucial terms in this discussion are *civitas* and *integrity*. Implicitly asserting a connection between the inclusive and exclusive definitions of lesbianism, these terms are crucial to Rich's attempt to reconcile the energies of autonomy and those of connection. Complementing Bulkin's description of the lesbian aesthetic as "personal, accessible, nonhierarchical," this constellation of concepts helps clarify the poetic process through which Rich has sought to expand the meaning of her love for women.

Rich's attempt to attain a sense of integrity which will contribute to the development of an expansive lesbian civitas involves both aesthetic and social considerations. In addition to reconsidering her underlying values in poems such as "The Mirror in Which Two Are Seen as One" (1971) and "Integrity" (1978), Rich considers their actual significance in regard to the idea of the common language. Attempting to disengage her own voice from the patriarchal aesthetic tradition, Rich sketches an "ideal" (though by no means abstract) process of communication in the brilliant sequence "Twenty-One Love Poems" (1974-76). This process is both derived from and tested against a range of women's experience, including that of foremothers such as Dickinson and H.D. Not limiting her consideration of the "lesbian continuum" to poets, Rich frequently meditates on the experience both of extraordinary "heroines" and of common women working in isolation. Alongside her historical excavations and her visionary mapping of the psychological, social, and mythic dimensions of lesbian space, Rich contributes to the growth of the actual civitas. Her participation in public forums and her continuing dialogs with Lorde, Grahn, Daly, and others seek to alter the actual conditions of life for younger writers who she hopes will not have to face the isolation experienced by the older lesbian writers, who, as Bulkin notes, wrote "without knowledge of such history and with little or no hope of support from a women's and/or lesbian writing community" (Bulkin, 1981, p. xxiii). As the lesbian community has developed a firmer sense of integrity, Rich has begun to concentrate on the problem of envisioning a lesbian approach—one consistent with the basic values of integrity and civitas—to the myriad problems of the patriarchal context, especially the problem of racism both within and beyond the women's movement.

As a comparison of "The Mirror in Which Two Are Seen as One" and "Integrity" shows, Rich refined her understanding of the relationship between integrity and *civitas* significantly during the 1970s. The sometimes anguished struggle to give birth to a new self in the earlier poem gradually gives way to the more confident vision expressed in the latter. The epigraph of "Integrity" defines the title term as "the quality or state of being complete; unbroken condition; entirety." Rich's attribution of this definition to "Webster" wryly challenges her readers to dissociate themselves from solipsistic patriarchal modes of thought. As used by Rich, "Webster" refers not to the patriarchal dictionary but to the mythic web-spinner/matrix builder described in Mary Daly's *Pure Lust*. Completeness, from this revisionary lesbian perspective, involves a full range of relationships with the many aspects of the self and of the *civitas*. The traditional definition of integrity as an essentially individualistic, frequently transcendent, state of being has little meaning within the developing common language.

"THE MIRROR IN WHICH TWO ARE SEEN AS ONE"

Yet Rich did not come to the Webster's definition easily. Influenced by American transcendentalism and Euro-American modernism, her early work conceives of integrity as a state attainable only in solitude. Marking a point of maximum tension in her process, "The Mirror in Which Two Are Seen as One" records the complexity of her struggle to accept the implications of her new perspective. Rich's reluctance to accept any incursion upon or connection with her personal integrity can be sensed in the line which opens both of its first two sections. Introducing the central problem of identity and relationship, the line reads: "She is the one you call sister." As the complex ambiguity of the title suggests, "she" and "you" may represent either aspects of a single woman's psyche, or two women involved in an unspecified relationship. In either case, "their" or "her" relationship to the poem's persona presents additional complexities. One reading of the image of the mirror would integrate "she" and "you" in a single "I" gazing at her own reflection; this concept of integrity seems distinctly individualistic and at least incipiently solipsistic. If, however, the poem is a mirror held up to its readers—a conceit as old as Thomas Wyatt—then the concept of integrity functions much more expansively, incorporating both characters and readers in its unifying reflection. This reading necessitates a shift in understanding of the syntax of the sentence. "Sister" changes from predicate adjective ("she" is being called a sister) to the object of address ("she" is being called by a woman the persona calls "sister"). The charged ambiguity which results from balancing these readings against one another seems most consistent with the emotional force of a poem which inspired Ostriker to image Rich as "a mirror in which multitudes are seen as one" (p. 105).

The overall movement of the poem—which culminates in the delivery of the baby of a dead mother by a midwife who is herself identified with the baby—suggests that, whatever the relationship of the women in the poem, they ultimately merge. It would in fact be possible to read the poem as an invocation of a lesbian muse. Transforming the aggressively patriarchal conception of the muse as feminine and other into a conception of the muse as "Familiar, maternal and sororal" (Carruthers, p. 295), Rich attempts to release the creative power of a female self which incorporates both self and "others" reconceived in terms of "familiarity and likenesses, rather than oppositions." In essence, Rich makes a very large, and perhaps unprecedented, gesture by claiming the stature of a muse not just for herself (a claim anticipated by Dickinson) but for other women poets. The use of "a" rather than "the" as the article preceding "muse" is important. Rich's communal conception of the muse challenges all women to discover in themselves the expansive integrity which, it could well be argued, is the identifying characteristic of powerful artists from Sappho and Shakespeare to Jane Austen and Gabriel Garcia Marquez.

If "The Mirror in Which Two Are Seen as One" calls for such a discovery, however, it expresses no illusions concerning the difficulties of the quest. Each segment of the poem identifies a barrier to its successful completion: the problem of accepting anger, especially anger over the failure of past efforts to harvest "the fruits of love"; the denial of passion for other women, whether physical, intellectual, or spiritual; and the difficulty of honestly confronting the brutalities of women's past treatment without succumbing to despair. The persona's fascination with the woman, or aspect of self, in the first section stems in large part from her apparent ability to combine feelings of love and anger in what appears to be a traditional domestic context. "Her simplest act has glamor" as she manipulates a scaling knife or talks of love while burnishing a kettle. Despite her attraction to this efficient feminine energy, the "you" of the section feels unable to respond fully. Even as she contemplates the theoretical plenty in her own domestic environment—the refrigerator is full, she is surrounded by ripe clusters of grain—she feels a "sudden emptiness." Despite her arduous attempts to fill the empty crate in the orchard—"your hands are raw with scraping"—the persona's energy deserts her. Unable to find a way of using the energy of the "she," especially the implicitly explosive energy imaged in the flashing knife, the "you" resigns herself to the feeling that "this harvest is a failure."

The second stanza again opens with an image of passionate energy, this time attributed primarily to the "you" who was unable to respond in section one: "you blaze like lightning about the room/ flicker around her like fire." Attesting to the presence of both active and passive principles in each individual woman, "she" in section two embodies more traditionally feminine attributes. Sensually moving "through a world of India print/ her body dappled/ with softness," "she" concerns herself primarily with responding to her companion's desires: "buying fresh figs because you love them/ photographing the ghetto because you took her there." Despite the reciprocity of feeling—"you" is "listing her unfelt needs"—which expands to include the persona who writes "we are sisters," the women in section two lack the common language which might enable them to progress from tentative connection to full acknowledgment of their love for one another. Ultimately, they retreat into the relative safety of indirect symbolic communication: "words fail you in the stare of her hunger/ you hand her another book."

Extending this progression toward felt connection, section three obliterates the distinction between "she" and "you," although it maintains the implicit tension between "you" and "I." Posing the question of integrity directly—"In this mirror, who are you?"—Rich catalogs historical manifestations of the separation portrayed in the first two sections. The nunnery, the nursery, the hospital: all appear as "dreams" centering on the death of women. Rising to an emotional intensity which expresses the anger imaged at the start of section one, Rich speaks with an integrated voice "of women who died in childbirth/ and women who died at birth." Bringing the anger to bear directly on the problems of the women (or woman) the poem centers on, Rich presents an anguished image of a bond between the "you" and her sister which entails the destruction of the mother, and therefore perpetuates the cycle of separation:

> Dreams of your sister's birth
> your mother dying in childbirth over and over
> not knowing how to stop
> bearing you over and over.

The final stanza of the poem incorporates the previously frustrated energies. Trapped like the persona of Arnold's "Dover Beach" between the "dead" and the "unborn," Rich's persona learns to manipulate the "blade of life" as she steadies herself for her own delivery, determined to resist the pressures which might frustrate the birth: "your nerves the nerves of a midwife/ learning her trade."

"INTEGRITY"

Midway through "Integrity," which culminates in the image of Rich as a fully accomplished midwife, Rich pauses to question the sense of integrity suggested by the preceding recapitulation of her earlier process: "*Nothing but myself? . . . My selves.*" Clearly acknowledging the expansive implications of "The Mirror in Which Two Are Seen as One," the shift to the plural cautions against an individualistic understanding of the Webster's definition which opens the poem. At this stage of her process, Rich interprets the emotional tensions presented through the juxtaposition of the "she" and "you" in the earlier poem as qualities present in each woman: "Anger and tenderness: my selves." Accepting this multiplicity enables her to resolve a number of the tensions which had haunted her earlier work. Where "The Demon Lover" and section two of "Snapshots of a Daughter-in-Law" present the urges to express anger and love for women as a battle between vaguely defined and deeply ambiguous demonic forces, "Integrity" presents the conjunction of these impulses as redemptive: "And now I can believe they breathe in me/ as angels, not polarities." Recognizing that her hands possess the full range of human abilities—they can hammer nails and slam doors without relinquishing the tenderness needed to nurture a clematis battered by a storm—she uses them to help put an end to the nightmarish cycle of childbirth and maternal death pictured in "The Mirror in Which Two Are Seen as One":

> they have caught the baby leaping
> from between trembling legs
> and they have worked the vacuum aspirator
> and stroked the sweated temples.

The combination of technological expertise and emotional support intimates one potential manifestation of the new integrity beyond the visionary context of the poem.

Rich portrays the process leading to this profound transformation as a traditional quest, shaping the poem around the image of the persona rowing a boat to the shores of an inland sea. Beginning *in medias res*, she invokes her own qualities in the opening line: "A wild patience has taken me this far." Cataloging the encounters she has survived, she emphasizes the pain caused by "some kind of sun" (an implicit reference to the patriarchal preference for the male child) which burns the "fore-arms," making effective use of her hands impossible. The first "plot" stanza concludes with the only grammatical indication of internal separation in the poem. Recalling the absence of the first person pronoun in "Snapshots of a Daughter-in-Law" and the fragmented pronouns in "The Mirror in Which Two Are Seen as One," Rich associates the pronoun "you" with the inability to accept and articulate the rage engendered by the "sun": "Your fore-arms can get scalded, licked with pain/ in a sun blotted like unspoken anger." The light she sees by "is critical: of me, of this long-dreamed, involuntary landing." Faced with the extreme difficulty of determining whether the criticism expresses the limitations of her sense of integrity or an imposed patriarchal system of values devaluing her quest, she determines to abandon all external systems of perception:

> really I have nothing but myself
> to go by; nothing
> stands in the realm of pure necessity
> except what my hands can hold.

The brilliant phrase "nothing but myself to go by" provides a fulcrum, enabling Rich to make full use of her hands in the second half of the poem. By embracing her individual experience and relaxing her concern with the criticism of the sunlight, she is able to perceive the necessity of going beyond the sense of a self engaged in a purely individual quest. Once she has accepted her "selves," Rich finds that she can "steer the boat in, simply," assuming the control that allows her to master her new trade as midwife/doctor. In addition, she sees clearly that her hands have possessed their power all along, that despite their burns, they

> steered the boat here through this hot
> misblotted sunlight
> critical light
> imperceptibly scalding
> the skin these hands will also salve.

Ironically, several of the antagonists faced by the questing heroine as she seeks salvation in her new sense of wholeness are themselves literary questers, most notably T. S. Eliot. The image of the boat being guided ashore echoes the fifth section of "The Waste Land," which, as I shall argue in my discussion of "Leaflets" in Chapter 5, has attracted Rich's re-visionary energies at least once before. Where Eliot, writing in a complex modernist style, sought salvation from his feelings of fragmentation in a constellation of transcendent forces, Rich creates a style designed to express the unified, concretely grounded, self who is able to "steer the boat in, simply." To be sure, Rich's conclusion in "Integrity" parallels Eliot's own; the boat in section five of "The Waste Land" responds "Gaily, to the hand expert with sail and oar." Eliot, however, extends the image in a way which Rich finds unacceptable, a major impediment to her own quest: "your heart would have responded/ Gaily, when invited, beating obedient/ To controlling hands." The problem with this passage for Rich is twofold. First, as a woman writing in a patriarchal tradition, she has been denied "controlling hands"; second, she has received no invitation to participate in the quest as an equal.

To attain the sense of integrity implied by the Webster's definition, she has no choice but to turn the "critical" light away from herself and point it toward her literary masters. The final stanza of "Integrity" extends the confrontation with Eliot from "The Waste Land" to "Little Gidding." The last of the *Four Quartets* presents Eliot's vision of a communal quest as follows:

We shall not cease from exploration
and the end of all our exploring
Will be to arrive where we started
And know the place for the first time.

Particularly in combination with the echoes of "The Waste Land," the
questing heroine's description of her arrival at the "cabin in the stand
of pines" where she expressed her anger and tenderness without realizing their significance reflects her refusal to join Eliot's version of the
communal "we." Simply and directly, Rich asserts her claim to a
knowledge unmediated by the criticism of masters: "I know this.
Know the print of the last foot . . . I know the chart." Rich's return to
the house serves as an emblem of her return to Eliot. No longer lacking control of her own direction or bound to the individualistic sense
of integrity, she can reconsider his vision, surrendering neither "anger"
nor "tenderness." Even as she insists upon the simplicity of expression
implicit in the concept of the "common language," she recognizes the
actual complexity of the task. Like the spider, the Webster spinning
out new definitions of old words and patterns, Rich recasts the conclusion of "The Waste Land" in feminist terms. Where Eliot's persona had
only "fragments . . . shored against my ruins," Rich implicitly
repudiates his resignation when she celebrates as her own "the spider's
genius/ to spin and weave in the same action/ from her own body,
anywhere—/ even from a broken web."

"THE KNOT"

The association of "unspoken anger" with "a casual mist" suggests
that "Integrity" completes a related re-visionary process begun in "The
Knot" (1965). Reflecting Rich's awareness of modernism as a many-
faceted movement, both poems revoice images from William Carlos
Williams, who anticipated many of Rich's criticisms of Eliot's abstract
modernism. Culminating in the image of the eye seeing "through a
mist of blood," "The Knot" responds directly to Williams' "Queen-
Anne's-Lace" (1921), and perhaps also to Robert Frost's "Design" (1936).
Recalling the "Whiteness of the Whale" chapter of *Moby-Dick*, both
Frost and Williams construct their poems around the metaphorical
significance of the color white. Frost speculates on the theological
significance of the coincidence which has brought together a white
spider, moth and flower; in accord with his aesthetic emphasis on particularity, Williams focuses on the flower. Like Shakespeare in "My
Mistress' Eyes Are Nothing Like the Sun," Williams uses the rhetorical

convention of negation to develop an extended analogy between the queen-anne's-lace and a woman's body. Images of subdued sexual violence occur throughout Williams' poem: the wild carrot takes "the field by force"; "wherever/ his hand has lain there is/ a tiny purple blemish." After denying the abstract purity of the flower/woman —"here is no question of whiteness,/ white as can be"—Williams concludes by suggesting that the flower desires its own destruction, its own violation:

> Each part
> is a blossom under his touch
> to which the fibres of her being
> stem one by one, each to its end,
> until the whole field is a
> white desire, empty, a single stem,
> a cluster, flower by flower,
> a pious wish to whiteness gone over—
> or nothing.

Although Williams may intend "Queen-Anne's-Lace" as a subtle critique of the lover/rapist's consciousness—his short story "The Use of Force" expresses a similar theme—"The Knot" responds to the poem as a patriarchal attempt to distract attention from the reality of sexual violence. Rich's opening lines read equally well as a nature poem or as direct commentary on Williams: "In the heart of the queen anne's lace, a knot of blood./ For years I never saw it." Reconsidering her perception of the flower's whiteness as "A foaming meadow; the Milky Way," she emphasizes the undertones of sexual violence in "Queen-Anne's-Lace":

> there, all along, the tiny dark-red spider
> sitting in the whiteness of the bridal web,
> waiting to plunge his crimson knifepoint
> into the white apparencies.

Although "The Knot" responds most directly to Williams, the spider at the center of the flower suggests an additional revoicing of Frost. Like Frost's use of "appall" in "Design," Rich's use of "apparencies" compresses presence and absence, vision and void. Rich's treatment of the paradox, however, emphasizes its concrete meaning in relation to the experience of women, suggesting an evasive quality in her male predecessors. The concluding abstraction of "Queen-Anne's-Lace"

—the flower literally wills itself into "nothingness"—veils the sexual implications of Williams' image; the speculative voice frequently distracts attention from the social context of Frost's life and work. Even at an early stage of the process, Rich realizes that recognizing the violence behind the aesthetic "apparencies" of the modernist "masters" will inevitably unleash the anger necessary to the development of her integrity: "Little wonder the eye, healing, sees/ for a long time through a mist of BLOOD."

"TRANSCENDENTAL ETUDE"

Returning to the "backroads fringed with queen anne's lace" in the final poem in *The Dream of a Common Language*, Rich feels the mist clearing. Even as it recapitulates the critique of American male modernism implicit in "The Knot," "Transcendental Etude" (1977) seems concerned primarily with re-vision rather than repudiation of the tradition (Diehl). As Gertrude Reif Hughes notes in her perceptive discussion of Emersonian elements in the poem, the opening descriptions of "hit-and-run hunters, glorying/ in a weekend's destructive power" seem relatively perfunctory beside the poem's intricate engagement with the subtleties of the transcendentalist tradition (in Cooper, p. 156). The second verse paragraph of "Transcendental Etude" marks a clear shift in Rich's focus from the destructive aspects of the American tradition to its philosophical underpinnings:

Later I stood in the dooryard,
my nerves singing the immense
fragility of all this sweetness,
this green world already sentimentalized, photographed,
advertised to death.

Recalling Whitman in vocabulary ("dooryard") and syntax (especially in the second line), Rich echoes the lament over the destructiveness of civilization sounded in *Democratic Vistas*, Cooper's Leatherstocking tales, Faulkner's "The Bear," and Hemingway's *The Sun Also Rises*. Although she suspects a "knot of blood" near the heart of at least some of these manifestations of the transcendental impulse, Rich shares their awe before the natural world: "a lifetime is too narrow/ to understand it all, beginning with the huge/ rockshelves that underlie all that life."

Even as she acknowledges the Whitmanesque/Emersonian impulse, however, Rich presents its previous expressions as impediments to women's apprehension of transcendent forces in relation to their own integrity. Repeatedly, Rich insists that each individual woman re(dis)cover her own relationship with her self/selves. This recovery, which provides the "rockshelf" supporting further growth, is complicated by the patriarchal language of previous descriptions: "nothing that was said/ is true for us"; "all the texts describe it differently." Demanding unmediated confrontation with "the undimensional solitudes," this process gives rise to feelings of absolute loneliness. Nonetheless, Rich interprets isolation as a crucial transitional stage in a progression from anger to "validation" (Pope) or "commitment" (Howard). The attempt to "disenthrall ourselves," which Rich portrays as a primary condition of survival, begins with a descent into "silence, or a severer listening, cleansed/ of oratory, formulas, choruses, laments, static/ crowding the wires." Paradoxically, attaining an integrity of relationship begins with the apparent destruction of all relationship. The quester "herself and all creation/ seem equally dispersed, weightless, her being a cry/ to which no echo comes or can ever come." The crucial term in this description, however, is *seem*. Rich emphasizes that the familiar noise (against which the quester measures the silence) in fact expresses a spiritual, social, and psychological void:

> the whole chorus throbbing at our ears
> like midges, told us nothing, nothing
> of origins, nothing we needed
> to know.

However frightening and intimidating the process, she insists that "No one who survives to speak/ new language, has avoided this:/ the cutting-away of an old force that held her."

Once she has experienced "the pitch of utter loneliness," however, the old force no longer dominates her consciousness. For the first time, she perceives the implications of the choral assault which insisted "that it is unnatural,/ the homesickness for a woman, for ourselves." To accept this definition is to surrender her integrity, to exclude herself from the process described in the old transcendentalist texts. This realization frees Rich to articulate the Webster's sense of integrity for the first time: *"This is what she was to me, and this/ is how I can love myself—/ as only a woman can love me."* Realizing that her alienation from her self cannot be separated from her alienation from other women, she celebrates "a whole new poetry beginning here." Subjecting Emerson's "Brahma" to a re-vision with far-reaching implications, she transforms the text of the master into a statement of lesbian aesthetics:

> *I am the lover and the loved,*
> *home and wanderer, she who splits*
> *firewood and she who knocks, a stranger*
> *in the storm.*

Where Emerson emphasizes the philosophical paradox of relationship, Rich grounds its meaning in concrete physical experience. As Hughes observes in her comment on the "transparent eyeball" epiphany in *Nature*: "When Rich transcends her ego boundaries, the negative capability she achieves has a different quality. Rather than becoming *nothing* as Emerson did, Rich experimentally becomes *anything*" (in Cooper, p. 157).

In addition, Rich specifically disavows any hierarchical or abstracting intentions which might be derived from her sense of "embodied transcendence":

> Such a composition has nothing to do with eternity,
> the striving for greatness, brilliance—
> only with the musing of a mind
> one with her body.

Following a catalog (which echoes Whitman in syntax—"not forgotten either"—though not in content) of objects being merged in a specifically female composition, Rich makes it clear that here, as throughout *The Dream of a Common Language*, she seeks a new language capable of

> pulling the tenets of a life together
> with no mere will to mastery,
> only care for the many-lived, unending
> forms in which she finds herself.

At once highly personal and expansive, the conception of integrity developed in "Transcendental Etude" encourages further exploration of a process of communication based on respect and love rather than domination.

The early sections of "Transcendental Etude" incorporate an awareness of the poem's own contribution to such a process. Describing an ideal progression from personal integrity through individual communication to social commitment, Rich meditates on the "music" of her "etude":

> we should begin
> with the simple exercises first
> and slowly go on trying

> the hard ones, practicing till strength
> and accuracy became one with the daring
> to leap into transcendence, take the chance
> of breaking down in the wild arpeggio
> or faulting the full sentence of the fugue.

Still, Rich recognizes two problems with such an idealized process. First, women have traditionally been excluded from serious developmental processes: "No one ever told us we had to study our lives." Second, ideal processes exist only on the abstract plane the poem rejects: "And in fact we can't live like that." All schematic processes, Rich believes, inevitably break down under the complex forces present in the actual world. As its title indicates, "Transcendental Etude" is simply a study of the idea of transcendence. It does not test the possibility of realizing its vision in a world where

> we take on
> everything at once before we've even begun
> to read or mark time, we're forced to begin
> in the midst of the hardest movement.

The actual test of her integrity, "the stone foundation, rockshelf further/ forming under everything that grows," is its ability to sustain communication in a society which cares little for transcendence of any type.

"TWENTY-ONE LOVE POEMS"

Adapting the form and conventions of the traditional love sonnet sequence, "Twenty-One Love Poems" (1974-76) provides just such a test. Rich acknowledges the difficulty of realizing an ideal process in the actual world:

> two women together is a work
> nothing in civilization has made simple,
> two people together is a work
> heroic in its ordinariness. [Poem XIX]

As Adrian Oktenberg observes, "Twenty-One Love Poems" is dialectical in nature; the dialectic, however, is somewhat more complex than Oktenberg implies. It is certainly true that the sequence "is concerned with not one but two civilizations" and that "patriarchal civilization is

only the starting point . . . Rich is equally concerned to grasp . . .
another conception of civilization—one that is woman-centered,
woman-identified, woman-created" (in Cooper, pp. 73-74). Rich is
equally concerned, however, with the dialectic between communication and solitude in the lives of two women whose experience is conditioned by the social dialectic Oktenberg emphasizes. Following Carol
Christ, who persuasively identifies the tarot deck as the source of the
imagery unifying the sequence, I would suggest that the core of the
"Twenty-One Love Poems" lies in Rich's ability to accept responsibility
for the painful collapse of what had seemed an ideal relationship
without surrendering her expansive sense of integrity. Courageous in
its simplicity, Rich's decision to accept her solitude and live "openly,
honestly, and with risk" (Christ, p. 93) reflects her awareness that the
real test of her process has little to do with patriarchal institutions: "If I
cling to circumstances I could feel/ not responsible. Only she who
says/ she did not choose, is the loser in the end."

  Without denying the accuracy and utility of Oktenberg's analysis of
"Twenty-One Love Poems" as anti-patriarchal argument, my discussion will focus on the ways in which the sequence adjusts the relationship between integrity and *civitas* envisioned in Rich's more
meditative poems. Whereas poems such as "Integrity," "The Mirror in
Which Two Are Seen as One," and "Transcendental Etude" focus
primarily on the psychology of the individual struggling to regain her
integrity, "Twenty-One Love Poems" focuses on the *use* of that integrity
by two women who share the "need to grasp our lives inseparable/
from [the] rancid dreams" of the patriarchal setting. Considering the
concrete implications of the other poems, Rich delineates the practical
attributes of the common language. Perhaps most importantly, it must
be nonhierarchical. The central line of poem III emphasizes the balance
of respect and desire in the lovers' responses to one another: "And
you, you move toward me with the same tempo." Anticipating the
image of the hand in "Integrity," poem VI credits the lover's hands with
the same anger and tenderness Rich finds in her own: "Your small
hands, precisely equal to my own . . . could turn the unborn child
rightways in the birth canal or . . . carry out an unavoidable violence."
In addition, Rich implies that a certain degree of shared experience
and/or perception helps provide the courage needed to maintain the
love of "women outside the law." In poem XIV, Rich describes a shared
perception as a crucial moment in the development of the relationship:
"It was your vision of the pilot/ confirmed my vision of you." Her
lover's ability to perceive the operations of patriarchal consciousness in
seemingly insignificant events is profoundly attractive. Hoping to be
freed from the need to continually justify basic modes of perception

and defend premises, Rich perceives an exhilarating potential for extended communication. The public touch of the two women—

suffering together
in our bodies, as if all suffering
were physical, we touched so in the presence
of strangers

—is a first tentative expression of an empowering common language. Shared perception contributes to the development of the language in part because the women can validate one another's sense of what experiences need naming: "I want to reach for your hand as we scale the path/ . . . never failing to note the small, jewel-like flower/ unfamiliar to us, nameless till we rename her." Recalling the free play of internal and external in the Webster's conception of integrity, Rich stresses the anti-solipsistic nature of the ideal process when she reflects on the naming of the flower: "that detail outside ourselves that brings us to ourselves,/ was here before us, knew we would come, and sees beyond us" (poem XI). Even when she senses the silence which subverts their relationship, Rich realizes the importance of her lover's ability to make "the unnameable/ nameable for others, even for me" (poem IX). Given this access to ways of naming consistent with her integrity, Rich feels able to reject inherited vocabularies which imply her victimization, committing herself "to go on from here with you/ fighting the temptation to make a career of pain."

Perhaps the most basic aspect of the common language in "Twenty-One Love Poems," however, is its approach to levels of experience which are not easily verbalized in any language. Projecting her own "animal thoughts" into her lover's dog in poem X, Rich writes of her belief "that creatures must find each other for bodily comfort,/ that voices of the psyche drive through the flesh/ further than the dense brain could have foretold." Seeking the tenderness without which "we are in hell," Rich communicates with her lover through the intensely erotic experience she celebrates in "THE FLOATING POEM, UNNUMBERED." In a world where all language is potentially evasive —"What kind of beast would turn its life into words?" (poem VII)—Rich asserts the importance of accepting sexuality as an aspect of integrity. The highly erotic lovemaking in "THE FLOATING POEM, UNNUMBERED" provides an emblem of a process of communication denied by received languages. Although the experience may be denied by those who consider lesbian sexuality unnatural or redefined by those who wish to universalize its meaning, Rich insists on its specific and untranslatable actuality: "whatever happens, this is."

If Rich presents an ideal process of empowering communication based on shared perception and mutual respect, she maintains her awareness of the antithetical forces both within and around the lovers. The early poems in the sequence establish the realities of pornographic violence (poem I), casual brutality in both political and personal forms (poem IV), and the historical oppression of women (poem V). Of more concern in regard to the dialectic between relationship and solitude, however, is Rich's consideration of the way these forces infiltrate the women's consciousness and subvert the ideal process. Paralleling the argument of the contemporaneous essay "Women and Honor: Some Notes on Lying" (1975), "Twenty-One Love Poems" emphasizes the danger of failing to express feelings and perceptions. Describing her lover's silence as "a pond where drowned things live," Rich says "I fear this silence,/ this inarticulate life" (poem IX). In the essay, Rich describes silence as a form of lying, a "danger run by all powerless people: that we forget we are lying, or that lying becomes a weapon we carry over into relationships with people who do not have power over us." Emphasizing that "When a woman tells the truth, she is creating the possibility for more truth around her," Rich argues that, however difficult the process of articulation, it provides the only alternative to the victimization she and her lover seek to escape: "Women have been driven mad, 'gaslighted,' for centuries by the refutation of our experience and our instincts in a culture which validates only male experience. The truth of our bodies and our minds has been mystified to us. We therefore have a primary obligation to each other: not to undermine each other's sense of reality for the sake of expediency; not to gaslight each other" (Rich, Lies, p. 190). The failure of the lovers in "Twenty-One Love Poems" to fulfill the promise of their process seems, at least indirectly, a form of "gaslighting." In poem XX, Rich thinks back on "That conversation we were always on the edge of having" and mourns the image of her lover "drowning in secrets,/ fear wound round her throat/ and choking her like hair." Ultimately, she realizes that the engulfing silence which drags the head "down deeper/ where it cannot hear me" also threatens her because, in expressing her deepest integrity to her lover, she "was talking to my own soul."

The dialectical process of "Twenty-One Love Poems" precludes simple retreat to the patriarchal perception of woman as victim or surrender to the romantic despair of Tristan und Isolde: "women at least should know the difference/ between love and death." Rather, she emerges from the experience with a strengthened commitment to expanding the meaning of her love for women. When her lover breaks her silence and says "the more I live the more I think/ two people together is a miracle" (poem XVIII), Rich feels herself returning to solitude and thinks *"There are no miracles"* (poem XIX). Unable to return to the romanticism of patriarchal love poetry, Rich reminds her lover of her continuing belief in a process capable of surviving tensions such as those described in poem XII:

> we have different voices, even in sleep,
> and our bodies, so alike, are yet so different
> and the past echoing through our bloodstreams
> is freighted with different language, different meanings.

The renewed experience of solitude reinforces Rich's perception that the common language must be able to express both similarity and difference, reflecting the diversity of individual apprehension of shared experience: "in any chronicle of the world we share/ it could be written with new meaning." Even faced with the relationship's collapse, she refuses to compromise the underlying values on which it was based: "I told you from the first I wanted daily life" (poem XIX).

Nor does she retreat to the feeling of victimization which had characterized her previous period of solitude. Repudiating the image of herself as isolated victim, Rich accepts the full implications of the credo presented in poem XV: "If I cling to circumstances I could feel/ not responsible. Only she who says/ she did not choose, is the loser in the end." Claiming control of her experience—"no one's fated or doomed to love anyone" (poem XVII)—Rich chooses to validate her personal integrity ("I am Adrienne alone," poem XVIII), the shared integrity of "THE FLOATING POEM, UNNUMBERED" ("whatever happens—this is"), and, above all, the integrity of the lesbian *civitas*. The final poem of "Twenty-One Love Poems" stakes out a specifically lesbian space—at once psychological, social, and mythological—which she refers to as "Stonehenge" (Christ, Carruthers). Rich associates this space both with her experience of intense relationship and with her refusal to deny her memory of that experience:

> this is not Stonehenge
> simply nor any place but the mind
> casting back to where her solitude,
> shared, could be chosen without loneliness.

Accepting the solitude which follows the end of her relationship with the specific lover, Rich affirms her belief in the expansive integrity which enables her to end the sequence with a simple statement of purpose: "I choose to walk here. And to draw this circle."

Part of the brilliance of "Twenty-One Love Poems" stems from Rich's awareness of their special position in the lesbian poetic tradition. As the relationship begins to decline, she realizes that part of the problem stems from the absence of an expressive tradition concerned with the problems she and her lover face. In place of romantic despair, Rich determines that her own perceptions should not remain entirely personal. She envisions a tape-recorder that "should have listened to us,/ and could instruct those after us" (poem XVII). "Twenty-One Love Poems" in effect transcribes the ideal process as it actually exists: "and these are the forces they had ranged against us,/ and these are the forces we had ranged within us,/ within us and against us, against us and within us" (poem XVII).

Rich and Dickinson

Seeking other models useful to women attempting to resist these complex forces, Rich frequently considers poetic predecessors, most notably Emily Dickinson. James Breslin hears echoes of Dickinson in Rich's work as early as "Vertigo" (1950); by "After Dark" (1964), Rich has begun to tap a Dickinsonian power which goes well beyond mere syntactical idiosyncracies. Between her first crucial consideration of Dickinson in "Snapshots of a Daughter-in-Law" and her "third and last address to you" in "The Spirit of Place" (1980), Rich has been largely successful in her attempt to see beyond what she described in the brilliant essay "Vesuvius at Home: The Power of Emily Dickinson" (1975) as the "legend [which] has gotten in the way of her being repossessed as a source and foremother" (Rich, *Lies*, p. 167). In defining the lesbian poetic tradition to include Dickinson, Rich explicitly rejects the exclusive definition of lesbianism. Rather than enmeshing herself in the critical-biographical argument over the identity and/or gender of Dickinson's supposed lover(s), Rich stresses the integrity of her personal process, her "mind engaged in a lifetime's musing on essential problems of language, identity, separation, relationship, the integrity of the self; a mind capable of describing psychological states more accurately than any poet except Shakespeare" (Rich, *Lies*, p. 167). Given the hostile circumstances surrounding its creation and the frequent distortions of its form and meaning by editors and critics, Rich finds in Dickinson an inspirational figure for herself and the lesbian *civitas*.

Rich's view of Dickinson as part of the lesbian tradition rests on the perception that she "is *the* American poet whose work consisted in exploring states of psychic extremity" (Rich, *Lies*, p. 176). Forced into a marginal position by the patriarchal tradition which defined the roles of woman and poet as mutually exclusive (Juhasz, 1976, p. 1), Dickinson accepted the risk of honestly confronting the forces ranged "within us and against us, against us and within us." Rich emphasizes the danger of Dickinson's choice, which entailed withdrawal to the single room where she was able to live life on her own premises: "It is an extremely painful and dangerous way to live—split between a publicly acceptable persona, and a part of yourself that you perceive as the essential, the creative and powerful self, yet also as possibly unacceptable, perhaps even monstrous" (Rich, *Lies*, p. 175). What fascinates Rich most in Dickinson's process are the strategies she developed to avoid being crushed by the tension inherent in her choice to affirm her own power. Above all, Rich perceives Dickinson as a poet highly conscious of the need to articulate experience, a woman determined to resist the silences which Rich sees as quite literally fatal. Describing the technical approach which enabled Dickinson to live "on *her* premises," Rich celebrates her ability to "retranslate her own unorthodox, subversive, sometimes volcanic propensities into a dialect called metaphor: her native language" (Rich, *Lies*, pp. 161-62).

Rich's discussion of poem 1062 ("He scanned it—staggered—") emphasizes the way in which Dickinson's ability to "retranslate" her psychological experience of suicidal impulses enables her to understand its relationship to the cultural context which seeks to alienate her from her powers: "the suicidal experience has been distanced, refined, transformed through a devastating accuracy of language. It is not suicide that is studied here, but the dissociation of self and mind and world which precedes" (Rich, *Lies*, p. 178). Recognizing Dickinson as a foremother whose process should be taken seriously by her contemporary daughters seems particularly vital in a century where many creative (and therefore marginalized) women—from Bessie Smith and Billie Holiday to Sylvia Plath and Anne Sexton—have been forced (or fallen) into self-destructive behavior. Again and again, Rich emphasizes Dickinson's awareness of her poetry as a stay against the forces raging about her: "Poetic language—the poem on paper—is a concretization of the poetry of the world at large, the self, and the forces within the self; and those forces are rescued from formlessness, lucidified, and integrated in the act of writing poems" (Rich, *Lies*, p. 181). Especially during the early transitional phase of her own career, Rich clearly took inspiration and solace from the presence of a predecessor whose work embodied this sensibility. For the young faculty wife, the existence of over 1700 poems, written by a nineteenth-century woman who felt the full force of the "woman-poet" dichotomy, affirmed the possibility of maintaining integrity through commitment to the work itself.

Equally important for Rich's long-term development was Dickinson's ability not just to survive but to develop an expansive vision of her integrity: "More than any other poet, Emily Dickinson seemed to tell me that the intense inner event, the personal and psychological, was inseparable from the universal" (Rich, *Lies*, p. 168). In her insightful book *An American Triptych: Anne Bradstreet, Emily Dickinson, Adrienne Rich*, Wendy Martin argues convincingly that the primary difference between Rich and Dickinson involves their treatment of this relationship between particular and universal. Martin argues that "Dickinson rejected male authorities and created a 'covered vision'; Rich has translated Dickinson's private cosmology into a public discourse" (p. 8). While this accurately identifies the central difference between the two poets—which, as Martin notes, develops inexorably out of the difference in their temporal and social contexts—it is important to note that Rich also finds inspiration for her own expanded role in Dickinson's work. As Paula Bennett notes in *My Life a Loaded Gun*, Rich's ability to complete the passage from "dutiful daughter" to "woman poet" represents a fruition of the Dickinsonian tradition of American poetry. Rich clearly identifies Dickinson as a source for her own sense of poetry as vision. Immediately after describing Dickinson's ability to integrate her own personality through the writing of poetry, Rich associates her with "a more ancient concept of the poet, which is that she is endowed to speak for those who do not have the gift of language, or to see for those who—for whatever reasons—are less conscious of what they are living through. It is as though the risk of the poet's existence can be put to some use beyond her own survival" (Rich, *Lies*, p. 181).

Throughout her career, Rich has put Dickinson to just such use, adapting her techniques and testing her attitudes against altered forms of patriarchal oppression. Rich shares many of Dickinson's general attitudes; as Martin notes, both poets depict "the male principle as an intrusion on the female process," endorse "a female poetic in which nature is not subordinate to reason and in which genius, literary or otherwise, is not perceived as male energy," and celebrate "female mutuality rather than male hierarchy" (p. 10). Reflecting Dickinson's ability to identify crucial issues concerning the woman writer, this list of shared concerns could be extended indefinitely. In more specific terms, Rich frequently invokes Dickinson through the use of specific images, many of them taken from poems Rich quotes in "Vesuvius at Home." For example, the image of the volcano as an emblem of female energy, which occurs in Dickinson's poems 601 ("A still—Volcano-Life—") and 1677 ("On my volcano grows the Grass"), recurs in several Rich poems including "Incipience," "Re-forming the Crystal," and "Love Poem XI," which opens: "Every peak is a crater. This is the law of volcanoes,/ making them eternally and visibly female."

The intricacy of Rich's dialog with Dickinson, an aesthetic analog of the process described in "Twenty-One Love Poems," can be seen in the three direct addresses Rich specifies in "The Spirit of Place." Although specific identification of the addresses is somewhat speculative, "Snapshots of a Daughter-in-Law," "I Am in Danger— Sir—" (1964), and "The Spirit of Place" all contain unambiguous Dickinsonian references. Beginning with an ambivalent perspective conditioned by patriarchal distortions of Dickinson's achievement, Rich gradually learns to put Dickinson's strategies to effective use. As she comes to terms with her own creative power, Rich ultimately vows to honor her foremother by extending her influence into the public sphere. Section four of "Snapshots of a Daughter-in-Law" opens with a clear statement of Rich's ambivalence concerning her identification with a woman who at that time was known to her in the "condescending, clinical, or sentimental" versions of traditional scholarship and bowdlerized editions. Distancing herself from the ambivalence through the use of third person pronouns for both Dickinson and the onlooker, Rich writes: "Knowing themselves too well in one another:/ their gifts no pure fruition, but a thorn/ the prick filed sharp against a hint of scorn." Portraying a Dickinson immersed in the minutiae of household chores, Rich nonetheless chooses specific images that attest to the poet's fierce attention—"dusting everything on the whatnot every day of life"—and to her transformative power—"the jellies boil and scum." Most importantly, Rich quotes a line which she interprets, in "Vesuvius at Home," as evidence of Dickinson's conscious knowledge of her potentially "lethal" power: "*My Life had stood—a Loaded Gun.*" Noting that the original version of "Snapshots of a Daughter-in-Law" quoted a different line from Dickinson—"This is the gnat that mangles men" —Rachel Blau DuPlessis observes that the change reflects a major shift (p. 229). Where the early version reflects Rich's perception of both herself and Dickinson as suffering a "diffusion of energy," the latter grants both an "explosive, possibly disciplined, power" (p. 229). In both versions, Rich tests her own perception and circumstances against Dickinson's.

Between the two versions of "Snapshots of a Daughter-in-Law," Rich had begun to employ Dickinsonian strategies in several of the poems published in *Necessities of Life*, the volume which elicited John Ashbery's ironically accurate description of Rich as "a kind of Emily Dickinson of the suburbs" (in Cooper, p. 217). Taking its title from a phrase from one of Dickinson's letters, "I Am in Danger—Sir—" marks a major advance in Rich's understanding of Dickinson's subtlety. Realizing that Dickinson's work has been available only "in garbled versions" and that the poet herself, "equivocal to the end," has been "mothballed at Harvard," Rich acknowledges the limitations of the perspective she had assumed in "Snapshots of a Daughter-in-Law." She poses the crucial question, ignored by critics and readers willing to accept Thomas Wentworth Higginson's description of Dickinson as "half-cracked": "who are you?" The answer Rich offers seems much less ambivalent than that implied in "Snapshots of a Daughter-in-Law." Deemphasizing, though not denying, the image of Dickinson as housekeeper attending to the details of daily life, Rich emphasizes her intellectual power. Even as she gardens and wipes dishes, Dickinson's

> thought pulsed on behind
> a forehead battered paper-thin,
> you, woman, masculine
> in single-mindedness,
> for whom the world was more
> than a symptom.

Ultimately, Rich arrives at a tentative understanding of Dickinson's choice of "silence for entertainment." Echoing poem 465 ("I heard a Fly buzz—when I died—"), Rich interprets Dickinson's "half-cracked" withdrawal as a response to the deathly "buzzing [of] spoiled language" in her uncomprehending environment. No longer perceiving Dickinson as a defensive victim, Rich understands that she was defending herself, attempting to alter the terms of the conflict with patriarchy. Anticipating her own choices of the next two decades, Rich honors Dickinson's determination "to have it out at last/ on your own premises."

Although "I Am in Danger—Sir—" addresses the Dickinsonian presence most directly, Rich returns to Dickinson in several other poems in *Necessities of Life*. By the time she was at work on the volume, Rich was familiar with Thomas Johnson's edition of Dickinson, the first complete edition which did not regularize Dickinson's punctuation. Given this relatively recent encounter with Dickinson's subversion of familiar verse forms through the use of an idiosyncratic prosody, Rich's frequent use of dashes to vary the rhythm of seemingly epigrammatic stanzas seems unlikely to have been purely coincidental. In addition to echoing several Dickinsonian images (the crown of self-assertion from poem 508—"I'm ceded—I've stopped being Theirs—"; and the crashing of dissolution from poem 997—"Crumbling is not an instant's Act"), "After Dark" (1964) uses dashes to emphasize the persona's rhythm of perception. Her sense of triumph, based on a new-found confidence in her own perception, vascillates with her fear that the confidence entails the destruction of the world she has known:

Alive now, root to crown, I'd give

—oh,—something—not to know
our struggles now are ended.
I seem to hold you, cupped
in my hands, and disappearing.

When your memory fails—
no more to scourge my inconsistencies—
the sashcords of the world fly loose.
A window crashes
suddenly down.

"Face to Face," the final poem in *Necessities of Life*, ends with a direct appropriation of the power Rich approached with caution in "Snapshots of a Daughter-in-Law." Although the poem can be read as a meditation on American patriarchal psychology, "the Early American figure . . . scanning the didactic storm in privacy" also resembles Dickinson. Especially in light of the opening line in which Rich determines "Never to be lonely like that," the final line expresses a growing understanding of her similarity to Dickinson: "behind dry lips/ a loaded gun."

Written after "Vesuvius at Home," when she no longer associated her creative power with masculine symbols such as the gun, Rich's final address to Dickinson in "The Spirit of Place" recapitulates her process. As if observing a meeting in Dickinson's house where scholars celebrate their "pious or clinical legends," Rich quotes a letter in which Dickinson anticipates the distortion of her process: "*and, as I feared, my 'life' was made a 'victim'.*" Reiterating the irrelevance of academic interpretations, especially those centering on Dickinson's supposed romantic/sexual experiences, Rich reemphasizes the extremity of Dickinson's perspective. Repudiating the "cult assembled in the bedroom," Rich asserts that Dickinson can be found only "in words/ (your own)." She quotes from a letter emphasizing the privacy of the poet's life, a privacy shared with other women: "*All we are strangers—dear—The world is not/ acquainted with us, because we are not acquainted/ with her.*" In a passage with extreme significance for the study of the relationship between literary mothers and daughters, Rich then offers a homage to Dickinson based on a perception of a *mutual* nurturing relationship. Acknowledging the privacy at the core of Dickinson's self-perception, Rich in her role as daughter surrenders all claim to knowing her mother better than her mother knew herself: "with the hands of a daughter I would cover you/ from all intrusion   even my own." Claiming an equality based on mutual respect, she continues: "with the hands of a sister I would leave your hands/ open or closed as they prefer to lie." Finally, in a passage which asserts a unique sense of literary influence, Rich determines to honor Dickinson in a manner implicitly compatible with Dickinson's own process. Like her foremother, Rich places the highest value on the continuation of her work: "with the hands of a mother I would close the door/ on the rooms you've left behind/ and silently pick up my fallen work." As Bennett and many other feminist critics have observed, this attitude toward the relationship with a literary mother raises serious questions concerning the applicability of Harold Bloom's theory of literary influence to women writers. Rich views Dickinson's influence as a source of empowerment, rather than anxiety. Understanding that the integrity of the mother in no way impinges upon her own ability to become a mother, Rich returns to her own work, her power increased by the knowledge that she is not alone.

Although Rich's ennumeration of three addresses cautions against overly zealous allusion hunting, "White Night" (1974) echoes "The Spirit of Place" in a manner that seems directly relevant to Dickinson. Transforming the romantic cliché of the "white knight" into an image of the redemptive relationship between two women, Rich expresses her determination to take up her own work, to test the lessons learned from such a relationship against the actual social context. Focusing on an unnamed neighbor, an "accurate dreamer" who, like Rich, works in "solitude," the poem compares their processes. Just as she was forced to reconstruct an image of Dickinson from the fragments of patriarchal distortions, Rich derives this comparison from her own speculations:

> I've had to guess at her
> sewing her skin together as I sew mine
> though
> with a different
> stitch.

In a sentence applicable to Dickinson's treatment by academic critics, Rich describes the unsuccesful attempts of those "who sleep the stone sleep of the past" to repress her neighbor's power:

> Somebody tried to put her
> to rest under an afghan
> knitted with wools the color of grass and blood
> but she has risen.

Inspired by this self-empowered resurrection, Rich feels a flow of energy connecting her with the neighbor's "darkness-lancing eye."

Anticipating "Twenty-One Love Poems," Rich does not content herself with this aesthetic bond; rather, she determines to test its strength against the hostile forces of the actual world: "Dawn is the test."

Part of Rich's work in the daily world involves her confrontation with the forces which kept Dickinson from pursuing the public or political implications of her process. Ironically, but fittingly, one of Rich's most significant successes has been her attempt to increase women's access to Dickinson's process. As Suzanne Juhasz notes in the introduction to the anthology *Feminist Critics Read Emily Dickinson*, Rich's essay was one of the earliest, and perhaps the most influential, work in the critical movement to recover Dickinson from the distortions of patriarchal criticism (Juhasz, 1983, p. xii). Feminist critics, working on Dickinson over the last decade, share "the same central premise: that Dickinson was a woman poet; that this identity brought her power. Rich's essay can serve to exemplify this first and crucial revision of traditional Dickinson criticism" (Juhasz, 1983, p. xii). In this sense, Rich has indeed become a "mother" of the Emily Dickinson presented by critics such as Karl Keller, Sandra Gilbert, and Margaret Homans, each of whom recognizes her as a poet whose process serves as inspiration for a *civitas* seeking to arrive at an expansive sense of its own individual and communal integrity.

Rewriting Women's History

Although Dickinson occupies a position of major importance in Rich's vision of the lesbian continuum, she is not a solitary presence. In fact, Rich's engagement with women's history has received thorough critical attention. In her essay "Mining the 'Earth-Deposits:' Women's History in Adrienne Rich's Poetry," Marianne Whelchel accurately describes Rich's progression "from poems focusing on the individual, named woman to those focusing on unnamed, 'ordinary' women or groups of women" (in Cooper, pp. 51-52). Carol Christ complements this description with an analysis of Rich's celebration of diverse types of women. In addition to the "woman alone" of "Twenty-One Love Poems," Rich writes "of extraordinary women who have defied patriarchy's strictures to create new kinds of lives for women . . . ordinary women—mothers, daughters, and grandmothers—the nurturers of life in an often violent society. . . . women lovers, creating new values through their choice of women" (Christ, p. 85). This sequence of heroic "types" parallels Rich's own process; after asserting her ability to use traditionally "masculine" capacities, Rich commits her energy to the creation of a specifically, though expansively, lesbian *civitas.* As Jane Vanderbosch observes, after *The Dream of a Common Language* "her journey into the female will be the only journey; the 'we,' which will be more directed, will have no detours into 'humanism' or 'androgyny'" (in Cooper, p. 114).

Among the studies of Rich's relationship with her aesthetic foremothers, Ostriker's *Stealing the Language: The Emergence of Women's Poetry in America*, Bennett's *My Life a Loaded Gun* (Dickinson, Plath, Rich), Martin's *An American Triptych* (Bradstreet, Dickinson, Rich), and Susan Stanford Friedman's "Adrienne Rich and H.D.: An Intertextual Study" stand out as particularly useful. Although Rich has taken issue with aspects of the essay, Friedman's sensitive reading of *The Dream of a Common Language* in relation to *Trilogy* celebrates the two poets' shared concern with "recovery of the Goddess—or, in Rich's terms, the 'female principle'" (in Cooper, p. 177). In a letter to *Signs* which raises the question of the underlying clash of feminist and academic criticism, Rich claims to have located a "hidden agenda" discrediting separatism in Friedman's essay. Acknowledging my own position within the academy, I would nonetheless agree with Friedman's response that Rich is, uncharacteristically, refusing to acknowledge a plurality of interpretations. Whatever the validity of Rich's criticism, Friedman presents a valuable Freudian perspective on Rich's attitude toward her literary foremothers, explicitly denying the relevance of Bloom's phallocentric theory of influence. In addition to emphasizing the importance of both H.D.'s and Rich's relationships with their mothers, Friedman presents an argument consonant with the reading of Rich's encounters with Dickinson described above:

> Rich's stance toward women writers is distinctly compassionate and noncompetitive. It embodies a feminist theory of reading in which the underlying receptivity inevitable in any literary influence overlaps with her desire to build a tangible women's culture. One writer's receptivity to the ideas of another depends upon a preexisting common bond, a conscious or subconscious identification of lives and ideas that allows the process of influence to proceed. Through her conscious search for a family of women who write as women, about women, Rich has intensified this process of bonding in order to transcend the divisions to which she believes the patriarchy determines women . . . . This approach reverses the family constellation Harold Bloom has identified for male writers whereby the "sons" regard previous writers as literary "fathers" with all the rivalry and ambivalence of a young boy in the throes of an Oedipus complex [in Cooper, pp. 172-73].

Supporting her position with a sensitive reading of "Sibling Mysteries," Friedman describes Rich's stance toward her predecessors as that of "the forgiving daughter or sister, simply emphasizing what she finds important and remaining silent about what she rejects. Consequently, Rich stresses H.D.'s matriarchal ethos and relationships with women and does not address her search for an androgynous male lover-companion or her belief in the potential transformation of men" (in Cooper, p. 198).

Rich's Heroic Poetry

This noncompetitive sororal attitude typifies Rich's approach in her poems on individual heroism. Although the concern with significant predecessors emerges as a dominant element in Rich's work only during the 1970s, early poems, such as "Mathilde in Normandy" (c. 1950), anticipate later portraits of women whose heroism differs sharply from the self-conscious individual assertion of the patriarchal mainstream. Like the semilegendary Mathilde, real women such as Natalya Gorbanevskaya in "For a Russian Poet" (1968) and "For a Sister" (1972), the two artists in "Paula Becker to Clara Westhoff" (1975-76), the writer Simone Weil in "A Vision" (1981), and Willa Cather in "For Julia in Nebraska" (1978, 1981) struggle with varying degrees of success for creative survival in societies which offer them little encouragement. Similarly, famous women from other fields of endeavor provide glimpses of the integrity Rich seeks. Among those who attract her attention are the physicist Marie Curie, in "Power" ("her wounds came from the same source as her power"); Ethel Rosenberg ("political in her ways   not in mine"); and the astronomer Caroline Herschel, in "Planetarium" (1968), who inspires Rich to perceive herself as

> an instrument in the shape
> of a woman trying to translate pulsations
> into images   for the relief of the body
> and the reconstruction of the mind.

Perhaps Rich's clearest statement on the mutually dependent heroism of individual women, "Culture and Anarchy" (1978) catalogs women who have influenced Rich's process: Harriet Tubman, Elizabeth Barrett, Elizabeth Blackwell, Frances Kemble, Ida Wells-Barnett, the Brontë sisters, Jane Addams, Sojourner Truth, and the list goes on. Like the poem on Cather which concludes with the bonding image of "a braid of hair/ a grandmother's strong hands plaited/ straight down a granddaughter's back," "Culture and Anarchy" concludes with a celebration of the lesbian continuum quoted from a letter from Elizabeth Cady Stanton to Susan B. Anthony: *"Yes, our work is one,/ we are one in aim and sympathy/ and we should be together."*

Gradually Rich shifts her attention from heroic women as individuals to heroic women in relation to the *civitas*. "Phantasia for Elvira Shatayev" provides a touchstone for Rich's changing conception of women's heroism by emphasizing the interdependence of the members of the all-woman Russian mountain climbing team, all of whom died in an attempt to scale Lenin Peak in 1974. Written from Shatayev's perspective, the poem acknowledges the reality of masculine love, addressing her husband as he climbs toward the bodies—"You come (I know this) with your love." Nonetheless, Shatayev directs her primary intensity toward the women who were able "to bring each other here/ choosing ourselves each other and this life." Moving beyond a purely individual sense of integrity, she speaks "with a voice no longer personal/ (I want to say *with voices*)." This communal voice transforms the apparent tragedy of her death into a source of inspiration:

> *We know now we have always been in danger*
> *down in our separateness*
> *and now up here together but till now*
> *we had not touched our strength.*

Ultimately, Rich claims this strength as the birthright, not simply of those who have performed heroic deeds, but of all women feeling what "Origins and History of Consciousness" describes as "the true nature of poetry. The drive to connect." Intimated in poems such as "Poem for Women" (c. 1967), "Women" (1968), and "To Judith, Taking Leave" (written in 1962 but withheld from publication until 1974, partially as a result of Rich's reluctance to acknowledge her love for women), the concern with "common" women emerges as a central theme in Rich's recent work. On one hand, Rich addresses individual women who have been important in her own life, including the lover in "Twenty-One Love Poems," the central figure of "A Woman Dead in Her Forties," and the title presence of "For Julia in Nebraska." Attempting to live with integrity and strength, these women encounter the same kinds of barriers and enjoy the same kinds of successes as their better-known sisters. Similarly, "Grandmothers" (1980) considers both the limitations and the wisdom of Rich's grandmothers, Mary Gravely Jones and Hattie Rice Rich, as they responded to the circumstances that shaped Rich's own consciousness.

Rich's second approach to the "unnamed, ordinary women or groups of women" concerns the mythic dimension of women's consciousness. Contrasting sharply with her realistic portraits of ordinary women, many of which attest to the difficulty of attaining the communal transcendence experienced by Shatayev and her companions, poems such as "Blood-Sister" (1973), "Natural Resources" (1977), and "Sibling Mysteries" (1976) articulate a visionary approach to the ideal of the lesbian *civitas* in which all women can experience their expansive integrity. Grounding its vision in the memory of how "we loved our mother's body," "Sibling Mysteries" envisions a *civitas*, situated in both dimly remembered past and visionary future, in which women perceive their integrity in terms of relationship rather than separation. In a passage echoing "The Mirror in Which Two Are Seen as One," Rich describes: "how sister gazed at sister/ reaching through mirrored pupils/ back to the mother." Explicitly repudiating patriarchal Freudianism (Stimpson), Rich concludes the poem with a vision of the lesbian continuum in which the energies of perception and physical being are not separated:

> The daughters never were
> true brides of the father
>
> the daughters were to begin with
> brides of the mother
>
> then brides of each other
> under a different law
>
> Let me hold and tell you.

Extending this vision in an exceptionally intricate manner, "Natural Resources" affirms the legacy of the woman "miner" described in section two in both realistic and visionary terms:

> The miner is no metaphor. She goes
> into the cage like the rest, is flung
>
> downward by gravity like them, must change
> her body like the rest to fit a crevice
>
> to work a lode.

Sharing a common lot with "the rest," this heroic figure inspires the credo with which Rich ends the poem:

> I have to cast my lot with those
> who age after age, perversely,

with no extraordinary power,
reconstitute the world.

"DISLOYAL TO CIVILIZATION"

In a society where rhetorical commitment to egalitarian ideals frequently masks indifference or hostility, Rich demands that all abstract
beliefs—including her vision of common women reconstituting the
world—be judged by their actual impact. As she observes in a 1985
book review published in *The Village Voice*: "At the core of these very
different essays is the present crisis in American politics, and the recognition that coalitions cannot survive without honest controversy, free
of liberal lip-service, labeling, self-indulgent posturing, self-abnegation,
or mutual wipeout. The belief that others can change, that we ourselves must go on changing through our work with others, keeps run-
ning aground in radical movements. Yet it is the great radical belief"
(Rich, 1985, p. 60). Appropriately, this statement concludes a review of
a collection of feminist writings on anti-Semitism and racism (*Yours in
Struggle*), a constellation of issues severely testing the abstract belief in
a mutually supportive community of women. Although the actual
impact and implications of the lesbian vision could be discussed in
relation to issues such as nuclear war, economic policy, and criminal
justice, race provides a continuing touchstone of Rich's political
activity. Her consideration of racism raises basic issues related to her
belief that the lesbian vision does not merely recast the structure of
patriarchal thought in different forms.

Rich places her discussion of racism in the context of a larger dialog
concerning the mutual distrust separating black and white feminists.
Near the beginning of her classic essay "Disloyal to Civilization: Feminism, Racism, Gynephobia" (1978), she writes: "I conceive this paper as
one strand in a meditation and colloquy among black and white feminists, an intercourse just beginning and charged with a history that
touches our nerve-ends even though we are largely ignorant of it"
(Rich, *Lies*, pp. 279-80). As Rich enters into this colloquy by raising the
twin problems of "white solipsism" and "false loyalty," she
acknowledges voices of importance to her own understanding of the
process. "Disloyal to Civilization" identifies Barbara Smith's essay
"Toward a Black Feminist Criticism," the Combahee River Collective's
"A Black Feminist Statement," and white feminist Gerda Lerner's
anthology *Black Women in White America* as important influences on her
theoretical perspective. In addition, Rich has repeatedly raised racial
issues in public forums. She read a statement, written with Alice

Walker and Audre Lorde, at the National Book Award ceremony in 1974; she has reviewed writing by black women in *Freedomways* and the *New Women's Times Feminist Review*; and she has carried on an extended public dialog with Lorde, several sections of which have been published. Both in her own books and in the lesbian journal *Sinister Wisdom*, which she co-edited with Afro-American lesbian writer Michelle Cliff, Rich has contributed to an awareness of racial issues in the lesbian community which matches that in any integrated or predominantly white segment of American society. As Lorde observed in a published conversation with Rich, this process has taken on almost emblematic dimensions: "Adrienne, in my journals I have a lot of pieces of conversations that I'm having with you in my head. I'll be having a conversation with you and I'll put it in my journal because stereotypically or symbolically these conversations occur in a space of Black woman/ white woman where it's beyond Adrienne and Audre, almost as if we're two voices" (Lorde, 1981, p. 103).

Rich's primary statement on race remains "Disloyal to Civilization," an essay which played a major role in the development of white feminism by advancing a number of positions (most of which had been previously recognized by black feminists) which have become guiding premises of many subsequent discussions. Recognizing that both blacks and women have been branded as "Other" by the patriarchal culture, Rich stresses the danger of white women failing to comprehend fully black women's experience of "double jeopardy": "It is far easier, especially for academically trained white women, to get an intellectual/political 'fix' on the *idea* of racism, than to identify with black female experience: to explore it emotionally as part of our own" (Rich, *Lies*, p. 281). The emphasis on the relationship between the experiences of black and white women leads to Rich's most original and useful contributions to the dialog. Understanding the futility of attempts to establish any hierarchy of suffering, Rich identifies two major forms of racial oppression: *"active domination"* and *"passive collusion"* (Rich, *Lies*, p. 299, italics Rich's). Rich's description of active domination, which involves both physical and institutional violence, echoes Mary Daly's description of the techniques used by patriarchy to discredit women's expression: *"Justification*: mythologizing, dehumanization through language, fragmentation (the token exception to 'prove' the rule)" (Rich, *Lies*, p. 299). Her description of passive collusion focuses on "White solipsism: to think, imagine, and speak as if whiteness described the world" and *"Internalized gynephobia*: if I despise myself as woman I must despise you even more, for you are my rejected part, my antiself" (Rich, *Lies*, p. 300).

This analysis has several practical consequences. First, it suggests that discussions of white women's responsibility for racism should focus on passive collusion because "An analysis that places the guilt for active domination, physical and institutional violence, and the justifications embedded in myth and language, on white women not only compounds false consciousness; it allows us all to deny or neglect the charged connections among black and white women from the historical conditions of slavery on; and it impedes any real discussion of women's instrumentality in a system which oppresses all women, and in which hatred of women is also embedded in myth, folklore, and language" (Rich, *Lies*, p. 301). Rich emphasizes that this does not absolve white women from the need to confront their racism. Rather, it removes a convenient rationale for failing to do so: "It also seems to me that guilt feelings—so easily provoked in women that they have become almost a form of social control—can also become a form of solipsism, a preoccupation with our own feelings which prevents us from ever connecting with the experience of others. Guilt feelings paralyze, but paralysis can become a convenient means of remaining passive and instrumental" (Rich, *Lies*, p. 306). By focusing on white women's contributions to active oppression (contributions which clearly form part of the historical record), black feminists may inadvertently encourage the passive collusion which Rich sees as the core of white women's actual racist activity. Further, Rich's argument implies that white feminists have no choice but to focus much of their energy on resisting patriarchy because the passive collusion which characterizes their historical relationship with black women depends in part on their ignorance of the impact of active domination on their own lives. In focusing on patriarchy as the source of racism, Rich does not establish a hierarchy of suffering or deny the reality of white women's racism. Rather, from her situation within white culture, she recognizes that any practical attempt to counter white solipsism and forge a political coalition of black and white women is doomed to failure so long as women continue to think in patriarchal terms.

Rich stresses the difference between attacks on white women's racism generated by patriarchal forces attempting to fragment the women's movement and those emanating from black women determined to protect their own integrity:

> The need to reject false guilt and false responsibility for the bedrock racism of American society may have evoked a kind of retreat from anything resembling rhetorical demands that white feminists "deal with our racism" as a first priority. But surely such demands have a different meaning and imperative when they come in bad faith from the lips of white—or black—males, whose intention is to discredit

feminist politics; and when they are articulated by black feminists, who are showing themselves, over time, unflagging and persistent in their outreach toward white women, while refusing to deny—or to have denied—an atom of their black reality [Rich, *Lies*, p. 290].

Ultimately, this demands that feminists take the expansive conception of integrity seriously, and resist the tendency to project the denied aspects of the self onto the "other." Requiring white feminists to actively study the history of black women, this expansion of the meaning of her love for women offers what Rich calls a "Real transcendence—and use—of the past [which] demands more difficult work. But it also brings into play that lightning-rod conductor between women which I think of as pulsing at the core of lesbian/feminism: love experienced as identification, as tenderness, as sympathetic memory and vision . . . a nonexploitative, non-possessive eroticism, which can cross barriers of age and conditions, the sensing our way into another's skin, if only in a moment's apprehension, against censure, the denial, the lies and laws of civilization" (Rich, *Lies*, p. 307). At its most intense, the engagement of black and white women with issues of racism and gynephobia— which inevitably raises disturbing issues such as the corrupt ideal of beauty propagated by white culture and the involvement of white women with black men during and after the Civil Rights Movement—helps clarify lesbian values, highlighting the need for an integrity based on relationship rather than solipsism. Underscoring the racial imperative facing the lesbian *civitas*, Rich writes: "We cannot hope to define a feminist culture, a gynecentric vision, on racist terms, because a part of ourselves will remain forever unknown to us" (Rich, *Lies*, p. 308).

Race in Rich's Poetry

Rich offers her own process of discovering the unknown parts of herself as her primary contribution to the actualization of a multiracial *civitas* based on "difference and identity." Although she recognizes the historical participation of women in the abolitionist and civil rights movements and draws on the examples of Mary Boykin Chestnut, Fanny Kemble, and Lillian Smith, Rich is acutely aware that very few white Americans have risked subjecting their attempts to eradicate racism from their own consciousness to public scrutiny. One of many poems on racial issues in *Leaflets*, The "Ghazal: 7/26/68/ii" reveals the limitations of Rich's early comprehension of racial issues. The poem invokes Afro-American leaders LeRoi Jones (Amiri Baraka) and

Eldridge Cleaver, both of whom have since been strongly criticized for their contribution to the subordination of women in the black nationalist movement of the 1960s. Uncomfortably close in stance to the exoticism of Norman Mailer's celebration of blacks as existential hero/criminals in "The White Negro," Rich montages her call to Jones and Cleaver with her feeling that white people have become "ghosts/ condemned to haunt the cities." The juxtaposition suggests that Rich had not yet overcome the influence of the conventional patriarchal treatment of blacks as "symbolic others." The title poem from the same volume imagines a kind of racial holocaust in which "the bodies come whirling/ coal-black, ash-white." Perhaps the most significant contribution to the dialog between blacks and whites in the volume, however, is "Ghazal: 8/1/68," in which Rich first recognizes the tendency toward abstracting blacks discernible in her references to Jones and Cleaver. Echoing Martin Luther King's "I Have a Dream" speech and Leslie Fiedler's commentary on *Huck Finn*, Rich writes: "Were you free then all along, Jim, free at last,/ of everything but the white boy's fantasies?" Having reached this perception, Rich immediately began to adjust the treatment of race in her poetry. The title poem of *The Will To Change* presents the black militant leader, in this case Bobby Seale, in terms of his own concrete experience ("chalked/ by the courtroom artist/ defaced by the gag") rather than as a symbolic reflection of her own. In "The Burning of Paper Instead of Children," she comments directly on the similarity between her own dilemma as an artist and that of Frederick Douglass. Most importantly, in the "Blue Ghazal: 9/23/68," she focuses for the first time on a black woman. Although she has not yet attained the clarity of "Disloyal to Civilization," her image anticipates the expansive integrity articulated in "Transcendental Etude": "An Ashanti woman tilts the flattened basin on her head/ to let the water slide downward: I am that woman and that water."

As she develops a Webster's integrity, Rich refers to black women with increasing frequency and force. The image of her sisters, "sold as breeding-wenches," in "From an Old House in America" is elaborated in "Heroines." The latter poem meditates on the paradox of white women's involvement in slavery, both as de facto victims:

> your husband
> > has the right
> of the slaveholder
> > to hunt down and re-possess you
> > > should you escape

and as passive collaborators:

THE LESBIAN VISION

You may inherit slaves
                    but have no power to free them
your skin is fair
          you have been taught that light
came
      to the Dark Continent
                with white power.

Two poems inscribed to Afro-American lesbians reflect Rich's awareness that she is not exempt from the criticism suggested in "Heroines."
Addressed to Lorde, "Hunger" includes Rich's challenge to herself to
feel the reality of suffering rather than distancing it through patriarchal
abstraction: "I live in my Western skin,/ my Western vision, torn/ and
flung to what I can't control or even fathom." Similarly, "The Spirit of
Place," dedicated to Cliff, stresses the insufficiency of any approach to
oppression which fails to take seriously the expansive ideal of integrity:

it was not enough to be for abolition
while the spirit of the masters
flickered in the abolitionist's heart

it was not enough to name ourselves anew
while the spirit of the masters
calls the freedwoman to forget the slave.

Rich's most intense personal confrontation with racism within the
women's movement, however, takes place in "Education of a Novelist"
(1983), a meditation on the relationship between Ellen Glasgow and her
black "Mammy," Lizzie Jones. Quoting several passages from Glasgow's autobiography *The Woman Within,* Rich reflects on the parallel
between that relationship and her own relationship with the woman
she described as her "black mother" in *Of Woman Born.* As she considers the problems she defines in her review of *Yours in Struggle* as
"difference - within - oppression" and "privilege - within - oppression"
(Rich, 1985, p. 57), Rich contrasts Glasgow's self-professed (and in
many ways actual) revolt against sentimentality with the extreme
sentimentality of her description of her relationship with the black
woman who incited her adventurous spirit during her childhood.
Observing that "the Black artist spent her genius on the white children," Rich makes it clear that she identifies strongly with Glasgow's
sense of creative power: "I, too, was always the one." The poem's central concern is with the tendency of even the most aware white women,
those determined not to accept their assigned places in a patriarchal

structure, to render their "black mothers" invisible. Quoting Glasgow's childhood pride over learning her letters on her own, Rich points out the reality of privilege-within-oppression: *"Nobody ever taught me to read/* (Nobody had to,/ it was your birthright, Ellen)."

Even more disturbing, however, is Glasgow's unfulfilled promise to teach Lizzie Jones to read. Particularly given the central importance of literacy in the Afro-American cultural tradition described by Robert Stepto in *From Behind the Veil,* this failure of courage or memory or love reveals the immense gap between the seriousness with which white women have taken what Glasgow called *"the sense of exile in a hostile world"* when applied to their own experience and when applied to that of black women. Quoting Glasgow's image of herself as a "caged bird"—an image popularized by Afro-American poet Paul Laurence Dunbar's poem "Sympathy" (1899)—Rich describes the invisible exile of Lizzie Jones: "Lizzie Jones vanishes. Her trace is lost./ She, who was winged for flying." The final section of "Education of a Novelist" focuses on Glasgow's frustration over her inability to find "the Revolution" at the end of the nineteenth century: *"In what mean streets and alleys of the South/ was it then lying in ambush? Though I suffered/ with the world's suffering."* Juxtaposing this with a reminder of Glasgow's promise to teach Jones her letters, Rich makes it clear that any real revolution must entail a true commitment to an integrity essentially incompatible with white solipsism. In addition, she underscores the relevance of her consideration of Glasgow to the stage of her own process, described in *Of Woman Born,* when her own "black mother . . . drifted out of reach, in my searches backward through time, exactly as the double silence of sexism and racism intended her to do. She was meant to be utterly annihilated" (Rich, p. 254-55). Refusing to absolve herself of responsibility, Rich concludes "Education of a Novelist" with a challenge to herself, to white feminists, to any individual seeking to realize an expansive conception of integrity:

> It's not enough
> using your words to damn you, Ellen:
> they could have been my own:
> this crisscross
> map of kept and broken promises
> *I was always the one.*

Rich intends this as a challenge to further "revolutionary" activity rather than a lament over past guilt. Similarly, the final section of "The Spirit of Place" suggests that the proper form of reparation for past sins is to honor those who did not survive "with grief   with fury   with action." Echoing the closing passages of "Natural Resources," Rich's meditation on the contradictions of the abolitionist mentality in "The Spirit of Place" leads directly to the question "*With whom do you believe your lot is cast?*" "Frame" (1980) reiterates Rich's answer in specifically racial terms. Focusing on the brutalization of a black college student by Boston police in 1979, the poem asserts the integrity of the woman's experience by assuming blackness as the "norm" for consideration of the events. The poem specifies color only in relation to the whiteness of the police and of Rich as onlooker. Acknowledging her perspective (social and aesthetic) "*just outside the frame,*" Rich perceives this distance, this inability to communicate with the black woman, as an aspect of the problem: "*I can see from this position there is no soundtrack/ to go with this and I understand at once/ it is meant to be in silence that this happens.*" The poem concludes with a statement of open defiance to anyone denying the connection, intrinsic to Rich's expansive lesbian conception of integrity, between her own experience and that of the black woman who has been maced and charged with assault and battery for attempting to get out of the cold: "*What I am telling you/ is told by a white woman who they will say/ was never there. I say I am there.*"

As her continuing involvement with racial issues suggests, Rich endorses no vision of the lesbian *civitas* which does not respect the integrity of black women's experience. Nonetheless, as the emphasis on silence in "Frame" suggests, she knows that realization of an acceptable vision requires continuing commitment to honest processes, both individual and communal. At the end of a published conversation with Lorde, Rich comments on her friend's work: "You had to understand what you knew and also make it available to others" (Lorde, 1981, p. 109). Rich's introduction to the tenth anniversary edition of *Of Woman Born* (1986) extends this principle to her own process. Acknowledging what she now sees as her earlier tendency to universalize black women's experience—which leads to an underemphasis on the specifically Afro-American cultural tradition—Rich makes available her knowledge of the inevitable limitations of even the most aware white perspective. Far from a cause for despair, this acknowledgment—especially combined with Rich's catalog of books by Afro-American women which have influenced her process since the original publication of *Of Woman Born*—simply reiterates the need for an ongoing process.

In one of the most significant passages from "Disloyal to Civilization," Rich implies that, finally, her most practical contribution to what Lorde called the "inseparable process" is her poetry itself: "If we have learned anything in our coming to language out of silence, it is that what has been kept unspoken, therefore *unspeakable*, in us is what is most threatening to the patriarchal order in which men control, first women, then all who can be defined and exploited as 'other.' All silence has a meaning" (Rich, *Lies*, p. 308). Attesting to the reality of the dialog between black and white lesbians, to the possibility of a common language, this passage closely parallels Lorde's assertion in "Poetry Is Not a Luxury" (which, like "Disloyal to Civilization," was originally published in *Chrysalis: A Magazine of Women's Culture*): "Within living structures defined by profit, by linear power, by institutional dehumanization, our feelings were not meant to survive . . . . But women have survived. As poets. And there are no new pains. We have felt them all already. We have hidden that fact in the same place where we have hidden our power. They surface in our dreams, and it is our dreams that point the way to freedom. Those dreams are made realizable through our poems that give us the strength and courage to see, to feel, to speak, and to dare" (Lorde, 1977, p. 39).

References

Addelson, Kathryn Pyne
1981. "Words and Lives: On 'Compulsory Heterosexuality and Lesbian Existence,'" *Signs* Autumn, pp. 197-99.
Bennett, Paula
1986. *My Life a Loaded Gun: Female Creativity and Feminist Poetics.* Boston: Beacon.
Breslin, James
1984. *From Modern to Contemporary.* Chicago: Univ. of Chicago Pr.
Bulkin, Elly
1977. "An Interview with Adrienne Rich," *Conditions: One* April, pp. 58-60.
1981. "Introduction—A Look at Lesbian Poetry" and "Lesbian Poetry in the Classroom," in *Lesbian Poetry*, ed. Bulkin and Joan Larkin. Watertown, Mass.: Persephone Pr., pp. xxi-xxxiv, 265-78.
Carruthers, Mary
1983. "The Re-Vision of the Muse: Adrienne Rich, Audre Lorde, Judy Grahn, Olga Broumas," *Hudson Review* Summer, pp. 293-322.
Christ, Carol
1980. *Diving Deep and Surfacing: Women Writers on Spiritual Quest.* Boston: Beacon.
Cooper, Jane Roberta
1984. (editor) *Reading Adrienne Rich.* Ann Arbor: Univ. of Michigan Pr.

Daly, Mary
1984. *Pure Lust: Elemental Feminist Philosophy.* Boston: Beacon.
Diehl, Joanne Feit
1980. "'Cartographies of Silence': Rich's *Common Language* and the Woman Poet," *Feminist Studies* Fall, pp. 530-46. Rpt. in Cooper, pp. 91-110.
DuBois, W. E. B.
1903. *The Souls of Black Folk.* Rpt. Greenwich, Conn.: Fawcett, 1961.
DuPlessis, Rachel Blau
1985. *Writing Beyond the Ending: Narrative Strategies of Twentieth-Century Women Writers.* Bloomington: Indiana Univ. Pr.
Ferguson, Ann
1981. "Patriarchy, Sexual Identity, and the Sexual Revolution: On 'Compulsory Heterosexuality and Lesbian Existence'—Defining the Issues," *Signs* Autumn, pp. 158-72.
Friedman, Susan Stanford
1983. "'I Go Where I Love': An Intertextual Study of H.D. and Adrienne Rich," *Signs* Winter,,pp. 228-45. Rpt. in Cooper, pp. 171-206.
1984. "Reply to Rich," *Signs* Summer, pp. 738-40.
Gelpi, Barbara Charlesworth
1979. "A Common Language: The American Woman Poet," in *Shakespeare's Sisters,* ed. Sandra M. Gilbert and Susan Gubar. Bloomington: Indiana Univ. Pr., pp. 269-79.
Gelpi, Barbara Charlesworth and Albert Gelpi
1975. (editors) *Adrienne Rich's Poetry.* New York: Norton.
Gilbert, Sandra M. and Susan Gubar
1979. *The Madwoman in the Attic: The Woman Writer and the Nineteenth-Century Literary Imagination.* New Haven: Yale Univ. Pr.
Grahn, Judy
1985. *The Highest Apple: Sappho and The Lesbian Poetic Tradition.* San Francisco: Spinsters.
Homans, Margaret
1983. "'Oh, Vision of Language!': Dickinson's Poems of Love and Death," in *Feminist Critics Read Emily Dickinson,* ed. Suzanne Juhasz. Bloomington: Indiana Univ. Pr., pp. 114-33.
Howard, Richard
1980. *Alone with America: Essays on the Art of Poetry in the United States since 1950.* New York: Atheneum, pp. 493-516.
Hughes, Gertrude Reif
1984. "'Imagining the Existence of Something Uncreated': Elements of Emerson in Adrienne Rich's 'Dream of a Common Language'," in Cooper, pp. 140-62.

Juhasz, Suzanne
1976. *Naked and Fiery Forms: Modern American Poetry by Women.* New York: Harper and Row.
1983. (editor) *Feminist Critics Read Emily Dickinson.* Bloomington: Indiana Univ. Pr.
Keller, Karl
1979. *The Only Kangaroo among the Beauty: Emily Dickinson and America.* Baltimore: Johns Hopkins Univ. Pr.
Lorde, Audre
1977. "Poetry Is Not a Luxury" in her *Sister Outsider.* Trumansburg, N.Y.: Crossing Pr., pp. 36-39.
1981. "An Interview: Audre Lorde and Adrienne Rich" in her *Sister Outsider,* pp. 81-109.
Milford, Nancy
1975. "This Woman's Movement," in Gelpi, pp. 189-202.
Oktenberg, Adrian
1984. "'Disloyal to Civilization': The *Twenty-One Love Poems* of Adrienne Rich," in Cooper, pp. 72-90.
Ostriker, Alicia
1983. *Writing Like a Woman.* Ann Arbor: Univ. of Michigan Pr.
1986. *Stealing the Language: The Emergence of Women's Poetry in America.* Boston: Beacon.
Piercy, Marge
1982. *Parti-Colored Blocks for a Quilt.* Ann Arbor: Univ. of Michigan Pr.
Pope, Deborah
1984. *A Separate Vision: Isolation in Contemporary Women's Poetry.* Baton Rouge: Louisiana State Univ. Pr.
Ratner, Rochelle
1984. *Trying to Understand What It Means to Be a Feminist.* New York: Contact II Publications.
Rich, Adrienne
1976. *Of Woman Born: Motherhood as Experience and Institution.* New York: Norton.
1976. "Vesuvius at Home: The Power of Emily Dickinson," *Parnassus* Fall/Winter, pp. 49-74. Rpt. in her *On Lies, Secrets, and Silence.* New York: Norton, pp. 157-83.
1977. "The Meaning of Our Love for Women Is What We Have Constantly to Expand." Brooklyn: Out & Out Books. Rpt. in her *On Lies, Secrets, and Silence* (1979), pp. 223-30.
1977. "Women and Honor: Some Notes on Lying." Pittsburgh: Motheroot. Rpt. in her *On Lies, Secrets, and Silence* (1979), pp. 185-94.
1978. "Power and Danger: Works of a Common Woman," in *The*

Works of a Common Woman: The Collected Poetry of Judy Grahn. Oakland: Diana Pr. Rpt. in her *On Lies, Secrets, and Silence* (1979), pp. 247-58.

1979. "Disloyal to Civilization: Feminism, Racism, Gynephobia," in her *On Lies, Secrets, and Silence* (1979), pp. 275- 310.

1979. "Foreword: On History, Illiteracy, Passivity, Violence, and Women's Culture," in her *On Lies, Secrets, and Silence*, pp. 9-20.

1979. "The Problem with Lorraine Hansberry," *Freedomways: A Quarterly Review of the Freedom Movement*, pp. 247-55.

1980. "Compulsory Heterosexuality and Lesbian Existence," *Signs* Summer, pp. 631-60. Rpt. in her *Blood, Bread, and Poetry* (1986), pp. 23-75.

1980, 1981. "'Wholeness Is No Trifling Matter': Some Fiction by Black Women," *New Women's Times Feminist Review* Dec. 1980/Jan. 1981, pp. 10-13, and Feb.-Mar. 1981, p. 12.

1984. "Comment on Friedman's 'I Go Where I Love': An Intertextual Study of H. D. and Adrienne Rich," *Signs* Summer, pp. 733-38.

1985. "Across the Great Divide," *Village Voice* May 28, pp. 57, 60.

1986. "Ten Years Later. A New Introduction," in her *Of Woman Born.* 10th anniversary ed. New York: Norton.

Stepto, Robert
1979. *From Behind the Veil: A Study of Afro-American Narrative.* Urbana: Univ. of Illinois Pr.

Stimpson, Catharine
1985. "Adrienne Rich and Lesbian/Feminist Poetry," *Parnassus* Spring/Summer/Fall/Winter, pp. 249-68.

Vanderbosch, Jane
1984. "Beginning Again," in Cooper, pp. 111-39.

Whelchel, Marianne
1982. "Mining the 'Earth-Deposits': Women's History in Adrienne Rich's Poetry," in *Toward a Feminist Transformation of the Academy: II, Proceedings of the Sixth Annual GLCA Women's Studies Conference,* ed. Beth Reed. n.p.: Great Lakes College Assn. Rpt. in Cooper, pp. 51-71.

Zita, Jacquelyn N.
1981. "Historical Amnesia and the Lesbian Continuum: On 'Compulsory Heterosexuality and Lesbian Existence'—Defining the Issues," *Signs* Fall, pp. 172-87.

CHAPTER 4

The Radical Voice: From Deconstruction to Reconstruction

Fully aware of the problematical and frequently self-contradictory sound of the "radical voice" in a culture convincingly described by Christopher Lasch as "narcissistic" and by Charles Newman as "inflationary," Rich has struggled since the mid-1960s to develop a poetic voice which poses a serious and self-renewing challenge to the dominant values of her political and aesthetic context. Even as she critiques entrenched institutions, she has remained remarkably free of long-term fixation on any single "alternative" approach. Rather, she has continually sought to deconstruct any ideological or aesthetic system attempting to establish fixed terms for perceiving self or context. Inextricably involved with her political critique of patriarchy, her radically subversive project depends on, and helps shape, the poetic voice she has been developing from *Leaflets* and *The Will to Change* through *Your Native Land, Your Life*. Despite lapses in individual poems, this voice speaks with an insistently decentering, politically focused, and ultimately self-critical power which intimates shared projects and useful connections between Rich's lesbian-feminism and several other forms of radical, or potentially radical, discourse.

Although her theoretical writings identify her with the "pragmatic American" rather than the "theoretical French" current of feminist thought, the deconstructive nature of Rich's sensibility has been recognized by several critics, most notably Charles Altieri and Rachel Blau DuPlessis. The fact that these temperamentally diverse but equally acute critics discuss Rich in relation to distinct movements—DuPlessis focuses on Anglo-American women writers, Altieri on American lyric poets of the 1970s and 1980s—adds significance to their agreement on one basic point: Rich's primary concern is with what DuPlessis calls the "critical attack on dominant patterns of perception and practice" (p. 127). Rich cares little whether these dominant patterns are manifested in the patriarchal romance plots described by DuPlessis, the "scenic mode" of lyric poetry identified by Altieri, or, as I shall argue below, "alternative" discourses such as academic deconstruction or "politically correct" feminism. Her abiding concern is to maintain the integrity of her process, to resist the power of any force which would establish a "center" of perception and circumscribe her exploration of the wild zone. (For the basic argument concerning the relationship between "center" and "margin," see the discussion of Elaine Showalter's theoretical model in Chapter 1).

Decentering Modern Poetry

Throughout most of Rich's career, the primary frame of reference for most Anglo-American criticism has been the technically innovative but socially conservative "high modernism" codified by Hugh Kenner's *The Pound Era* and Frederick Karl's *Modern and Modernism*. Developed in part as a response to the perceived decay of traditional culture and values, this strain of modernism concentrated on various attempts to reestablish coherence, frequently through invocation of "universal values" or the "sovereignty of the artist." From the perspective of marginal groups, this movement often seems little more than a half-conscious attempt to reestablish the traditional power structure which exploited and excluded "others" from participation in the "lost" tradition. Even critics who have revealed the inadequacy of Kenner's formulation (Friedman, Gilbert, Benstock) acknowledge the massive influence of Pound, Eliot, and to a lesser extent Williams and Stevens during the first half of the century. By the start of Rich's career, however, the influence was fading. The major works of the high modernists had been published. Although critical discussion of "contemporary" poetry would continue for several decades to center on "The Waste Land," *The Cantos*, and *Paterson*, the works gradually ceased to exert a strong influence on the practice of younger poets. Auden's discouragement of innovation in the preface to *A Change of World* simply reflected what had become a dominant attitude among poets and would soon become a dominant attitude among critics. In the wake of high modernism, James Breslin argues in *From Modern to Contemporary* that younger poets, including Rich, developed a highly polished but thematically and experientially cautious approach to poetry which reinforced the "basic assumptions reflected in the social and political consensus of their time" (p. 45). In the course of an excellent discussion of *A Change of World* and *The Diamond Cutters*, Breslin describes the central values of this mode as follows: "The imagination is valorized—by being dehistorized. [The poems] do not confront historical pressures in evolved forms that are disjunctive and heterogeneous; instead they step back and circumscribe delimited areas of experience in stable forms" (p. 39).

Culminating in the publication of Donald Hall, Robert Pack, and Louis Simpson's influential anthology *New Poets of England and America* (1957), which included a selection of Rich's early work, the formalist movement seemed, at least as seen in academic context, to have established a new center. Where the high modernists maintained their aesthetic centrality for nearly a half century, however, the formalists were challenged almost immediately by various "schools" (Beat, New York, Black Mountain, etc.), represented in Donald Allen's iconoclastic anthology *The New American Poetry* (1960), which brought increased attention to various forms of "Open Poetry" or, in Charles Olson's phrase, "composition by field." By the appearance of Stephen Berg and Robert Mezey's anthology *Naked Poetry: Recent American Poetry in Open Forms* (1969), it seemed clear that the "radicals" of a decade earlier—whose commitment to raw experience and repudiation of traditional prosody quickly developed into various forms of counter-dogma—had established a claim to the center at least as compelling as that of the formalists. By the beginning of the 1970s, the rise of poetic movements such as the Black Arts Movement and the first wave of feminist poetry, alongside continuations of each earlier "post-modernist" school, had created a situation in which the question had shifted from "Who occupies the center?" to "Does the concept of a center have meaning?" In 1950 it clearly made sense to speak of what Altieri calls a "dominant mode" which "organize[s] discourse in such a way that even those with very different commitments find themselves compelled to shape their work so that it addresses these central issues" (p. 5). Two decades later, however, very few poets or critics would venture to identify such a mode for any save polemical reasons. Although Altieri argues for a new dominant mode in the "scenic" poetry of the 1970s—which probably does come as close to dominance as possible, given the developments of the 1920s and 1960s—the absence of any obvious academic consensus concerning the existence of the mode or any codifying anthology with widespread influence (A. Poulin's pluralistic *Contemporary American Poetry* seems to be used at least as widely as Dave Smith and David Bottoms' "scenic" *Morrow Anthology of Younger Poets*) suggests strongly that the center has not held.

There are, of course, alternative ways of presenting the history of modern poetry. Each alternative, if viewed from outside its own premises, would probably yield the conclusion that no unquestionable center has survived the dislocations of the postwar era. Because it developed in this "decentered" matrix, Rich's commitment to resisting dominant systems has generated shifting and increasingly complex stances which are comprehensible only in the context of her on-going process. After her early formalist period, Rich's work explored several ways of decentering other "modes" with pretensions to centrality. In effect, Rich's experiments with metonymic forms, such as the ghazal, during the 1960s (a selection of her work was included in *The New Naked Poetry*, the 1976 sequel to the Berg-Mezey anthology) decenter the formal mode. Conversely, the more discursive voice of her early feminist work deconstructs the entrenched forms of 1960s "radicalism" which had failed to repudiate its patriarchal substructures. As Terry Eagleton notes, the result of this radical failure was a general collapse into nihilism and political cynicism following the defeat of the Parisian leftists in 1968 (p. 142).

Rich's lack of interest in academic deconstruction is an extension of her response to this retreat. A brief survey of the intellectual premises of American academic deconstruction, which grew out of the French movement, superficially echoes many of Rich's deepest beliefs. Eagleton's chapter "Post-Structuralism," in *Literary Theory: An Introduction*, and Jonathan Culler's chapter, "Critical Consequences," in *On Deconstruction*, two works which diverge sharply in their views of the larger significance of the movement, highlight the consensual understanding which developed in nondeconstructionist academic discourse during the mid-1980s. Both understand deconstruction as a philosophically grounded approach to thought which (1) emphasizes the problematic relationship between the linguistic signifier and the "transcendent signified" (Eagleton, p. 131; Culler, p. 188); (2) challenges, and ultimately decenters, hierarchies of thought or expression based on binary oppositions which privilege one term over its ostensible opposite (Culler, p. 213; Eagleton, p. 132); (3) focuses on the "marginal" terms excluded from the discourse in order to recognize the way in which the text subverts its own meaning (Culler, p. 215; Eagleton, pp. 132-33); and (4) recognizes that all signifiers derive their meaning from "traces" of other signifiers and concentrates on the "play of signifiers," creating a theoretically endless chain which frustrates attempts at closure (Eagleton, p. 134; Culler, p. 188).

Rich's use of subversive forms from the ghazals of the 1960s to the discursive montages of the 1980s suggests that she would find much of interest in Eagleton's summary of the deconstructive project: "Deconstruction tries to show how such oppositions, in order to hold themselves in place, are sometimes betrayed into inverting or collapsing themselves, or need to banish to the text's margins certain niggling details which can be made to return and plague them . . . . The tactic of deconstructive criticism, that is to say, is to show how texts come to embarrass their own ruling systems of logic" (p. 133). Generalizing this approach in a manner which would seem to echo Rich's emphasis on the contextual determinants of textual meaning, Culler asserts "One could, therefore, identify deconstruction with the twin principles of the contextual determination of meaning and the infinite extendability of context" (p. 215).

The Politics of Deconstruction

Nonetheless, Rich has never explicitly endorsed either the goals or methodology of academic deconstruction, which she perceives as withdrawn from its actual social context. Critics with an interest in literary theory evince almost no interest in her work. Those who do—Cary Nelson, Margaret Homans and Marjorie Perloff are the most prominent examples—frequently present Rich's use of a discursive voice in her lesbian-feminist poetry as a retreat from the radical implications of deconstruction (or other post-modernist insights into the nature of language). Yet the criticisms, and the more frequent silences, seriously underestimate Rich's awareness of the underlying concerns and implications of post-structuralist thought. Although Homans criticizes the "poetically terminal" commitment to simplifying metaphors in Rich's recent work (p. 229), Rich has in fact adapted the radical structures of the 1960s to the values (not simple, but clear) of the lesbian civitas, generating a new voice unlikely to repeat the entropic patterns of the earlier "radical" movement. Charles Altieri's suggestion that, in responding to Rich, we seek not "foundations" but a "position" helps clarify her idiosyncratically deconstructive sensibility (p. 28). Defining "foundations" as the values or techniques a poet assumes as a fixed basis for her discourse, Altieri suggests that we seek instead her "position": "a place from which someone speaks, but the place itself is positioned by the cultural practices and the personal history and needs of the speaker. This means, ultimately, that all authority is at best provisional: No one discourse can claim to speak for or over another since there are enormous difficulties in translating between positions or deciding how they might be commensurable" (p. 28).

Adapting deconstructionist insights to her political concerns, Rich creates a position resembling that developed by Foucault, post-Brechtian Marxist critics (Eagleton, Jameson), and Jean-Luc Godard, whose influence she acknowledges. Among the concerns she shares with this stream of post-structuralist thought are her commitment to the decentering of dominant discourses, which involves both the identification of the unstated premises of social discourse which support dominant group interests at a given historical moment (the historical emphasis, it should be noted, significantly modifies the "universalist" claims of structuralist theorists working in the wake of Levi-Strauss); her recognition that marginalized elements (the "wild zone" experiences of lesbians, for example) unveil the internal contradictions of dominant discourses; her understanding of the discrepancy between signifier and signified; her awareness of the "intertextuality" linking even ostensibly radical statements to the systems of thought against which they claim to rebel; and, although she develops the concept in ways which contrast sharply with those most common in theoretical discourse, her rejection of the concept of an "essential" self separable from its historical context.

In practice, Rich's poetry supports Derrida's concern with politics. Derrida's recent writing on issues such as racial discourse supports Eagleton's claim that "Derrida is clearly out to do more than develop new techniques of reading: deconstruction is for him an ultimately *political* practice, an attempt to dismantle the logic by which a particular system of thought, and behind that a whole system of political structures and social institutions, maintains its force" (p. 148). Ultimately, Rich uses deconstructive methodologies as part of the process leading to the reconstruction of the integrity of the lesbian *civitas*. Her conception of reconstruction does not imply a re-centering on an essential, unified self, somehow freed from its intertextual relationship to social codes. Rather, it implies an alternative means of conceiving the self as a conscious *manifestation* of ever-shifting relationships. Deconstructing the "scripts" of patriarchal romance (DuPlessis), Rich seeks to reconstruct alternative scripts, aware of their own contingency even as they resist the centers of power which discourage such processes. My examination of the development of Rich's poetic voice since the mid-1960s, then, will focus on her continuing commitment to decentering dominant modes of discourse and on her growing insistence on the need for reconstruction (not recentering) of a contingent or relational self committed, at least provisionally, to the expansive integrity of the lesbian *civitas*. While understanding that these values, like all values, are ultimately mediated through linguistic and trans-linguistic codes, Rich nonetheless insists that there is an actual and substantial difference in their cultural significance. To the greatest extent possible, she seeks to reconstruct her voice as an alternative to the discourses which, at this historical moment, enforce the destructive values of the dominant power structure.

Rich's Provisional Voice

Rich's attempt to discover and maintain a position from which she can speak with the "provisional authority" described by Altieri revolves around her use of two seemingly contradictory types of poetic voices. On the one hand, the characteristic voice of the "Ghazals" and recent sequences such as "North American Time" reflects a self-consciously deconstructive position, employing techniques of juxtaposition which emphasize the discontinuity of experience and resist attempts to impose limitations on perception. To describe this aspect of Rich's aesthetic approach in terms familiar to recent theoretical discourse, her deconstructive voice revels in the loosely organized, metonymic "play of signifiers" in order to reduce the shaping power of patriarchal linguistic and formal structures. On the other hand, the characteristic voice of *The Dream of a Common Language* and, to a lesser extent, *A Wild Patience Has Taken Me This Far* speaks from a reconstructive position, employing techniques designed to reveal the relationship between seemingly diverse aspects of experience: personal, political, spiritual, physical. From an academic post-structuralist perspective, this voice, metaphorical rather than metonymic, marks a retreat to an untenable belief in the literal identification of signifier and signified. Such an understanding of Rich's reconstructive voice, however, fails to consider adequately its position in her overall process. As Breslin suggests, her earliest work probably is grounded in a naive belief in the power of poetic language; her return to metaphor, however, does not, as Homans suggests, reassert a belief in literal identification of signifier and signified. Rather, it furthers a dialectical process intended in part to decenter Rich's own metonymic discourse and check against the movement into pure contemplation visible in the work of some academic theorists (a movement which, ironically, reasserts the binary opposition of life and art). Understanding the complex relationship between structures which appear to exist in fixed forms and linguistic acts designed to interact with and ultimately alter those structures, Rich oscillates between the metonymic and metaphorical voices in a dialectical process conceived as a basic aspect of a tenable lesbian-feminist position.

Hearing the full richness of Rich's voice in any text requires recognition of this dialectical quality. While Breslin, Nelson, and Homans respond sensitively to certain strains in Rich's voice, the problems each encounters with other strains reflect the danger of extracting any aspect of Rich's work from her on-going process. Even as Breslin emphasizes the importance of discontinuity to an understanding of recent American poetry, he fails to recognize the radical transformation of Rich's voice of the 1960s. While I would accept his comment that the emphasis on "control, technical mastery and intellectual clarity" in her early work reveals a belief in poems as "extensions of the human will," careful analysis of the deconstructive techniques of poems such as "Shooting Script" renders problematic his assertion that "the author of *The Will to Change* has never abandoned, only complicated, this view" (p. 45). Similarly, Nelson's blindness to aspects of Rich's lesbian-feminist poetry relates directly to his insight into earlier work. Although he recognizes Rich's "deconstructive force" and sees that "the whole tone of formal control [in *The Will to Change*] is toward increasing our uncertainty, not toward containing it" (p. 169), he reduces "Not Somewhere Else, but Here" and "THE FLOATING POEM, UNNUMBERED" to essentially literal statements, asserting a "privileging of sexuality" when they can be more fully understood as explorations of contingent forms of unity which derive their meaning from their place in her dialectical process. Applying a similar perspective to *The Dream of a Common Language*, Homans assails what she sees as Rich's "naive wish for a literal language and . . . belief in poetry's capacity for the duplication of experience" which "foster a conception of the feminine self in poetry that is, paradoxically, even more egotistical than some of the masculine paradigms from which it intends to free itself" (p. 239). While her brilliant reading of "Phantasia for Elvira Shatayev" in relation to "Transcendental Etude" clearly points to the dialectical nature of Rich's work, Homans fails to acknowledge the interdependence of voices. Casting the two poems in stark opposition, Homans reads the closing image of "Transcendental Etude" as an attempt to "destroy figuration" by directly identifying women with the purely physical, nonsentient bedrock. This in turn leads Homans to accuse Rich of endorsing a dangerously simplistic literal view of language which does nothing more than "ratify women's age-old and disadvantageous position as the other and the object" (p. 234). Again, this is a very difficult reading to uphold in light of the lengthy struggle against such reductions in Rich's work both before and after the image in question, which can be better read as part of Rich's on-going deconstruction of the transcendental current of patriarchal thought.

The most adequate discussions of Rich's voice are those of DuPlessis and Altieri, both of whom are aware of the dialectical nature of her recent work. As DuPlessis argues, the real key to understanding Rich's approximations of a "unitary world where word does equal thing, and where women 'tell the truth' about their lives as if a 'truth' that exists beyond the fictions and languages in which it is told could be reached" (p. 139) lies in recognizing the position of the assertion in Rich's larger project. Two of DuPlessis' comments seem particularly insightful in relation to this issue: first, that Rich's "postulating of monistic discourse is, then, a poetics that signals ideological critique, the valorizing of oppositional in contrast to dominant" (p. 134) and, second, that such a postulation, accompanied by the "self-scrutiny [that] is one part of Rich's generally existentialist project" is intended to help "transform the static polarization of (male) Self and (female) Other that has structured Western ideology" (p. 141). Complementing this approach, Altieri identifies Rich's explicit acceptance of the "self-division," which he sees as the most striking aspect of *A Wild Patience Has Taken Me This Far*, as "the prologue to whatever freedom may be possible" (p. 189). Recognizing that she has come to view discourse not as a literal version of reality but as a useful tool for modeling various responses to reality, Altieri concludes his discussion with an insightful comment on the relationship between Rich's aesthetic and political positions: "Discourse becomes the poet's paradigm for accepting things as they are without resigning herself to what we have made of them. If she can at once accept and criticize her own stances by risking the divisions of self-consciousness, she has every right to hope society can pursue that same endless, tauntingly gradual process of self-revision. Even male poets may follow" (p. 190).

"The Roofwalkers," "The Trees"

The development of Rich's dialectical aesthetic can be traced through two sequences of poems, one focusing on metonymy, the other on metaphor. The first sequence, focusing directly on poetic stance and voice, considers the problems Rich experienced writing within what she perceived at the time as the "dominant modes" of the 1950s and 1960s. Expressing an intense concern with figuration, this sequence contrasts with a second sequence which, although it does not focus directly on poetry, provides insight into Rich's reconstructive explorations. Beginning with "The Roofwalker" (1961) and "The Trees" (1963) and receiving its most powerful articulation in "A Valediction Forbidding Mourning" (1970), the explicitly aesthetic sequence reveals Rich's gradual disillusionment with the dominant modes. An important transitional poem which can be read in relation to either sequence, "The Fact of a Doorframe" (1974) connects Rich's meditations on poetic voice with the images of women's creativity which recur from "Aunt Jennifer's Tigers" and "Mathilde in Normandy" through "Necessities of Life" to "From an Old House in America" and "Transcendental Etude." Juxtaposed with the questions concerning metonymic figuration, posed most powerfully in "A Valdediction Forbidding Mourning," Rich's emphasis on the direct, predominantly metaphorical, aspects of women's expression seems a considered aspect of a complex aesthetic position rather than a retreat to naive literalism.

Rich's early meditations on poetry introduce disquieting questions concerning the positions available to women poets within the dominant modes. Employing the central image of the poet as a housebuilder, "The Roofwalker" (which was presented as a statement of Rich's aesthetic in the first edition of Poulin's *Contemporary American Poetry* but dropped in subsequent editions) emphasizes, both thematically and figuratively, the inadequacy, especially for a woman poet, of the confessional mode which provided a transition between formalism and the "open" poetry of the early 1960s. The poem opens with the image of larger-than-life builders standing on the roofs of "half-finished houses," a group of "Giants" who recall the major figures of high modernism and perhaps the male "founders" of the confessional movement. Described in the heroic quest imagery invoked by Pound at the start of "Canto I" and Eliot throughout "The Waste Land," these "Giants" remain half-seen, reflected against a sky "where figures pass magnified, shadows/ on a burning deck." Implying both the persona's awe and her doubts concerning these "roofwalkers," this passage is followed by a "confessional" passage asserting both Rich's identification with and her distance from the poetic "Giants": "I feel like them up there:/ exposed, larger than life,/ and due to break my neck." This tentative identification, however, gives way almost immediately to a strong statement of alienation from the entire enterprise of housebuilding, of poetry. Questioning the "blueprints,/ closings of gaps,/ measurings, calculations" characteristic of her work in the late modernist mode, Rich identifies the results as inadequate to her needs, "a roof I can't live under." Perceiving herself as the victim, rather than the architect, of her discourse, she dismisses her image of herself as heroic quester along with her belief in her vocation as a poet employing the familiar techniques of the dominant mode:

> A life I didn't choose
> chose me: even
> my tools are the wrong ones
> for what I have to do.

The final, and in relation to the development of Rich's dialectical aesthetic most significant, expression of disaffection occurs in the final sentence of the poem in which Rich describes herself as a "naked man fleeing,/ across the roofs," who might almost as easily have been sitting comfortably inside "reading—not with indifference—/ about a naked man/ fleeing across the roofs." Ostensibly focusing on the tension between the risks of participation and the safety of observation—a common issue in confessional poetry—the concluding figure highlights the sources of the disaffection expressed previously in the poem. Rich's description of herself as a naked *man* suggests the profound inadequacy of the figurative vocabulary available within the dominant mode. This acceptance of an "undeconstructed" image dictates further dislocations of meaning, since the position of the male within the house is not, as many of Rich's earlier poems recognize, interchangeable with that of a woman occupying the same space. Following her central figure to its logical conclusion, Rich, probably unconsciously at this stage, reveals the inadequacy of the figure as an expression of the female quest. While this could be taken as evidence of the inevitable limitation of all forms of signification, and Rich would probably not argue the point, its significance for Rich clearly relates more directly to the position of the woman poet in patriarchal discourse.

Similarly "The Trees," which Deborah Pope uses as a touchstone for her discussion of Rich's developing aesthetic, emphasizes the inadequacy of available figures for the persona's experience. Describing "the diminution, indeed the wholesale decampment of the vital imagination . . . that sustains creation" (Pope, p. 118), Rich employs the central figure of trees abandoning the poet's house to move into an empty "forest." Although the poem presents the exodus of the trees (a common modernist image of feminine generative power) as a cataclysmic event, the persona of "The Trees" is unable to articulate its reality, let alone its significance: "I sit inside, doors open to the veranda/ writing long letters/ in which I scarcely mention the departure." Ultimately, the inadequacy of her voice threatens to destroy the poet's access to the sources of her power: "My head is full of whispers/ which tomorrow will be silent." Alienated from her unconscious—the images recur in "Women and Honor"—she can perceive even the moon, perhaps the most powerful emblem of womanly power, only through modernist figures implying narcissism and fragmentation: "The moon is broken like a mirror,/ its pieces flash now in the crown/ of the tallest oak." The paradox of such a description, of course, is that it resists precisely the phenomenon it describes. Rich employs figures which imply a potential unity between the persona and the sources of women's creativity in a way which implies that the specific approach to figuration may render such unity inexpressible. Framing Rich's critique of received modes in terms compatible with those modes, "The Trees" intimates the need for the dialectic of literal and figurative which emerges in her later work.

"A VALEDICTION FORBIDDING MOURNING"

The dissatisfaction with dominant modes implicit in "The Roof-walker" and "The Trees" emerges as a fully articulated theme in "A Valediction Forbidding Mourning," which Betsy Hirsch has identified as one of Rich's most important aesthetic statements. The first line of the poem—which both criticizes and draws power from Donne's "model"—expresses a clash between kinetic female experience ("My swirling wants") and static masculine expression ("Your frozen lips"). Although she has withheld any explicit linguistic or conceptual connection between the two images, the second line reveals her awareness of the impossibility of such "separation": "The grammar turned and attacked me." The simple juxtaposition, the presence of the masculine and feminine "figures" within a single structure, plunges her into an antagonistic relationship with the masculine presence of both Donne and the "you" of the poem, perhaps the husband she is preparing to leave in an inversion of Donne's original. Looking back at her previous writing, she finds only "Themes, written under duress./ Emptiness of the notation." Significantly, Rich employs a nonfigurative discursive voice to explain her departure, which she attributes to the inability of the system she has been living and writing within to respond to her most basic needs: "I want you to see this before I leave:/ the experience of repetition as death/ the failure of criticism to locate the pain." Having attempted repeatedly to articulate her experience in dominant modes, she now attempts to develop a voice which, as Altieri observes, must not be judged in relation to modes of figuration which do not help deal with the pain in concrete practical terms: "The single norm for the person speaking the poem is the power she dramatizes that the writer can wield as a historical agent. If we are to appreciate [Rich's later] work fully, we must read it not by aesthetic criteria, but from the inside, as a project for exploring the interconnections between poetry and life" (p. 167).

The last two stanzas of "A Valediction Forbidding Mourning" suggest that by 1970 Rich had developed a fairly clear conception of the dialectical voice which would develop over the next decade. Unwilling to abandon her attempt to communicate with the masculine world, she makes one "last attempt," explaining in as direct a voice as the concept will allow: "the language is a dialect called metaphor." I understand this phrase as a statement that the language in which Rich writes, described in "The Burning of Paper Instead of Children" (which, like "A Valediction," was published in *The Will to Change*) as the "oppressor's language," bears no special relationship to a "transcendent signified."

Rather, it is simply a "dialect," the expression of a particular cultural group, in this case composed primarily of Euro-American males with some degree of economic and social power. Typically presented as a universally valid language, this dialect asserts its values through "metaphors" encoding the values which relegate women to marginal positions. No longer content to struggle against this voice, Rich devotes the remainder of the poem to a description, which is at once an example, of her emerging voice: "These images go unglossed: hair, glacier, flashlight." Although this might at first appear to mark a retreat into a naive literalism, the next lines indicate that Rich understands its position in a dialectical process. Emphasizing the historical and kinetic quality of her new departure, Rich claims access to the traditional quest pattern which was unavailable to her as long as she mediated her voice through masculine figures: "When I think of a landscape I am thinking of a time./ When I talk of taking a trip I mean forever." She concludes the stanza with a self-conscious refusal to return to naive figuration: "I could say: those mountains have a meaning/ but further than that I could not say."

This "silence" intimates the alternative concept of women's creativity expressed in the second sequence of Rich's aesthetic meditations. Although it anticipates both the emphasis on "unglossed objects" and the association of women with natural forces present in "Transcendental Etude," the alternative voice introduced in "A Valediction Forbidding Mourning" does not, as Homans suggests, "uncritically [accept] what amounts to the male paradigm of the woman who merges with nature" (pp. 234-35). Rather, it helps Rich resist the modes of figuration which had alienated her from her creative powers and abandoned her to the "emptiness of the notations." Responding to "Transcendental Etude," Homans, who somewhat uncritically argues that a "belief in figuration is life-giving" (p. 223), claims that the woman who identifies herself with the "rockshelf further/ forming underneath everything that grows" can never be a poet (p. 229). The response intimated in "A Valediction Forbidding Mourning" is that, while the specific forms of Dickinsonian figuration Homans describes may in fact be life-giving, for Rich the situation differed substantially. To employ figuration as it existed in what she still experienced as the dominant, implicitly patriarchal, poetic modes would enable her to identify herself as a "poet" in the professional sense, but it would not enable her to articulate her pain or to express her expanding sense of integrity as relationship, both crucial aspects of her developing position. "A Valediction Forbidding Mourning" closes with a rhymed couplet—"but further than that I could not say./ To do something very common, in my own way"—which suggests the dominant tones of the voice Rich will adapt as she gradually shifts her attention away from the deconstructive aspects of her position following *The Will to Change*.

"THE FACT OF A DOORFRAME"

Combining silence and voice, individual and communal concerns, this resolution signals a clear movement toward the aesthetic suggested as early as "Aunt Jennifer's Tigers" and explicitly endorsed by the choice of "The Fact of a Doorframe" as the title for Rich's second volume of selected poems. Establishing a point of reference for her recent work, Rich challenges the current of theoretical thought which implies that the inherent rupture between signifier and signified precludes "meaning" as the term is usually understood. The opening lines of "The Fact of a Doorframe" assert the possibility of communicable understanding while reemphasizing the psychological importance of allowing objects such as the doorframe to exist apart from the mediations of patriarchal figures, to remain, at least momentarily, "unglossed images": "The Fact of a Doorframe/ means there is something to hold/ onto with both hands." Whether or not use of this alternative mode ultimately leads to similar philosophical problems—and Rich seems aware that it does—these objects provide a temporary ground for the expression of "wild zone" experiences. Holding the doorframe, Rich describes herself "slowly thrusting my forehead against the wood/ and taking it away/ one of the oldest motions of suffering." Focus on the "literal" enables her to articulate pain suppressed by "oppressor's language." Where Homans implies that the rejection of figuration entails silence (p. 229), Rich concludes the first stanza with an image underlining the reality of forms of expression which may be more useful than their linguistic counterparts: "music is suffering made powerful." Following a cautionary parable of the "goose-girl" who unthinkingly passes through a gate in ignorance of the reality of female suffering—the head of her mare is nailed over the arch and chastizes her in the name of her mother—Rich reiterates her belief in poetry as "violent, arcane, common, hewn of the commonest living substance." Refusing to compromise the suffering, which she perceives as the necessary ground for the "common language," Rich directly addresses a "you" which can be understood as "poetry," as the physical doorframe, or as any individual in a position analogous to her own: "I grasp for you, your bloodstained splinters, your/ ancient and stubborn poise." Paradoxically grounded on the status of the doorframe as fact *not* figure, this elaborate figure prefigures the voice of

Rich's most recent poetry, a voice which simultaneously resists and acknowledges its own potential deconstruction.

Ghalib and the Ghazal Form

Perhaps the most significant influence on the development of Rich's dialectical voice has been her encounter with the ghazal form, especially as used by the Urdu poet Ghalib (Mirza Asadullah Beg Khan, 1797-1869). Rich's interest in the form originated in the late 1960s, when Aijaz Ahmad solicited poetic versions of his literal translations of Ghalib's ghazals from prominent American poets, including Rich, W. S. Merwin, William Stafford, and Mark Strand. Rich contributed ten versions to a Ghalib centennial booklet published by the *Hudson Review* and eighteen versions to Ahmad's anthology *Ghazals of Ghalib*, which, despite its scanty selection of thirty-seven ghazals chosen from a canon of hundreds, remains the best English-language introduction to Ghalib's work. In working with Ghalib's poetry, Rich attempted to remain faithful to the formal nature of the ghazal form, which Ahmad describes as

> the basic poetic form in Urdu from the beginnings of the language to the middle of this century. The ghazal is a poem made up of couplets, each couplet wholly independent of any other in meaning and complete in itself as a unity of thought, emotion, and communication. No two couplets have to be related to each other in any way whatever except formally. . . . and yet they can be parts of a single poem. The *only* link is in terms of prosodic structure and rhymes. All the lines in a ghazal have to be of equal metrical length. The first is a rhymed couplet, and the second line of each succeeding couplet must rhyme with the opening couplet. The unit of rhyme repeated at the end of each couplet may be as short as a single syllable or as long as a phrase of half a line. The convention is that a ghazal should have at least five couplets. Otherwise it is considered a fragment. There is no maximum length [pp. xvi-xvii].

Describing her approach to the form with obvious excitement, Rich wrote to Ahmad:

> I've been trying to make the couplets as autonomous as possible and to allow the unity of the ghazal to emerge from underneath, as it were, through images, through associations, private and otherwise . . . . For me, the couplets work only when I can keep them

from being too epigrammatic; what I'm trying for, not always suc-
cessfully, is a clear image or articulation behind which there are
shadows, reverberations, reflections of reflections. In other words,
something that will not remind the Western reader of haiku or any
other brief, compact form, such as Pope's couplets in English, or the
Greek anthology [in Ahmad, pp. xxv-xxvi].

Rich's emphasis on the distance between the ghazal and familiar
Western forms seems particularly significant in light of her adaptation
of the form in the "Ghazals: Homage to Ghalib" section of *Leaflets* and
"The Blue Ghazals" and "Shooting Script" in *The Will to Change*. Written
against the backdrop of the anti-Vietnam War movement and the rise
of black nationalism, Rich's letter to Ahmad makes it clear that she saw
the ghazal as a way of articulating a sense of reality frustrated by her
work in dominant modes: "I needed a way of dealing with very complex and scattered material which was demanding a different kind of
unity from that imposed on it by the isolated, single poem: in which
certain experiences needed to find both their intensest rendering and to
join with other experiences not logically or chronologically connected
in any obvious ways" (Rich, 1969, p. 59). In the headnote to the
"Homage," Rich describes her desire for a freedom of voice based on
"the continuity and unity flow[ing] from the association and images
playing back and forth among the couplets." For Rich, the ghazal
intimated the possibility of deconstructing the implicitly patriarchal
control-oriented forms of Western poetry without surrendering her
desire to reconstruct a contingent relational integrity.

Rich's use of the ghazal is at once profoundly attuned to and
ultimately distinct from Ghalib's. The Urdu poet, who lived most of
his life in the Indian city of Delhi during the transition from the Mus-
lim Moghul empire to British rule, shared Rich's sense of "writing in an
age of political and cultural break-up." After Britain's brutal suppres-
sion of the revolt of 1857, Ghalib, particularly in private letters which
sometimes contradict the more tempered public diary he directed to
the British authorities, evinces an acute awareness of the constituting,
but generally unacknowledged, violence at the core of the British
empire. Rich, of course, was arriving at similar perceptions concerning
violence in American culture at precisely the time she encountered
Ghalib's ghazals (which, for reasons which will be discussed below,
raise political issues only indirectly). Despite this general temperamen-
tal similarity, however, several elements distinguish Ghalib's ghazals
from Rich's adaptations. As Ahmad comments, "the movement in
Urdu poetry is always *away* from concreteness. Meaning is not
expressed or stated; it is signified" (p. xv). Conversely, the movement

in Rich's Vietnam-era poetry is toward immediacy, "an ungridded area of human activity without ideology—giving access to an epiphanal or purely experiential truth" (DuPlessis, p. 128). In addition, the prosodic rigidity of the Urdu ghazal was of very little interest to Rich, who had long since abandoned the strict metrics of her work in the formalist mode. Nonetheless, particularly if one accepts Ahmad's argument that the essence of Ghalib's sensibility lies in his refusal to accept a distinction between the particular and the universal, the most profound connection between the nineteenth-century Urdu and the twentieth-century feminist positions may be intimated by Ahmad's elaboration of Ghalib's sense of universality: "The particular *is* the universal: a man's history is the history of his intelligence, *plus* his emotions, *plus* his times" (p. xxiv). The fact that Rich's descriptions of the ghazal form stress its conception of unity suggests that she was aware of its relevance to her reconstructive interests.

The immediate impact of the form, however, was to expedite the development of Rich's deconstructive voice. Section two of the "Shooting Script" sequence, a translation/adaptation/response to Ghazal V from the Ahmad collection (which does not include her version), highlights Rich's sense of the tension between her voice and Ghalib's. Ghalib's ghazal is an elaborate reworking of a common Sufi teaching tale concerning the drop of water which merges its own identity with that of a river in order to transcend the illusion of individuality. Ahmad locates the center of the story in the Urdu conception of *Fana Hona*, which he glosses as "to die, to be consumed, to become so much a part of something that separateness is overcome" (p. 23). Ahmad's analysis of Ghalib's use of the concept continues: "The whole ghazal, it seems to me, is about the process of change. The drop falls into the river and dies; this is the ultimate joy for it. . . . The final couplet is . . . a celebration of change and acceptance of it as the eternal, joyous process" (p. 24).

Without the explicit acknowledgment at the head of the section, Rich's adaptation would not be easily recognizable as a version of the same material. The single clear point of connection lies in Rich's allusion to the Sufi tale in her third couplet: "Grief held back from the lips wears at the heart; the drop that/ refused to join the river dried up in dust." Rich's tone and development of the image, however, differ greatly from Ghalib's. Where Ghalib celebrates the joy of dissolution—"The happiness of the drop is to die in the river" (Ahmad's literal translation, p. 22)—Rich emphasizes the isolation of the individual drop: "Even when I thought I prayed, I was talking to myself." Similarly, her presentation of the central image stresses the refusal of the drop to join the river and hints at an ultimate destruction. Conversely, Ghalib stresses the inevitable union, paradoxically brought about by the individual suffering: "Spring cloud thinning after rain: Dying into its own weeping" (Thomas Fitzsimmons version, p. 25). Ghalib's original concludes with a celebration of openness; Rich's poem ends with a couplet concerning her emotional identification with the isolated drop. The first phrase of the couplet—"To see the Tigris in a water-drop"—suggests the unification of macro- and microcosmic perspectives. But Rich is unable to complete the celebratory thought. Broken off abruptly by an ellipse, the promise of unification collapses into an angry assertion of separation: "Either you were playing/ games with me, or you never cared to learn the structure of my/ language."

The third line in the final "couplet" (which has been maintained in every reprinting of the poem with which I am familiar, strongly suggesting it is not simply a typographical by-product of line length) focuses attention on the word "language." The disruption of the ghazal structure parallels Rich's revision of Ghalib's reconstructive sensibility. The full meaning of the disruption and the second person address emerges only in the overall context of "Shooting Script," which I will discuss below. The preceding "couplet," however, links Rich's dissatisfaction with her feeling that the language of unification omits elements of experience vital to her developing sense of integrity: "Now tell me your story till the blood drips from your lashes. Any/ other version belongs to your folklore, or ours." Looking beyond the celebratory surface of Ghalib's ghazal, Rich insists on the need for articulating the political/personal suffering of the brutalized individual, whether colonized British subject or contemporary American woman.

RICH'S GHAZALS

The ghazals included in *Leaflets*, Rich's most successful experiments with the form, frequently emphasize the silences underlying discourse, the gap between expression and experience. The ghazal of 8/4/68, inscribed to Ahmad, begins with an acceptance of what seems, in contemporary terms, a deconstructive sensibility: "If these are letters, they will have to be misread." Culminating in a direct address to Ghalib, the conclusion reiterates the inevitable "absences" of language and anticipates the emphasis on unglossed images in "Transcendental Etude": "When they read this poem of mine, they are translators./ Every existence speaks a language of its own." The language of "Ghazals: Homage to Ghalib" reflects both Rich's disgust with the language, which leaves "part of my life cut out forever," and her desire to "see the world reformed." Many of the ghazals conclude with bitter addresses to men ("You were American, Whitman, and those words are yours" [7/14/68: i]; "I hope you are rotting in hell, Montaigne, you bastard" [7/16/68: ii]; "What are you doing here at the edge of the death-camps, Vivaldi?" [7/23/68]) who represent a hostile tradition: "I can't live at the hems of that tradition—/ will I last to try the beginning of the next?" (7/24/68: i). In general, Rich's criticism of the European representatives of the tradition is much harsher than that of the Americans—Whitman and Melville are invoked directly, Frost and Stevens through allusion— whom she credits with some understanding of the elusive nature of the correspondence between words and event. Echoing "Thirteen Ways of Looking at a Blackbird," she describes her struggle for meaning: "Our words are jammed in an electronic jungle;/ sometimes, though, they rise and wheel croaking above the treetops" (7/23/68).

Thematically, these poems do not differ greatly from those of the early 1960s. Rich's earlier poems, including those in the "Night Watch" section of *Leaflets*, rarely question their own premises. In contrast, "Homage to Ghalib," and to a lesser extent the poems in the "Leaflets" section, draw attention to the deconstructive issues of absence and negation affecting their own composition. The first ghazal (7/12/68) inscribes the paradoxical (and perhaps unwritable) message that its message cannot be transmitted through language. Addressing an absent friend, Rich writes "When I look at that wall I shall think of you/ and of what you did not paint there." She concludes "When you read these lines, think of me/ and of what I have not written here." The ghazal of 7/14/68: ii generalizes this observation in specifically deconstructive terms: "For us the work undoes itself over and over." Connecting philosophy with politics, Rich interprets this linguistic absence as a tool of the oppressive system which thrives on destroying communication: "The mail came every day, but letters were missing;/ by this I knew things were not what they ought to be" (7/16/68: ii). Placing this sense of dislocation in its immediate political context, Rich invokes Afro-American militants LeRoi Jones and Eldridge Cleaver (both of whom, ironically, would draw well-founded attacks from both black and white feminists during the 1970s). More symbolic than actual, Jones and Cleaver represent potential presence on a landscape Rich experiences in terms of absence: "we are ghosts/ condemned to haunt the cities where you want to be at home." Although the nature of the tension precludes clarity, Rich senses that the dislocation (like the tendency to perceive blacks symbolically) originates in her perceiving consciousness: "The white children turn black on the negative./

The summer clouds blacken inside the camera-skull" (7/26/68: ii). An earlier ghazal casts this politically resonant image in psychological terms: "In the red wash of the darkroom, I see myself clearly;/ when the print is developed and handed about, the face is nothing to me" (7/14/68: ii). Expression, whether personal or political, devolves into a self-negating mass of contradictions.

Rich does not retreat into pure contemplation of the nihilistic implications of this cluster of perceptions; nor does she attempt to dismiss their validity. Rather, she attempts to turn them to practical use. The first couplet of the ghazal of 7/24/68: ii anticipates DuPlessis' reading of Rich's recent poetry as an attempt to "write beyond the ending": "The friend I can trust is the one who will let me have my death./ The rest are actors who want me to stay and further the plot." Focusing attention on externally imposed plots which impose a narrow coherence on perception, Rich turns the deconstructive quality of language to the "undoing" of the connections on which traditional narrative depends. Exploiting the disruptive potential of the ghazal form, Rich juxtaposes images in a seemingly random manner. Nearly every sequence of couplets in the ghazals illustrates the complex effect of this rhetorical strategy. The following three have been chosen randomly. The first is from the ghazal of 7/17/68:

Two hesitant Luna moths regard each other
with the spots on their wings: fascinated.

To resign *yourself*—what an act of betrayal!
—to throw a runaway spirit back to the dogs.

From the ghazal dated 7/26/68: ii:

Someone has always been desperate, now it's our turn—
we who were free to weep for Othello and laugh at Caliban.

I have learned to smell a *conservateur* a mile away:
they carry illustrated catalogues of all that there is to lose.

From the ghazal dated 7/14/68: i:

In Central Park we talked of our own cowardice.
How many times a day, in this city, are those words spoken?

The tears of the universe aren't all stars, Danton;
some are satellites of brushed aluminum and stainless steel.

While elaborate readings of the consistency and progression of these couplets could be constructed (Caliban and/or Othello as *conservateurs*; the Luna moths as embodiments of the spirit destroyed by denial of self; the cowardice manifested in technological retreat from concrete realities, etc.), such connections, like the "linked analogies" of the cetology chapters of *Moby-Dick*, fit equally well into any number of conceivable structures. Similarly, while there are certain thematic "developments" in the "Homage" as a whole—from philosophical to political, from deconstructive to reconstructive concerns—there are numerous contradictions which subvert any confident assertion of "meaning." Frustrating all attempts to construct a coherent unified plot from the materials of the ghazals, Rich challenges her readers to increase their awareness of their sense-making process. Unlike John Ashbery, who shares many of these concerns, however, Rich grounds her process in a complex political commitment. Her materials are those of the political world; she is concerned with the concrete quality of experience, including that of people who are not aware of the complexities which fascinate Ashbery. For Rich, freeing perception from the constraints of received modes of coherence is a first step toward imaging new forms of relationship rather than a plunge into solipsism. Still, like Ashbery, she understands that both local "coherence" and overall "plot" are artifacts of consciousness. The "Homage" communicates by imaging the return of an individual consciousness to a core set of concerns rather than by articulating a preconceived position.

This sense of uncertainty, of developmental freedom, differentiates the "Homage" from "The Blue Ghazals," a slightly later sequence published in *The Will to Change*. While many individual couplets share the power of those in the earlier sequence, most of the later ghazals are too carefully structured to tap the associational power of their predecessors. The ghazal of 9/28/68: ii, inscribed "For Wallace Stevens," for example, begins with an allusive tribute: "Ideas of order . . . Sinner of the Florida keys,/ you were our poet of revolution all along." Where the ghazal alluding to "Thirteen Ways of Looking at a Blackbird" drew power from the juxtaposition of Stevens with Vivaldi and a sexual encounter, the later ghazal is essentially a traditional meditation on a poetic predecessor. Enforcing a center of perception, the fourth stanza alludes to the "Anecdote of the Jar" and the final couplet creates a sense of thematic closure which the "Homage" casts into doubt: "The use of force in public architecture:/ nothing, not even the honeycomb, manifests such control." The irony of this conclusion seems obvious in light of Rich's reassertion of control in "The Blue Ghazals." Still, her reconstructive drive differs radically from that of the coercive, implicitly patriarchal, attitude of the architect.

Although it makes use of deconstructive strategies, "Ghazals: Homage to Ghalib" is by no means thoroughly committed to deconstruction. Like Rich's later poetry, the sequence refuses to apply deconstructive insights into language to issues of personal identity. Rather than decentering the self, Rich insists on the reconstituted, though not essential, self as the base for reconstruction: "To resign *yourself*—what an act of betrayal!" (7/17/68). Contingent truths, she suggests, may be found in immediate experience and should be mediated as little as possible through imposed metaphors: "I tell you, truth is, at the moment, here." The following line of this zen-like couplet emphasizes the importance of embodied experience, the truth that is felt rather than thought: "burning outward through our skins" (7/16/68: i). The use of "our" rather than "my," repeated frequently in the "Homage," anticipates the collective emphasis of Rich's reconstructive program of the 1970s. The final ghazal of the "Homage" shows Rich's application of the aggressive "masculine" energies she had reclaimed in "Orion," the opening poem in *Leaflets*. Echoing the aesthetic of "Aunt Jennifer's Tigers" and "Transcendental Etude," the first couplet combines the "magic" of women's arts with a violent determination to reconstruct the fragments of a deconstructed linguistic and cultural pattern: "A piece of thread ripped-out from a fierce design,/ some weaving figured as magic against oppression" (8/8/68: ii).

Rich and Godard

The ghazal form provided Rich with a formal approach compatible with her continually self-renewing process. The limitation of the form, reflected in Rich's inability to endorse Ghalib's sense of transcendent unity, was that it offered relatively little practical help in making the transition from deconstruction to reconstruction. As a result, the poems in *The Will to Change* explore several alternative forms: the letter form of "Letters: March 1969"; the dream form of "I Dream I'm the Death of Orpheus"; the collage approach of "The Burning of Paper Instead of Children"; and, most importantly, the cinematic style of Jean-Luc Godard in "Images for Godard," "Pierrot Le Fou," and "Shooting Script." At the same time Rich was transforming her voice in *Leaflets*, which includes poems written between 1965 and 1968, Godard was responding to the political turmoil in Paris, which gave rise to deconstruction as a major international movement, by transforming his approach to cinema. Progressing rapidly from the relatively commercial and comparatively conservative narratives of *Breathless* (1959) and

A Married Woman (1964), Godard (whom Rich first directly addressed in her poetry in 1969) produced an influential sequence of radically deconstructive films, including *Alphaville* (1965), *Masculine/Feminine* (1966), *The Chinese* (1967), and *Sympathy for the Devil* (1968). Transmuting Brechtian theatrical aesthetics, these films sought to alienate their audience from received modes of perception and conventional narrative expectations. In contrast to Ghalib's metaphysical conception of unity, Godard offered a vision of reconstruction based on an "anti-ideological" politics of perception. Clearly alienated from the dominant bourgeois culture which had dictated the form of his earlier films, Godard nonetheless resisted alternative ideological or cultural movements which failed to subject their own premises to constant re-vision. Significantly, this did not result in a politically quiescent posture. Rather, Godard sought to deconstruct the forms of aesthetic discourse supporting the oppressive economic, social, and political systems and to highlight the extreme difficulty of cleansing perception sufficiently to allow a reconstruction of real significance. Godard's awareness of his own complicity in an oppressive aesthetic (visible in the coercive interrogations of actresses in *Masculine/Feminine* and *Sympathy for the Devil* and his awareness of the patriarchal substructures of radical movements, reflected in his deconstruction of texts by both Jones and Cleaver in *Sympathy for the Devil*) were particularly attractive to Rich. Although the specific direction of Rich's process toward lesbian-feminism differs from Godard's sexual explorations of the late 1970s and 1980s, the intensity of her response to his work of the late 1960s clearly identifies Godard as one of the most powerful influences on the development of her sensibility.

The opening lines of part two of "Images for Godard" identify the basis of Rich's interest in Godard's process: "To know the extremes of light/ I sit in this darkness." Grounded in the theater where she watches the film, these lines meditate on the relationship between deconstruction and reconstruction. Deconstructing received structures of thought, Rich plunges into an extreme darkness in order to accompany Godard on his journey back to a newly conceived form of enlightenment contingent on the experience of negation. Both "Images for Godard" and "Pierrot Le Fou," which shares a title with Godard's improvisational 1965 film, recapitulate the deconstructive insights introduced in Rich's ghazals. "Pierrot Le Fou" stresses the negation of perception, expression, and experience: "your unlived life," "the unseen film," "an empty room stacked with old films." As the persona, fragmented between first and second person pronouns, scans reels of film, she experiences an encompassing sense of absence: "the light is failing/ and you are missing." Again, Rich rejects received plots: "if you know how the story ends/ why tell it." Similarly, "Images for Godard" opens with an acknowledgment of shared perception. Following Wittgenstein, both Rich and Godard investigate "Language as city." Rich imagines "driving to the limits/ of the city of words" to explore the limits of her vision. Her commitment to the light of meaning—implicitly resisting the extension of the deconstructive metaphor—is expressed as an awareness of the power relationships, like those in the Godard interviews, inherent in her own expression:

> When all conversation
> becomes an interview
> under duress
>
> when we come to the limits
> of the city
>
> my face must have a meaning

Rich's Godard poems consistently seek meaning in the type of reconstructive project which would lead her to the vision of a common language. In "Pierrot Le Fou," she asks what stories would be worth telling if "we had time/ and no money." Underlining her connection with Godard, she replies that she would tell the story of Pierrot Le Fou, which serves as an emblem of

> . . . all the stories I knew
> in which people went wrong
> but the nervous system
>
> was right all along

Using the traditional connective device of full rhyme to stress the insufficiency of traditional modes of perception, Rich emphasizes the dangers of abstraction; Pierrot's tragedy is that he "trusted/ not a woman/ but love itself." Recasting Rich's critique of language, section four envisions a reconstructed Utopia in which two people learn to speak a language grounded in physical realities:

> The island blistered our feet.
> At first we mispronounced each other's names.
> All the leaves of the tree were scribbled with words.
> There was a language there but no-one to speak it.

Repeatedly, Rich emphasizes the importance of embodiment to the reconstructed vision she seeks. The key to the "meaning" of the self in "Images for Godard" lies in the physical body: "To love, to move perpetually/ as the body changes."

Both "Pierrot Le Fou" and "Images for Godard" are structured to reflect the reality and necessity of change. Developing the basic techniques she would use in "The Burning of Paper Instead of Children," "The Phenomenology of Anger" (1972), and "Meditations for a Savage Child" (1972), Rich adapts the ghazal's emphasis on free-flowing juxtaposition to the needs of her increasingly political voice. Extending her "control" (which she now distinguishes from the technical control of the dominant modes of her earlier work), she begins to develop perceptions at whatever length seems appropriate within individual sections. The juxtaposition of sections, however, is carried out in a manner similar to the juxtaposition of couplets within the ghazals. Each section revises those preceding it and is subject to revision by those following, creating a simulacrum of Rich's poetic process. The final section of "Images for Godard" states this aesthetic of change directly, emphasizing the necessity for incorporating the deconstructive perceptions within a reconstructive vision. Transmitting the "interior monologue of the poet," Rich observes her own "mind, collecting, devouring/ all these destructibles." In the process, she offers three seemingly proscriptive but cumulatively self-deconstructing definitions of the nature of her work: "the notes for the poem are the only poem"; "the mind of the poet is the only poem"; "the moment of change is the only poem." In relation to her later development, the final formulation would seem most inclusive, incorporating contextual as well as textual and biographical perspectives. Rich's most serious disagreement with Godard, in fact, hinges on what she perceives as his failure to pursue this extension of context far enough. Although she honors his ability to create intense images of "horror & war & sickness," capable of changing the audience's perception of reality, she determines to move beyond the self-imposed limits which keep him from articulating the connection of "meaning: love." Responding to the absence expressed in the typography of the line, Rich seeks to create images of concrete love even as she understands that they must be realized outside the aesthetic confines of the theater:

> to touch the breast
> for a woman
>
> to know the sex of a man
> That film begins here

yet you don't show it
we leave the theatre

suffering from that

"SHOOTING SCRIPT"

Rich's fascination with Godard culminates in "Shooting Script," a powerful fourteen-part sequence which marks an important transition to her lesbian-feminist work. The ambiguities of the poem's title reiterate Rich's concern with the disjunction of language and meaning which can be understood only partially in terms of academic deconstruction. "Shooting Script" can be decoded as a film scenario, an attack on language, an attack of language, or a suicide note (the poem's intensity probably derives from Rich's response to her husband's suicide). Perhaps because these levels are difficult to "resolve," perhaps because Rich's focus was shifting rapidly to explicitly feminist concerns, no critic has addressed the dynamics of the poem as a whole. (As I complete revisions of this study, Claire Keyes has published an extended discussion in *The Aesthetics of Power: The Poetry of Adrienne Rich*. Previously, only Cary Nelson, whose reading of the "Newsreel" section is among the strongest readings of any Rich poem of the period, had dealt extensively with individual sections.) As much as any poem written by a politically active poet during the period, "Shooting Script" resembles the deconstructive lyrics of Ashbery and Mark Strand, which simultaneously invite and resist the operations of the ordering mind. As a result, any critical description of the poem reveals at least as much of the reader/critic as it does of Rich. As in the ghazals, the juxtaposition of lines, couplets, or stanzas in an individual section encourages the creation of patterns which may be frustrated, encouraged, or revised by subsequent combinations. As in the Godard poems, relatively cohesive sections are juxtaposed in a similarly associative manner. Extending the principle to larger units, the two seven-section "parts" of "Shooting Script" subject one another's smaller juxtapositions to another level of self-reflexive revision. More than any other poem in Rich's canon, "Shooting Script" asserts the never-ending nature of the deconstructive process. All readings, like all statements, whatever level they choose to focus on, are partial, their internal contradictions revealed through juxtaposition with contrasting perspectives which themselves present readings which can be seen as partial when juxtaposed, etc.

Inevitably partial and subjective, the following discussion encodes my personal response to "Shooting Script" as an aesthetic unit, however elusive and self-deconstructing. As a result, my use of traditional terminology—terms such as "structure" and "meaning," always problematical when approaching a poet of process—is intended to provide a base for future discussion which does not depend on deep familiarity with a particular methodology or critical vocabulary. As Rich wrote in the ghazal of 8/4/68: "If these are letters, they will have to be misread./ If scribblings on a wall, they must tangle with all the others." Echoing this image, the final section of "Shooting Script" transforms the tangle into an image of deconstructive/reconstructive process. Gazing at the "web of cracks filtering across the plaster," Rich attempts "To read there the map of the future, the roads radiating from the/ initial split, the filaments thrown out from that impasse." Seeking to internalize her awareness of the continuing interdependence of deconstruction and reconstruction, she approaches the relationship from both directions. On the one hand, she indicates that the deconstructive impulse, grounded in the suffering she experienced within a culture based on an oppressive discourse which refuses to acknowledge its own limitations, does not obliterate all possibility of meaning: "the/ lifeline, broken, keeps its direction." Immediately thereafter, however, she reverses the emphasis, indicating that, in the midst of the light-seeking reconstructive endeavor, she must maintain her awareness of the gaps and silences requiring the deconstructive approach: "to know in every distortion of the light what fracture is." The process leading toward this awareness in "Shooting Script" involves two general movements, reflected in the poem's two seven-section sequences. The first movement, in which the word "woman" never occurs, focuses primarily on deconstruction, emphasizing the experience of silence as torment. The second movement, which begins with the image of "a woman waking," focuses on the reconstruction, emphasizing the experience of silence as a potentially useful base for new forms of expression. Where the first movement focuses on the breakdown of "personal" communication and includes little direct political reference, the second movement insists on the connection between the personal and the political, especially as imaged in the war in Vietnam.

The first movement begins with a direct recognition that the process being initiated cannot be brought to a final point of rest: "We were bound on the wheel of an endless conversation." Juxtaposing images of speech ("The dialogue that lasts all night or a whole lifetime") with images of tide ("The dialogue of the rock with the breaker"), Rich images communication as a natural process entailing continual change: "The wave changed instantly by the rock; the rock changed by the wave returning over and over. . . . A cycle whose rhythm begins to change the meanings of words." As this cycle progresses, internal coherences emerge, constantly changing suggestions of structure. The third line of the section—"A monologue waiting for you to interrupt it"—metamorphoses, three lines from the end, into "a monologue that waits for one listener." The antagonistic listener concerned with the sound of his own voice is transformed into the poet contemplating the zen-like voice of the ocean: "An ear filled with one sound only./ A shell penetrated by meaning." A reader familiar with Rich's earlier work may perceive connections between this section and the opening poem of "Ghazals: Homage to Ghalib," the penultimate couplet of which reads: "To mutilate privacy with a single foolish syllable/ is to throw away the search for the one necessary word."

Subsequent poems in the first part of "Shooting Script" elaborate the problems Rich experiences with the conversation. Section two, the adaptation of Ghalib's Ghazal V discussed above, reveals her frustration with structures which underestimate the difficulty of attaining the unity imaged in the first section. After a section juxtaposing the failure of the conversation between a married couple with images of snow and cold, sections four and five reconsider the tension between the deconstructive and reconstructive impulses. The opening line of section four envisions destruction as part of a reconstructive project: "In my imagination I was the pivot of a fresh beginning." Almost immediately, however, Rich emphasizes the political context, especially the war in Southeast Asia, in which destruction is simply destruction: "It is all being made clear, with bulldozers, at Angkor Wat . . . . the baring of the stones is no solution for us now . . . . Defoliation progresses." Recalling and varying this complex of perceptions, section five invokes the reconstructive implications of "Aunt Jennifer's Tigers" by juxtaposing pieces of "broken pottery" with the process of "turning the findings out, pushing them/ around with a finger, beginning to dream of fitting them together."

At this point, however, the impulse remains a dream; the "rhythms of choice" remain "lost methods." Returning to the origins of the deconstructive impulse in the failure of individual communication, the final two sections of the first part of "Shooting Script" reiterate the realities of personal alienation. Anticipating the specific direction of Rich's post-1968 process, section six strongly implies the need for deconstructing patriarchal sex roles. As "the light eats away at the clarities I had fixed on," Rich recognizes the inadequacy of a language which invests either sex with transcendent qualities. If the conversation is to attain meaning, both sexes must deconstruct their assumptions: "No, I don't invest you with anything; I am counting on your weakness as much as on your strength." And again: "It is to know that I too have no mythic powers; it is to see the liabilities of all my treasures." Read in light of Rich's later process, this section asserts a process of attaining integrity which requires a period of separation between the sexes. Significantly, Rich emphasizes the importance of this stage to men as well as women: "You will have to see all this for a long time alone." The sense of alienation—from self, other, political context, language—permeating the first movement culminates in section seven, where Rich portrays the changes expressed throughout the movement as "Picking apart the strands of pain," a process in which "the change leaves you dark." Although glimmers of reconstructive light flicker through the first seven sections of "Shooting Script," the movement concludes where "Images for Godard" began, with the poet sitting in darkness thinking of light.

The second movement opens in darkness, with the "woman waking behind grimed blinds." Almost immediately, however, Rich expands her frame. Contrasting "the subversion of choice by language" with "the alternative: to pull the sooty strings to set the window bare to purge the room with light to feel the sun breaking in," she invokes an energy, reflected in the rhythm of the line, which moves from abstraction to an immediacy of perception. This energy taps a specifically feminine power suppressed in the generalized meditations of the first movement: "The woman is too heavy for the poem." Throughout the section, Rich expresses a deep distrust of aesthetic modes which undervalue concrete experience: "Entering the poem as a method of leaving the room." Complementing the focus on "this time, this place" in the final stanza of section eight, "(Newsreel)" brings the connection between aesthetic evasion and political oppression into momentary focus. Rich draws parallels between poetic modes which separate personal experience from political context and the distortions of "documentary" films which omit the personal presence. Her response to the newsreel superficially resembles the negations which began "Ghazals: Homage to Ghalib": "This would not be the war we fought in." Where before she explored the nature of the disjunctions, however, she now attempts to reestablish connections. Recognizing the impossibility of returning to a pre-deconstructive stance, she phrases her reconstructive impulse in terms of negation: "But I find it impossible not to look for actual persons known/ to me and not seen since; impossible not to look for myself."

Although she acknowledges the carnage portrayed in films of the war—"the dead look right, and the roofs of the huts, and the crashed fuselage burning among the ferns"—she insists that the images omit elements of her experience: "this is not the war I came to see, buying my ticket, stumbling through the darkness, finding my place among the sleepers and masturbators in the dark." Rich's use of specific images, which would recur in her analysis of sexual violence in "The Images," reflects her growing awareness of the parallel between the military violence directed against Vietnam and the psychological violence directed against women in "personal" relationships, such as those portrayed in the first movement of "Shooting Script." Acknowledging the deconstructive experience of discourse as absence, the final stanza of "(Newsreel)" emphasizes Rich's complex position. Although she shares the guilt of the passive American audience, whose discourse is in need of deconstruction, she is also a woman victimized by that discourse: "somewhere my innocence is proven with my guilt, but this would not be the war I fought in." Despite her dissatisfaction with the available public expressions of her experience, Rich makes a major advance in perception as she recognizes absence not as a denial of experience and/or the possibility of reconstruction, but as an indication of the limitations of dominant modes. Extending the emphasis on the political dimension of personal alienation, section ten echoes the image of patriarchal oppression from "Aunt Jennifer's Tigers." Addressing Valerie Glauber, Rich associates the dominant discourse's "descriptions of your soul" with "rings they want to fasten on you." The section concludes with the image of Glauber as "a letter written, folded, burnt to ash, and mailed in an envelope to another continent."

The possibility of a reconstructive communication rising up out of the ashes becomes a central concern in the next two sections. Section eleven begins by emphasizing the connection between deconstruction, significantly imaged in terms of a dead female animal, and reconstruction: "The mare's skeleton in the clearing: another sign of life." Sensing a message, equivalent to that embedded in the ashes of Glauber's letter, in the mare's "pelvis, the open archway, staring at me like an eye," Rich refuses to equate silence with an ultimate impossibility of meaning: "So many questions unanswered, yet the statement is here and clear." Again, the use of rhyme hints at a connection not readily discernible in the deconstructive context. Although the final stanza of the section articulates a joy of release extremely rare in Leaflets or The Will to Change, it also evinces an awareness of danger. The immediate joy, Rich cautions, recalls that of the American forefathers whose own rebellion against British oppression devolved inexorably into the war in Vietnam: "With what joy we left the woods, swinging our sticks, miming the speech of noble savages, of the fathers of our country, bursting into the full sun of the uncut field."

Envisioning a voice capable of articulating the joy without descending into solipsistic oppression, section twelve contains several "clauses" which lose their identity as subordinate in "sentences" devoid of "main" organizing clauses. Like the experimental work of Gary Snyder, George Oppen, and Robert Creeley (all of whom extend the tradition of William Carlos Williams and Charles Olson, whose poem "The King-fishers" provided Rich with the title image of *The Will to Change*), stanzas such as the following suggest a possible voice for a poetry of contingency:

When I give up being paraphrased, when I let go, when the
beautiful solutions in their crystal flasks have dried up in the sun,
when the lightbulb bursts on lighting, when the dead bulb rattles
like a seed-pod.

Anticipating the critique of patriarchy that would emerge as a dominant concern in her next volume, Rich's image of Manhattan makes it clear that she no longer feels the temptation of "buying/ these descriptions at the cost of missing every other point."

The determination to move beyond old modes of perception and develop a poetic voice which will be of use emerges as a major focus in the final two sections of "Shooting Script." Section thirteen opens with Rich's decision to embark on a night-sea journey, a quest which eventually culminates in the landing at the start of "Integrity." Rich recognizes the necessity of deconstructing her own attitudes toward such endeavors: "A long time I was simply learning to handle the skiff; I had no/ special training and my own training was against me." Nonetheless, she realizes that, given the uncertainty of her position and the absence of practical images of the reconstructive process, she has no choice but "to try any/ instrument that came my way. Never to refuse one from conviction of incompetence." Surpassing her previous sense that "darkness and water were a threat," she transforms obstacles into aids: "In spite of this, darkness and water helped me to arrive here." Rich concludes "Shooting Script" by reiterating her commitment to change which involves both deconstruction and reconstruction: "To pull yourself up by your own roots; to eat the last meal in/ your old neighborhood."

"THE PHENOMENOLOGY OF ANGER"

During the first stages of the journey from her old premises to the lesbian *civitas*, Rich expressed her critique of patriarchy in the voice she had developed in *Leaflets* and *The Will to Change*. *Diving Into the Wreck* includes two poems, "The Phenomenology of Anger" and "Meditations

for a Savage Child," which montage images and sections to develop the
specifically anti-patriarchal implications of "Shooting Script" and "The
Burning of Paper Instead of Children." While each contains powerful
passages, neither finds effective ways of uniting the deconstructive
power of the earlier work with the pointed political/cultural insights of
contemporaneous poems such as "Trying to Talk with a Man," "Rape,"
or "The Ninth Symphony of Beethoven Understood at Last as a Sexual
Message." Rich's rhetorical problem contributes to simplistic critical
responses such as that of M. L. Rosenthal and Sally M. Gall, who
dismiss "The Phenomenology of Anger" as a "song of hatred toward a
particular man and toward male insensitivity" (p. 492). Although their
book *The Modern Poetic Sequence* offers many insights relevant to an
understanding of Rich, they fail to engage either the complexity or
development of her form. Rather, applying the standards of the dominant modes against which Rich had rebelled, they accuse her of a
retreat to a simplistic rhetoric in which "the didactic and rhetorical pre-
dominate and diminish the affective purity and authority of the work"
(p. 494).

To an extent, Rich invites this type of misreading. Opening with the
image of "the freedom of the wholly mad," "The Phenomenology of
Anger" does unleash an embodied anger unprecedented in Rich's
work. Where previously she had evinced a strong interest in revolutionary figures such as Cleaver and Che Guevara, she has come to see
"the world/ as no longer viable," as a stage where both the openly
imperialistic defoliation carried out by the United States in Vietnam
and hypocritical "revolutionary bills . . . they sell at battlefields" simply
reinforce patriarchal power. Although this anger remains almost
entirely conceptual, Rich seems aware of the inadequacy of her stance:
"Fantasies of murder: not enough." As the juxtapositions—though not
the individual sections which Rosenthal and Gall criticize
—demonstrate, Rich sees release of the anger as a transitional stage
toward action in the political world. Although she can now articulate
her "woman's confession" that "*The only real love I have ever felt/ was for
children and other women,*" she is haunted by the feeling that her consciousness still resides in her old neighborhood: "awake in prison, my
mind/ licked at the mattress like a flame." The tension between com-
peting impulses in "The Phenomenology of Anger" devolves into a
solipsistic focus on consciousness which Rich links to patriarchal discourse: "Every act of becoming conscious/ (it says here in this book)/
is an unnatural act." While the anger in "Meditations for a Savage
Child" is more specific, Rich again fails to connect her perception that
the patriarchal scientists "teach you names/ for things/ you did not
need" with a vision of effective communal, or even individual,

response. Withholding pity from the oppressor, a central theme of the final section, provides little of actual use to the reconstructive endeavor. "Yet you don't show it:" Rich's practical critique of Godard identifies the problem with the sequences in *Diving Into the Wreck* much more accurately than the primarily aesthetic complaints of critics grounded in academic modes.

"Natural Resources": Toward Reconstruction

Given this impasse, it does not seem surprising that most of the poems in which Rich initially develops her reconstructive vision of the lesbian *civitas* make relatively little use of the self-deconstructing voice. Although she continues to work in multisection poems ("Natural Resources," "Twenty-One Love Poems," "Sibling Mysteries," "Hunger"), the internal dynamic of these poems resembles that of contemporaneous lyrics ("Transit" or "Integrity") more than that of her ghazals or "Shooting Script." Exploring the specifically feminine power veiled by the patriarchal discourse against which she directed her earlier deconstructions, Rich writes in a manner which refocuses attention on an alternative which must be glimpsed before it can be seen in its full complexity. In "Natural Resources," Rich writes that for a poet educated in the system which indoctrinated the wild boy in "Meditations for a Savage Child," the first step toward effective reconstruction is simple recognition that she shares a common situation with other women: "The miner is not metaphor. She goes/ into the cage like the rest." Turning away, at least momentarily, from the complex politics of consciousness inherent in her deconstructive poems, Rich determines

> . . . to cast my lot with those
> who age after age, perversely,
>
> with no extraordinary power,
> reconstitute the world.

Eventually the process of reconstitution created a new use for deconstructive techniques. A crucial passage in Rich's movement to the lesbian *civitas* involved her reaction against *Diving Into the Wreck*; in "Natural Resources" she declares "There are words I cannot choose again:/ *humanism androgyny*." As DuPlessis observes, this response hinges on Rich's perception that "the universalizing assumptions of humanism about the needs and aspirations of all '(hu)mankind' are found to be bereft of meaning because they do not acknowledge people's formation as specific, historically rooted subjects" (p. 136). At the same time, DuPlessis identifies a curious tension in Rich's "unmediated appeal to myth" which "can be seen as a sacred or primal verity touched within the poem, a statement that by its very nature offers an unmediated gist beyond social grids and ideological expectations. . . . Mediation of any sort, including the social practices of language and literary convention, tends then to be overlooked or minimized" (p. 136). This accurately identifies an important source of tension in Rich's work of the 1970s; her deconstructive sensibility insists on the contingency of expression at the same time her reconstructive sensibility desires a foundation immune to the historically contingent denials of feminine power.

The key to understanding Rich's contingent resolution of this tension lies in DuPlessis' distinction between "archetype" and "prototype" in contemporary feminist poetry. Discussing the mythic sensibilities of Rich, Denise Levertov, and Muriel Rukeyser, DuPlessis argues that their most effective use of myths "are nonstatic and nonarchetypal . . . historically specific inventions" (p. 133). These inventions are compatible with the poets' deconstructive commitment to the "rupture of sequences, the 'splitting open and delegitimation of constituted stories'" (p. 133). Building on the discontinuity which both Breslin and Altieri see as central to contemporary poetic consciousness, the feminist myths DuPlessis describes "replace archetypes with prototypes. . . . Prototypes are original, model forms on which to base the self and its action—forms open to transformation and forms, unlike archetypes, that offer similar patterns of experience *to* others, rather than imposing these patterns *on* others . . . . A prototype is not a binding, timeless pattern, but one critically open to the possibility, even the necessity, of its transformation. Thinking in these terms historicizes myth" (pp. 133-34). This crucial distinction clarifies the nature of the spiritual journey Carol Christ finds in Rich's recent poetry. Rather than simply revising an obsolete ahistorical abstraction, Rich creates a dynamic pattern, seeking to integrate consciousness with action. Emphasizing Rich's reconstructive attempt to present a "vision of the path toward the integration of spiritual vision into social reality," Christ describes a prototypical process involving four distinct but interrelated stages "in which experiences of nothingness, awakenings, insights, and namings form a spiral of ever-deepening but never final understanding" (p. 14). Contrasted with the ahistorical tendencies of academic deconstruction, the prototypical commitment of the lesbian *civitas* to the integration of the spiritual and the social, of the personal and the political, is itself a radical act. The process of integration, however, requires a continual awareness of the need for self-renewal. Experiences of nothingness inevitably follow the process leading from awakenings through insights to namings. Deconstruction must follow reconstruction if prototypes are to be kept from ossifying into archetypes. It is in the context of this process that Rich reclaims—in significantly revised form—her deconstructive voice in the later sections of *A Wild Patience Has Taken Me This Far* and *Your Native Land, Your Life.*

"Turning the Wheel"

The title of the final poem in *A Wild Patience Has Taken Me This Far* recalls the opening line of "Shooting Script": "We were bound on the wheel of an endless conversation." Like the earlier poem, "Turning the Wheel" deconstructs received certainties and static perceptions through the juxtaposition of images and sections. Unlike the earlier poem, it directs its deconstructive energies at a conception of feminine mythic energy which Rich had only begun to perceive in 1968. Several sections, particularly those with even numbers, focus on emblems of mythic feminine power as it has existed in the American Southwest: the burden baskets of "young women's puberty dances" in section two; the Colcha embroidery expressing "our ancient art of making out of nothing" in section four; an "Apparition" of female power in section six; the Grand Canyon, "the female core/ of a continent" in section eight. Rich finds each of these images fascinating; each contains something of real value to the development of the lesbian *civitas.* The primary concern of the poem, however, is with the problem of transforming this potential into actuality. As a result, Rich focuses on the particular circumstances in which the power must be utilized. Insisting on a realistic apprehension of the problem, sections one and three attack the "nostalgia" which amounts to nothing more than "amnesia turned around." Emphasizing the difficulty of imagining the prehistoric inhabitants of the land, Rich juxtaposes the commercialization of the desert in section one with the "amnesia-language" which subverts the reconstructed female power in section three: "the shamaness could well have withdrawn her ghost." Suspended between these images of loss, the expressive power of the baskets in section two becomes difficult to tap, even for those explicitly committed to its recovery: "the lesbian archaeologist watches herself/ sifting her own life out from the shards she's piecing,/ asking the clay all questions but her own." Similarly, the embroidery of section four resists simplification into an emblem of pure feminine power. Rather, Rich sees in it evidence of the inevitable corruption of all expression, the need to deconstruct rather than romanticize. Acknowledging the difficulty of perceiving the full impact of patriarchal consciousness on her sensibility—"To understand colonization is taking me/ years"—she perceives the embroidery not as archetypal alternative to but as prototypical analog of her situation:

> . . . here we have a scene of flagellants,
> each whip is accurately self-directed. . . .
> What rivets me to history is seeing
> arts of survival turned
> to rituals of self-hatred.
> This is colonization.

Recalling the dense ambiguities of *Leaflets* and *The Will to Change*, "this" could refer equally well to the actual contents of the embroidered image or to Rich's imposition of her own sensibility upon the material.

In place of the generalized commitment to the reconstructive process in her earlier deconstructive poems, Rich makes specific suggestions concerning the process in "Turning the Wheel." Titled "Particularity," section five opens with a direct statement on the relationship between archetype and prototype: "In search of the desert witch, the shamaness/ forget the archetypes. . . ./ do not pursue/ the ready-made abstraction, do not peer for symbols." Intimating the need for continual deconstruction of any mode of thought which abstracts feminine power from the body which urinates, scratches, snores, Rich concludes the section with a direct statement unlike any in the poetry of the late 1960s:

> so long as you try to simplify her meaning
> so long as she merely symbolizes power
> she is kept helpless and conventional
> her true power routed backward
> into the past, we cannot touch or name her
> and, barred from participation by those who need her
> she stifles in unspeakable loneliness.

The deprivation of voice clearly implies the need for deconstructing the voice of the deprivers, in this case the members of the lesbian *civitas* who, ironically, destroy the power they most need.

Despite the general similarity of method in which each perception is revised by each subsequent section, "Turning the Wheel" differs sharply from "Shooting Script" and "The Phenomenology of Anger" in its willingness to build gradually toward a reconstructive statement in the final sections. Combining the ambiguities of Rich's deconstructive voice with the concrete, common voice of the reconstructive poems, section six of "Turning the Wheel" cautions its readers to deconstruct their own perception at the same time that it asserts the actual power of the shamaness: "look at her closely if you dare/ do not assume you know those cheekbones/ or those eyesockets; or that still-bristling hair." This leads to the meditation in section seven on the realistic heroism of Mary Jane Colter, an architect who, during the early part of the twentieth century, designed eight buildings which still stand near the Grand Canyon. Acknowledging Colter's attempt to incorporate the local arts of the desert tribes into her designs, Rich comments in her note on the poem that "her life-work—remarkable for a woman architect—was framed by the contradiction that made it inseparable from the violation and expropriation by white entrepreneurs of the original cultures she respected and loved." Framing her meditation on Colter in an imaginary letter from Colter to her mother, Rich balances this paradox with her respect for Colter's commitment to her own vision, her continuing concern for her relationship with other women, and, above all, her recognition of her prototypical status: "I am here already, trying to make a start." The final section of the poem, in which Rich turns the wheel of her car away from the Grand Canyon, responds to Colter's prototypical example by emphasizing her realistic engagement, rather than her symbolic association, with the archetypal power of "the female core of a continent." Refusing the journey to a "world beyond time," Rich rededicates her energy to the imperfect world imaged in her connection with an unnamed, but clearly "real," friend "with whom I talked for hours/ driving up from the desert though you were far away/ as I talk to you all day whatever day."

"North American Time"

The final poem in The Fact of a Doorframe, "North American Time" (which anticipates the emphasis of other poems—particularly "Contradictions: Tracking Poems"—published alongside it in Your Native Land, Your Life), reiterates this commitment to concrete engagement specifically in relation to Rich's primary form of action: the writing of poetry. Restating the positions articulated in "Blood, Bread, and Poetry: The Location of the Poet," the nine-part poem opens by emphasizing the danger of using abstractions, however laudable their political purpose, to evade confrontation with the full range of experience. Reflecting on her involvement in lesbian-feminist politics in an image equally applicable to other ideological systems, Rich feels a profound disturbance

When my dreams showed signs
of becoming
politically correct
no unruly images
escaping beyond borders.

She connects this tendency toward abstraction with the repressive
silence against which she had struggled through much of her life:

when walking in the street I found my
themes cut out for me
knew what I would not report
for fear of enemies' usage.

It matters little whether the themes are "cut out" by a patriarchal system which refuses to acknowledge the reality of women's experience or
by the "politically correct" individual demanding a solid front against
that system.   Silence, as Rich emphasizes in section six, amounts to
little more than a failure to testify to the particular realities of oppression and suffering. Although in an abstract sense it is "no use protest-
ing" the fact that the poet's words may be distorted, Rich underlines
the fact that the failure to protest is not at all an abstract action in the
current political context:

I wrote that
before Kollontai was exiled
Rosa Luxembourg, Malcolm,
Anna Mae Aquash, murdered,
before Treblinka, Birkenau,
Hiroshima, before Sharpeville,
Biafra, Bangla Desh, Boston,
Atlanta, Soweto, Beirut, Assam.

Without the testimony of voices such as her own, Rich observes, those
events will be lost to history, "sheared from the almanac/ of North
American time."
    Intensely aware of her implication in the oppressive system against
which she testifies, Rich nonetheless challenges her audience to political commitment. In sections two and four, she concludes discussions
of the nature of language with the line "and this is verbal privilege."
Recognizing that the abstraction of her concern reflects the privileged
position which enables her to ignore, even momentarily, the realities of

South Africa or Lebanon, Rich acknowledges two inescapable aspects of her situation. First, her own words will inevitably be impure, in need of deconstruction. Second, this impurity does not, at this stage of her process, justify refusal to engage the issues. As she writes in section two, "Poetry never stood a chance/ of standing outside of history." As a result, any expression can be deconstructed, revealed as a function of the system against which it ostensibly rebels. This means that "Everything we write/ will be used against us/ or against those we love." Despite the fact that "our words stand/ become responsible/ for more than we intended," Rich sees only two alternatives:

Words are found responsible
all you can do is choose them
or choose
to remain silent.

To allow the abstract deconstructive insight to silence her, Rich reiterates in section eight, would be to surrender to the oppressive system. As she contemplates her desire to "engage/ this field of light and darkness," she realizes the connection between her relatively abstract urge, which resembles the original statement of the deconstructive-reconstructive problem in section two of "Images for Godard," and her evasive tendencies:

underneath the grandiose idea
is the thought that what I must engage
after the plane has raged into the tarmac
after climbing my old stairs, sitting down
at my old window
is meant to break my heart and reduce me to silence.

This understanding of the inevitable impurity of her own words, both in abstract terms and in particular situations where "anything we write/ can be used against those we love," simply reinforces Rich's belief in the need for prototypical images. As she testifies to the reality of oppression in "a country/ where words are stolen out of mouths/ as bread is stolen out of mouths," she reminds her readers that poetry must be understood as part of a larger process. In order to protect even the most "apolitical" forms of communication against political distortion, the poet must focus insistently on the particular circumstances of which she writes; to write of one woman braiding another's hair, Rich observes, it is necessary to know not only the pattern of the braid but also "what country it happens in/ what else happens in that country."

Commenting on the mechanics of distortion, Rich observes that when the oppressors use the words of the oppressed to further the oppressive system, "the context is never given." Invoking the prototypical figure of Julia de Burgos, Rich places herself in the position of the prototypical audience. Rather than responding to de Burgos in aesthetic terms, she determines to act on the example of the Puerto Rican revolutionary poet who was shot down on the streets of New York City. Having deconstructed her "politically correct" lesbian-feminist position, Rich makes it clear that she has by no means repudiated the basic values of that position, the values expressed in the quotation from de Burgos which hangs over her door. Acknowledging that elements of patriarchal discourse inevitably taint her reconstructive impulses, she nevertheless closes the poem, the graph of her process to date, with a synthetic renewal of her commitment to process:

> The almost-full moon rises
> timelessly speaking of change
> out of the Bronx, the Harlem River
> the drowned towns of the Quabbin
> the pilfered burial mounds
> the toxic swamps, the testing-grounds
>
> and I start to speak again.

Invoking the rising but still unfulfilled power of the moon, the power of the lesbian *civitas* which, like all other power, remains in constant need of renewal, Rich remains the prototypical poet of process, her reconstructed voice resounding amid the toxic waste.

References

Ahmad, Aijaz
  1971. *Ghazals of Ghalib.* New York: Columbia Univ. Pr.
Allen, Donald
  1960. *The New American Poetry 1945-1960.* New York: Grove.
Altieri, Charles
  1984. *Self and Sensibility in Contemporary American Poetry.* New York: Cambridge Univ. Pr.
Benstock, Shari
  1986. *Women of the Left Bank: Paris, 1900-1940.* Austin: Univ. of Texas Pr.
Berg, Stephen, and Robert Mezey
  1976. (editors) *The New Naked Poetry.* Indianapolis: Bobbs-Merrill.

Breslin, James
1984. *From Modern to Contemporary: American Poetry 1945-1965.* Univ. of Chicago Pr.
Christ, Carol
1980. *Diving Deep and Surfacing: Women Writers on Spiritual Quest.* Boston: Beacon.
Culler, Jonathan
1982. *On Deconstruction: Theory and Criticism after Structuralism.* Ithaca: Cornell Univ. Pr.
DuPlessis, Rachel Blau
1985. *Writing Beyond the Ending: Narrative Strategies of Twentieth-Century Women Writers.* Bloomington: Indiana Univ. Pr.
Eagleton, Terry
1983. *Literary Theory: An Introduction.* Minneapolis: Univ. of Minnesota Pr.
Hall, Donald, Robert Pack, and Lewis Simpson
1957. *New Poets of England and America.* New York: Meridian.
Homans, Margaret
1980. *Women Writers and Poetic Identity.* Princeton: Princeton Univ. Pr.
Jameson, Fredric
1981. *The Political Unconscious.* Ithaca: Cornell Univ. Pr.
Karl, Frederick
1985. *Modern and Modernism: The Sovereignty of the Artist 1885-1925.* New York: Atheneum.
Kenner, Hugh
1971. *The Pound Era.* Berkeley and Los Angeles: Univ. of California Pr.
Keyes, Claire
1986. *The Aesthetics of Power: The Poetry of Adrienne Rich.* Athens, Ga. and London: Univ. of Georgia Pr.
Lasch, Christopher
1978. *The Culture of Narcissism.* New York: Norton.
MacCabe, Colin
1980. *Godard: Images, Sounds, Politics.* Bloomington: Indiana Univ. Pr.
Nelson, Cary
1981. *Our Last First Poets: Vision and History in Contemporary American Poetry.* Urbana: Univ. of Illinois Pr.
Newman, Charles
1985. *The Post-Modern Aura: The Act of Fiction in an Age of Inflation.* Evanston: Northwestern Univ. Pr.

Perloff, Marjorie
  1983. "Private Lives/Public Images," *Michigan Quarterly Review* Jan.,
  pp. 130-43.
Pope, Deborah
  1984. *A Separate Vision: Isolation in Contemporary Women's Poetry.*
  Baton Rouge: Louisiana State Univ. Pr.
Poulin, A.
  1980. (editor) *Contemporary American Poetry* (3rd ed.).   Boston:
  Houghton Mifflin.
Rich, Adrienne
  1969. *Leaflets.* New York: Norton.
Rosenberg, Liz
  1986. "The Power of Victims," *New York Times Book Review* July 20, pp.
  21-22.
Rosenthal, M. L., and Sally M. Gall
  1983. *The Modern Poetic Sequence: The Genius of Modern Poetry.* New
  York and Oxford: Oxford Univ. Pr.

CHAPTER 5

Adrienne Rich in the American Grain

Traceable to Coleridge, Shakespeare, Dante, Heraclites, Rich's process-oriented aesthetic assumes its quintessential American form from Walt Whitman. Whitman recognized two principles which would become leitmotifs for Rich: that all teachings, including his own, inevitably became old forms; that the discovery of sufficient forms demands immersion in extraliterary experience. In *Leaves of Grass*, Whitman wrote: "I am the teacher of athletes;/ He that by me spreads a wider breast than my own, proves the width of my own;/ He most honors my style who learns under it to destroy the teacher" ("Song of Myself," section 47). And again, "I bequeathe myself to the dirt, to grow from the grass I love;/ If you want me again, look for me under your bootsoles" ("Song of Myself," section 52).

In her long conversation with the elders, Rich frequently adapts Whitman's voices. In *Leaflets* (Section 5), she writes:

> I want this to be yours
> in the sense that if you find and read it
> it will be there in you already
> and the leaflet then merely something
> to leave behind.

But Rich is not simply a feminist Whitman. She knows that the elders—Yeats, Whitman, Dickinson, H.D.—offer much; she also knows that the terms of the offer demand refusal of the proferred terms. Further, she knows, and has known since "Snapshots of a Daughter-in-Law," that what she accepts and what she refuses determines who she is, who she can become.

In each phase of her career, Rich interweaves acceptance and refusal. On July 14, 1968, Rich wrote two ghazals. The first concludes with an oblique acceptance of one of Whitman's most oblique lessons: "'It may be if I had known them I would have loved them.'/ You were American, Whitman, and those words are yours." Perhaps the most basic democratic lesson, incorporated in the value structure of the lesbian *civitas*, is (to paraphrase James Baldwin, one of Rich's chosen ancestors) that "One can despise no one without despising one's self." Accepting the possibility of love, the second ghazal honors the teacher with a vow of refusal: "Did you think I was talking about my life?/ I was trying to drive a tradition up against the wall." For an American poet, for a woman unintentionally excluded by a language which assumes a male student—"*He* most honors me"—Whitman stands near the center of the tradition. Destroying her teacher, Rich celebrates a process deeply inimical to centers: "The field they burned over is greener than all the rest."

For Rich, this process takes place in an American field—physical, aesthetic, political—radically transformed since Whitman's time. Only in the darkest moments of "Democratic Vistas" did Whitman envision the waste land which was to overshadow Rich's early development. As he introduced Rich to the literary world, Auden claimed that the old forms (which for him had been the new forms of the modernist assertion) *would* suffice for the polite young woman who accepted her teachers' words. For Auden's Rich, T. S. Eliot—as inevitable (which, given the veiled presences of Emily Dickinson and H.D., is *not* to say as necessary) a presence as Whitman in the lineage of an American poet—had articulated the essentials: the reduction of old certainties to fragments in the ruins of "unreal cities"; the impossible agony of creation after the Great War: "I had not thought death had undone so many." Eliot's artist, as complexly contradictory as Whitman, contemplated fragments "shored up against my ruins"; realized his (the pronoun had not changed) own madness; envisioned reintegration in a vocabulary foreign to the lands of his birth and exile: "Datta. Dayadhvam. Damyata. Shantih. Shantih. Shantih."

Sympathizing profoundly with the plight of the undone, Rich (who, like Eliot, began her career at Harvard, America's last best attempt to prove the old forms would suffice) at first studiously surrendered herself to the Eliotic quest for "a way of controlling, of giving a shape and a significance to the immense panorama of futility and anarchy which is contemporary history." To Rich, confronting the Civil Rights Movement, Vietnam, the threat of nuclear catastrophe—experiencing what Henry Adams called the "law of acceleration"—the anarchy seemed obvious. But the old forms, whether the fragments of "The Waste Land" or the meditations of "The Four Quartets," offered Rich no adequate means of establishing control. Honoring Eliot as she honors Whitman, Rich again refused the terms of his offer. Asserting independence as she pays homage, she transforms a quintessentially Eliotic gesture—the weighted allusion—into a repudiation of patriarchal solipsism. Where Eliot buried his dead by quoting Baudelaire—"You! Hypocrite lecteur!—mon semblable—mon frère!" Rich resurrects her silenced sisters: "ma semblable, ma soeur!" Attempting to connect the diverse elements of her personal genealogy, Rich teaches the necessity of articulation, tentative and subject to change. She requires only that her readers accept the challenge posed by "From a Survivor," which envisions life as "a succession of brief, amazing movements/ each one making possible the next." Among Rich's most significant lessons are:

1. *The complexity of evasion.* Rich recognizes that the truth of one moment can be used to evade the truths of the next. She distrusts words—abstractions, professions and explanations, regrets and promises—which are not grounded in action. All can be used to mask, rather than reveal, realities.

2. *The suspicion of structure.* Like Baldwin and Whitman, Rich distrusts all systems, even, or especially, those based on ideas with which she sympathizes. Even the most sensitive systems can serve to distance or distort the experiences they theoretically embrace.

3. *The acceptance of processes.* Recognizing the inherent limits of fixed principles, Rich sees that an attitude which may be extremely destructive when asserted by a member of a dominant group may signify something very different when adapted as a survival strategy (psychological or physical) by a member of a marginal group. The marginal group must acquire much that the dominant group must surrender, above all the belief in the reality of its experience. As Rich discovered through her involvement with lesbian separatism, such a belief, once assumed, may metamorphose into cultural solipsism. Like all other stages of a process, such a stage serves as the base for further growth.

4. *Embodied anger.* Rich demonstrates, as intensely as Richard Wright or Malcolm X, the necessity of acknowledging, articulating, and, at times, acting on rage. Her horrifying picture of the effects of unacknowledged and misdirected patriarchal rage on women intimates a vortex of destructive energies. No abstraction, no politically correct idea, can tame or control these energies, safely abstracted into Jungian shadows.

5. Finally, Rich insists on *a return to the world.* The question raised in "From an Old House in America" echoes through her work: *"what will you undertake?"* Many of Rich's most powerful poems—including those discussed in the remainder of this chapter—respond directly to this question, in a constantly changing, re-visionary process.

"Leaflets"

The title of "Leaflets" (Winter/Spring 1968) recalls Whitman, revising *Leaves of Grass* in an America diminished, radicalized. Anticipated by "Snapshots of a Daughter-in-Law," "Leaflets" demands pluralistic reading. Its multiple ways of knowing the world resist reduction to a unified "reading." Among Rich's central themes are her attempt "to drive a tradition up against the wall"; her determination to assume a power still conceived as masculine; her meditation on rebellion against rulers who based their authority on a tradition of rebellion; and her insistence on the "Now" which, like Whitman, she knew would have become a part of history for her readers.

"Leaflets" opens as an insomniac persona gazes out at "The big star, and that other/ lonely on black glass/ overgrown with frozen lesions." In a culture obsessed with stardom, the star suggests the greats of the tradition; the title specifies Whitman. The first section closes with a meditation on the history of the democratic vision:

> the steamer edging in toward the penal colony
> chained men dozing on deck
> five forest fires lighting the island
>
> lifelong that glare, waiting.

Founded by convicts, shaped by the labor of slaves, America transforms itself more frequently through wanton destruction than through prophetic vision. Over the burning fields described in "The Burning of Paper Instead of Children," Rich recalls the visionary Whitman, not yet the "big star" ensnared by his own myth:

> I want this to reach you
> who told me once that poetry is nothing sacred
> —no more sacred that is
> than other things in your life—
> to answer yes, if life is uncorrupted
> no better poetry is wanted.

The subjunctive—*if* life is uncorrupted—reiterates Rich's belief in the connection between poetry and life, a belief shared in radically different form by T. S. Eliot, the second "big star" (or perhaps the "other lonely" star subjected to "frozen/ lesions, endless night"). Like Eliot, Rich guides us through a blasted landscape in a poem of five parts incorporating multiple voicings. More specifically, the imagery of "The

Waste Land" recurs remotely, but repeatedly, in parallel sections of
"Leaflets."

I. *The Burial of the Dead*—Voices, fading in midsentence, testify to a
pervasive human misery, to frustrated desires juxtaposed with the
hope of resurrection:

> *that I can live half a year*
> *as I have never lived up to this time—*
> Chekhov coughing up blood almost daily
> the steamer edging in toward the penal colony.

Chekhov and Kafka (who wrote of the metaphysical/political penal
colony) assume the role of ritual gods. Fragmented into the dual per-
sonae of suffering romantic and pedantic academic, the Eliot who
identified the "dissociation of sensibility" (which has developed into a
definitionless image of alienation) would certainly have recognized
Rich's "seasick neon/ vision, this/ division." Transfixed by his own
vision of death ("I had not thought death had undone so many"), Eliot
wanders "unreal cities" in the aftermath of the Great War while Rich
attempts to break away from its paralyzing effects:

> the head clears of sweet smoke
> and poison gas
>
> life without caution
> the only worth living

II. *A Game of Chess*—"*Who'd choose this life?*" "*Tell me what you are
going through—*" The second section of each poem describes the characteristic agonies of contemporary life. Eliot envisions Cleopatra, transcribes his wife's complaints, confronts the apocalypse in the closing of
a bar ("It's time, It's time, It's time"); Rich writes of Telemachus while

> the bodies come whirling
> coal-black, ash-white
> out of torn windows
> and the death columns blacken

Again, Rich attempts to transform the waste land through an act of
will. Where Eliot's figures—unaware even that they have been
sacrificed—merge with the blasted ground, Rich sounds a rallying cry

in oddly Catholic tones: "We're fighting for a slash of recognition,/ a piercing to the pierced heart."

III. *The Fire Sermon*—Like the Eliot who assumed the androgynous form of Tiresias at the exact center of "The Waste Land," Rich focuses her third section on the ambiguous fire which compresses oppositions: purification and punishment, passion and denial, Christianity and Buddhism. Called by the "Dahomeyan devil" to "enter the fire" in order to effect the resurrection of "the young man," the "girl" in section III of "Leaflets" accepts the sacrificial role: "If, the girl whispers,/ I do not go into the fire/ I will not be able to live with my soul." By entering the fire, claiming her identity as "someone," the girl becomes an androgynous quester, assuming her identity with the young man of part II, whose tears are "burning/ as the tears of Telemachus/ burned."

IV. *Death by Water*—Rich opens the section with the image of "Crusaders' wind glinting/ off linked scales of sea." Unresurrected, like Eliot's Phlebas the Phoenician, she drains even the killing ocean, anticipating the images of the final section in her vision of dessication:

gray strangers still straying
dusty paths
the mad who live in the dried-up moat
of the War Museum.

Just as Eliot insists that his readers acknowledge their identity with the aimless dead, Rich concludes: "what are we coming to/ what wants these things of us/ who wants them."

V. *What the Thunder Said*—Meditating in the subjunctive ("If there were water, If there were water"), Eliot returns to the "unreal cities." Acknowledging the fragmentation, Rich opens the final section: "The strain of being born/ over and over has torn your smile into pieces." She shares Eliot's desire for a regenerative rain: "I want to hand you this/ leaflet streaming with rain or tears." Like the girl of section III, like Eliot, Rich feels the limitations of her own power even as she asserts its reality:

What else does it come down to
but handing on scraps of paper
little figurines or phials
no stronger than the dry clay they are baked in
yet more than dry clay or paper
because the imagination crouches in them.

The subjunctives remain crucial as both poets prepare fragments to shore up against the ruins. Where Eliot recapitulates the images of his poem and invokes the archetypal timeless past, Rich meditates on the destructive impact of the Eliotic consciousness on the present:

> If we needed fire to remind us
> that all true images
>   were scooped out of the mud
> where our bodies curse and flounder
>   then perhaps that fire is coming
> to sponge away the scribes and time-servers
>   and much that you would have loved will be lost as well
> before you could handle it and know it
>   just as we almost miss each other
> in the ill cloud of mistrust, who might have touched
>   hands quickly, shared food or given blood
> for each other

Alluding briefly to Yeats, Rich repudiates the abstraction which alienates us from the source of truth in the "foul rag-and-bone shop of the heart." She warns that the abstraction breeds the reality ("then perhaps the fire is coming"). Addressing Yeats and Eliot, Whitman and her readers, she observes the "cloud of mistrust" which obscures the value of the tradition bearers, against whom—rather than for whom—she asserts her individual talent. It hardly seems paradoxical that she images the loss by translating the first two virtues articulated by Eliot's thunder ("Datta." Give. "Dayadhvam." Sympathize.) into a common language: "who might have touched/ hands quickly, shared food or given blood/ for each other." As its victim, she does not endorse control. Extending the resolve of Eliot's questing hero/poet, she concludes her quest with a determination to use the fragments not for defense but for engagement: "I am thinking how we can use what we have/ to invent what we need."

For Rich, much of what she needed was to be found in the work of her poetic, political, and personal mothers. Although her (re)engagement with H.D. was still several years away, the sensibility, though not the specific imagery, of "Leaflets" resembles that of *Trilogy* as much as that of "The Waste Land." Perhaps "that other/ lonely" star is H.D.'s Osiris (or H.D. herself). Perhaps the resurrection of section V anticipates a maternal force, a vision capable of seeing Dickinson as clearly as Whitman. Apparently directed to the young man introduced in section II—though the imagery of birth and the Osirian re-membering assert a powerful female presence—section V resonates with Rich's growing awareness of patriarchy:

The strain of being born
 over and over has torn your smile into pieces
Often I have seen it broken
 and then re-membered
 and wondered how a beauty
 so anarch, so ungelded
 will be cared for in this world.

Although she perceives their inadequacy, the old definitions still command her attention: "I'm too young to be your mother/ you're too young to be my brother." Unable to conceive of alternative relationships possible in the reality she perceives, Rich knows that her perceptions remain fragmentary. Recalling the malaise of "The Demon Lover"—"Seasick, I drop into the sea"—she acknowledges her "seasick neon/ vision, this/ division."

Rich's rebellion in "Leaflets" seems suspended by its own contradictions, the tension between her desire to repudiate patriarchy and her desire to assume "masculine" powers. The resolve of section I restates an American patriarchal archetype:

life without caution
the only worth living
love for a man
love for a woman
love for the facts
protectless

The undertones are aggressive: "that self-defense be not/ the arm's first motion." But Rich realizes that the striking out of women is not the striking out of men, that, most certainly, given the divided vision endemic to patriarchal culture, the "love for a woman" cannot be confused with "love for a man."

"Leaflets" marks Rich's recognition that rebellion in America requires that the rebel repudiate abstract rebellion. Winthrop was a rebel, as were Washington, Emerson, Whitman, Melville, Faulkner, Malcolm, Hemingway, Mailer: her list is endless. The gallery engenders seasickness. In "Leaflets," a rebel speaks of a rebel as Rich bears witness to the spreading disease:

Your face
 stretched like a mask
 begins to tear
as you speak of Che Guevara

One of the most striking aspects of Rich's meditation on rebellion is the complex beauty of the music emerging from the noise. The following lines exemplify the intricate prosody of even Rich's most rebellious voice: "(Her face calm and dark as amber/ under the dyed butterfly turban/ her back scarified in ostrich-skin patterns)." Rich's description of the young woman entering the fire is patterned as densely and as appropriately as her simultaneous experience of victimization and transcendence. The poetic signatures of "Aunt Jennifer's Tigers" or "Necessities of Life" remain. The *er* sounds (introduced by the reiterated and specifically feminine "her") build to the final recognition of "pattern." Even as she assumes her hierarchical position under the *tur*ban, she is an amber butterfly. Further, the sounds of "butterfly" ground her beauty in her social context. The *u* echoes "under"; the long *i* rhymes with the multifaceted "dyed" and "scarified," both of which reflect her ornamentation and her reduction to ritual object. Examples of thematically resonant sound texturing could be multiplied indefinitely ("The crusader's wind glinting/ off linked scales of sea"). But, as Rich had come to know clearly by 1968, aesthetic beauty could provide only a momentary, and ultimately illusory, relief from the present dangers.

Asserting Rich's commitment to actual engagement with the world, the crucial word in "Leaflets" is the "now," set off to the right at the midpoint of the second section. Rich insists that the meaning of the leaflet derives intimately from the moment of its reading. In 1968, the poem drew energy from and gave energy to Vietnam protests, racial rebellion. In 1986, its potential energy challenges the patriarchal premises of those protests and that rebellion, as well as American policy in Central America or renewed (and not always more subtle) forms of racism. Its conclusion remains valid in its present tension: "I am thinking how we can use what we have/ to invent what we need."

"Diving Into the Wreck"

Rich's repudiation of "Diving Into the Wreck"—"There are words I cannot choose again:/ *humanism   androgyny*"—obscures the poem's uses, the role it played in the development of Rich's vision of "what we need." Like "Natural Resources," the poem in which the repudiation occurs, it reflects a moment of process, essential and, like all other moments, incomplete. The humanistic androgyny of its resolution—"I am she: I am he" (and it is important to observe that this is only the start of a sentence which extends through the last two stanzas)

—assumes its meaning as much from the disorienting "masculine" assertions of "Leaflets" and "Orion" as from the lesbian clarity of her later work.

"Diving Into the Wreck" clarifies Rich's past, anticipates her future. The poem's syntax, which alternates between didactic directness and suggestive elusiveness, subjects every perception, every impression to immediate and continuing revision. The poem opens with a simple catalog of preparations, implying a degree of self-knowledge which will be challenged repeatedly as the immersion progresses: "First having read the book of myths,/ and loaded the camera/ and checked the edge of the knife-blade," the persona arms her(?)self with her knowledge of tradition (she has certainly read "The Waste Land"), instruments to record her perceptions (recalling the cinematic obsessions of her previous volumes), and a tool, or weapon (recalling the phallic sword of "Orion" and the midwife's instrument of "The Mirror in Which Two Are Seen as One"). She seems sure of what she has done. But as soon as the poem shifts to the present, uncertainty infects the syntax. The comma after "knife-blade" is followed by the seeming simplicity of a main clause: "I put on/ the body-armor of black rubber" (no period). However gently, the absence of punctuation in the remainder of the first sentence introduces uncertainty, the breakdown of the familiar sense-making process:

> I put on
> the body-armor of black rubber
> the absurd flippers
> the grave and awkward mask.

Her confidence dissolves into a slightly strained list of present-tense actions which contrasts with the ordered, punctuated list of past preparations. She puts on (assumes) not only a diving suit but also a complex rhetorical mask, a persona incorporating both the certainty and the confusion of the moment. To forget this tension, implicit in the style of the first sentence, is to render "Diving Into the Wreck" nearly incomprehensible.

Recognizing Rich's rhetorical approach highlights the moments of certainty which occur periodically in the poem. Essentially anti-ideological, many of these moments involve minimally glossed observations of the world: "There is a ladder." "This is the place." Others center on her knowledge that she is engaged in a process: "I go down." "I go down." "I came to explore the wreck." One is a brief, surprisingly clear judgment: "The words are purposes./ The words are maps." Embracing the clarity of limitation, Rich leaves all else subject to revision, focusing on moments of testing, of process:

I am she: I am he

whose drowned face sleeps with open eyes
whose breasts still bear the stress
whose silver, copper, vermeil cargo lies
obscurely inside barrels
half-wedged and left to rot
we are the half-destroyed instruments
that once held to a course
the water-eaten log
the fouled compass

We are, I am, you are
by cowardice or courage
the one who find our way
back to this scene
carrying a knife, a camera
a book of myths
in which
our names do not appear.

The line "I am she: I am he" is too frequently, and often without qualification, presented as the "message" of "Diving Into the Wreck." Read as simple endorsement of androgyny (and to a degree Rich's repudiation encourages the reading), it implies an identity between "he" and "she" which the syntax resists. "I am she:" the colon introduces a gloss on the preceding words, not the second term of a parallel series. Far from repudiating her feminine identity, Rich revises her understanding of that identity to incorporate the masculine qualities claimed in "Leaflets." The next three lines qualify her understanding of the masculine attributes. Not a stereotypical "pseudo-male," she recognizes in herself the questing hero, the drowned, but still perceptive (note the line break on "eyes") fisher king from part IV of "The Waste Land." Immediately, she qualifies this traditionally masculine figure by describing his eyes as breasts. Employing her line break to emphasize that these feminine qualities exist under stress, she immediately interprets the stress as a source of value, as a "cargo." The line break on "lies," in turn, intimates the deceptive sense of value derived from the standard myths; the subsequent adverb "obscurely" resists an easy understanding of the lie. The introduction of "we," without a comma

or period, claims the experience of the isolated quester for the larger
community. She seeks not to obliterate distinctions (the punctuation of
the introductory line remains vital), but to invite her readers, male and
female, to test their certainties. The instruments she perceived in the
first lines of the poem as external aids, she now identifies with the self
in progress. Aware that we have been damaged by our experiences (of
patriarchy, the waste land, Vietnam, solipsism), she asserts our potential: we once were capable of holding a course. Our sense of direction
"fouled," but not destroyed, we are suspended between stanzas; Rich
does not assert the closure of the period. So that "We are, I am, you
are" the compass, capable of finding "our way back to the scene." Both
in syntax and in statement, Rich acknowledges the multiplicity of process. We are what we are "by cowardice or courage," but we are not
ourself, at any moment, multiple: we are "the one." But the verb is
plural, acknowledging our internal plurality, the plurality of a self
changing through process. We/I arrive. And we arrive, like Eliot in
the "Four Quartets," precisely where we began: with the preparation
for the descent which we are, then and now and perpetually, just
beginning. Reversing the initial order, we are "carrying a knife, a
camera/ a book of myths." Only now, knowing the place for the first
time, we know that it is a book "in which/ our names do not appear."
Now, with Rich, we can begin.

Rich's repudiation was directed at the word "androgyny": a slogan, a
fixation. The recovery of the feminine, the recovery of the masculine,
remain necessary if we are to tap our potential energies. Rich knows
that the real wreck is our own; she describes "the wreck and not the
story of the wreck/ the thing itself and not the myth/ . . . this threadbare beauty/ the ribs of disaster." The ribs which, in the patriarchal
myth without our names, separated male from female, Adam from
Eve.

The most thickly woven beauty in "Diving Into the Wreck"—not
threadbare but quilted richly as "Aunt Jennifer's Tigers" or "Transcendental Etude"—occurs at precisely the moment when the diver dis-
covers her androgynous complexity:

This is the place.
And I am here, the mermaid whose dark hair
streams black, the merman in his armored body
We circle silently
about the wreck
we dive into the hold.
I am she: I am he

patterns of structure

The *s* sounds characterize the diver's arrival at and contemplation of the central image: "This," "is," "place," "streams," "circle," "silently." *M* sounds underscore the claim to a fluid, androgynous identity: "am," "mermaid," "streams," "merman," "armored," "am," "am." Hard *ck*'s reassert the danger even as they discover a submerged beauty in darkness: "dark hair streams black," "circle," "wreck." *R* sounds, mostly internal, link the darkness with both the setting and the diver's androgynous identity: "her," "mermaid," "dark," "hair," "streams," "merman," "armored," "circle," "wreck." The long, open vowel sounds—"place," "mermaid," "streams," "silently," "dive," "hold" —complement the beauty of the consonants, culminating in the luminous rhyme of "he" and "she."

relation

But, as in "Leaflets," Rich explicitly presents her process as partial: "The words are purposes./ The words are maps." As always, for Rich, "Diving Into the Wreck" marks the beginning of a process, not an end.

"Cartographies of Silence"

"Cartographies of Silence," which treats the same set of issues as Rich's essay "Women and Honor: Some Notes on Lying," provides a gloss on the complex sequence of Rich's maps. The poem begins with a doubt:

A conversation begins
with a lie. And each

speaker of the so-called common language feels
the ice-floe split

The map is subjunctive, an estimation of what the world might look like if it could be perceived without mediation. Drifting apart, the speakers of the common language, the members of the lesbian *civitas* Rich was just beginning to envision, feel "as if powerless, as if up against/ a force of nature." Later, the subjunctives return, transformed into images of possibility as the victim regains her equilibrium and recognizes the artificiality of her victimization. In section five (recalling a crucial image from "The Burning of Paper Instead of Children"), Rich contemplates the "mutely surveyed" image of Falconetti's face in Dreyer's *Passion of Joan*:

If there were a poetry where this could happen
not as blank spaces or as words

stretched like a skin over meanings
but as silence falls at the end

of a night through which two people
have talked till dawn

The "then" clause, as yet, remains unthinkable. The common language
remains, potentially and actually, linked to the contradictory, partial
world: "A poem can begin/ with a lie." But Rich recognizes the crucial
difference between the common language of poetry and the common
language of human speech. At least in the early stages, the poet retains
control, can revise and reconsider the impact of her words.
Understood and used, the distance between poet and audience can
become a source of power:

A poem can begin
with a lie. And be torn up.

A conversation has other laws . . .

. . . Cannot be torn
up. Infiltrates our blood. Repeats itself.

Inscribes with its unreturning stylus
the isolation it denies.

Paradoxically, isolation lurks in contact, and isolation (that of the poet)
possesses a unique power for establishing contact. But the power rests
on the unfulfilled subjunctive, on the struggle for a poetry, common
but perpetually revised, capable of articulating the experience rendered
silent.
    Repeatedly, Rich insists that silence, which has nothing to do with
sound, does not signify absence. Experience retains its reality even in
the unmapped wild zone:

the blurring of terms
silence not absence

of words or music or even
raw sounds

The silence filling most speech creates a sense of vertigo. Rich perceives words losing their ground in experience: "How calm, how
inoffensive these words/ begin to seem to me/ though begun in grief

and anger." The abstraction of words torments her: "Can I break
through this film of the abstract/ without wounding myself or you."
Music, "the classical or the jazz music station," seems momentarily "to
give a ground of meaning to our pain." But the section ends with a
question mark. The next section shifts from music to film—the image
of Joan embodying a "silence that strips bare"—but the phrase "film of
the abstract" filters the perception. The issue, for the poet, remains the
subjunctive.

Rich maps "Cartographies of Silence" by using a form similar to the
ghazal. Although not self-enclosed, most of the lines occur as couplets
which take their meaning from juxtaposition with those around them.
As in "Shooting Script," each section assumes meaning from similar
juxtaposition. Two lines, however, are typographically isolated. In
section three, after considering the possibility that "silence can be a
plan," Rich writes: "the blueprint to a life." In section six, contemplating the horror of "an illegitimate voice" which "has ceased to hear
itself," she emphasizes the question by placing it in a stanza by itself:
"How do I exist?" The following line—"This was the silence I wanted
to break in you"—again grounds experience in the world. Consistently, Rich pressures us to fulfill the subjunctive. Having asked the
question, articulated the silence of the sufferer who experiences her
voice as illegitimate (the absence of the mother as serious as the
absence of the father), Rich reiterates the limitations of the common
language, conceived in purely aesthetic terms: "I had questions but
you would not answer/ I had answers but you could not use them/
This is useless to you and perhaps to others."

Using the ghazal-based form to open the poem to new energies, Rich
attempts to clarify potential uses, reentering old territory: "It was an
old theme even for me:/ Language cannot do everything—." As she
begins to fold the map in upon itself, in the final two sections, Rich
reiterates the subjunctives: "If at the will of the poet the poem/ could
turn into a thing." She envisions the silence, embedded in the common
language, the shared experience, of which she dreams:

> If it could simply look you in the face
> with naked eyeballs, not letting you turn
>
> till you, and I who long to make this thing,
> were finally clarified together in its stare

The section ends, the subjunctive again suspended and suspending.

The final section opens with a denial of the previous formulation, a
repudiation of abstract salvation, an acceptance of the waste land

without rain: "No. Let me have this dust, these pale clouds dourly lingering." Rich, of course, does not abandon her quest. Rather, she accepts her words for what they are: instruments of ambiguous change, capable of discovery despite their limitations: "these words/ moving with ferocious accuracy/ like the blind child's fingers." Accepting the actuality of her life, her choices, she renews her integrity, accepts her responsibility: "No one can give me, I have long ago/ taken this method." When she returns to the subjunctive in the final five stanzas (the final ghazal?) of "Cartographies of Silence," it has been transformed into commentary upon itself, its own implicit evasion of the actual:

> If from time to time I envy
> the pure annunciations to the eye
>
> the *visio beatifica*
> if from time to time I long to turn
>
> like the Eleusinian hierophant
> holding up a simple ear of grain
>
> for return to the concrete and everlasting world

Both abstract and concrete simplify. Rich fulfills the syntactical promise of the subjunctive by embracing her process, as embodied in her present act: "what in fact I keep choosing/ are these words, these whispers, conversations/ from which time after time the truth breaks moist and green."

"Sources"

The most recent work of a living poet, particularly one committed to process, can only be partially read. To approach "Sources" as a rewriting of "Abnegation" (1968), "The Knot," "At the Jewish New Year" (written 1955, published 1984), or "Jerusalem" (1966) would provide shadows of its depths. Rich returns to the "Shape of the queen anne's lace, with the drop of blood," emblem of the hidden violence at the heart of patriarchy, as prelude to her atonement with father and husband; hearing new reverberations, she reexamines her repudiation of the "chosen people," identified with New England Puritans rather than Jews; the "blasted walls" of "Jerusalem" give way to "YERU-SHALAYIM: a vault of golden heat." Rich reconsiders her past as the source of her strength: "Everything that has ever/ helped me has come through what already/ lay stored in me.   Old things, diffuse, unnamed, lie strong across my heart."

By Jewish law, Rich, daughter of a Jewish father, is not a Jew. By law of "that dangerous place/ the family home," she was heir to her father's "rootless ideology," encouraged "to become/ a citizen of the world/ bound by no tribe or clan." *"Split at the root,"* Rich claimed an unlikely kinship with the New Englanders

> . . . who hung on
> here in this stringent space
>
> believing their Biblical language
> their harping on righteousness

Realizing that the New Englanders "are not my people by any definition," Rich locates the point of connection between her two half-imagined heritages in their fierce belief in Zion, *"a city on a hill."* Refusing to simplify her past, Rich recognizes that this city, too often, has been founded on silence and dedicated to solipsism. Rich identifies the silence of the Southern Jews:

> If they played the flute, or chess
> I was told   I was not told what they told
> their children when the Klan rode
> how they might have seen themselves . . .
>
> . . . clinging by strategy to a way of life
> that had its own uses for them

This is the silence of women, unwilling (unable?) to name over the necessities of life, to know themselves as source.   Rich remembers the Southern Jews, "proud of their length of sojourn in America/ deploring the late-comers   the peasants from Russia." How, she asks, did they differ from the New Englanders who

> . . . persecuted, pale with anger
> know how to persecute
>
> those who feel destined, under god's eye
> need never ponder difference?

If Jew and Puritan play out similar scenarios as they seek the city on the hill, what of the lesbian *civitas*? Is the pattern inexorable? As Rich phrases the question, "is this a law of history/ or simply, *what must change?*"   .

Rich's response, "Sources" is a poem of destiny and atonement. Rich acknowledges destiny as "a thought often peculiar to those/ who possess privilege."   She has deconstructed the concept often, and well. Out of the recognition, she reconstructs of destiny a source: "the faith/ of those despised and endangered/ that they are not merely the sum of damages done to them."   Using silence—a given in their world—as resource, the chosen people, the common women, are artists like Aunt Jennifer, having "kept beyond violence the knowledge/ arranged in patterns like kente-cloth/ unexpected as in batik." The knowledge is common; knowledge

> of being a connective link
> in a long, continuous way
>
> of ordering hunger, weather, death, desire
> and the nearness of chaos.

Accessible to all, the destiny Rich describes recapitulates the process she has discovered arduously throughout her life. Its stages include (1) surviving within a hostile order;   (2) repudiating that order;   (3) imagining a new order; (4) testing the new order against the world; (5) beginning again with the knowledge gained.   At times, she believes, the common people can, if they will, glimpse the city on the hill.

Seeking to cleanse her vision of destiny, Rich seeks a complex atonement. Rich returns to her father, her husband. She becomes Jewish as she has previously become much else, embracing the most adequate becoming she can now conceive, surrendering none of the old becomings. To reach the patriarch, she must discover a way "of being a connective link/ in a long, continuous way." Denied knowledge of his alienation, his suffering, without the concrete clues needed to forge the chain, Rich accepted her role as "she who must overthrow the father, take what he taught her and use it against him."   Ironically and appropriately, Rich used her knowledge of patriarchal abstraction to abstract her father: "After your death I met you again as the face of patriarchy, could name at last precisely the principle you embodied, there was an ideology at last which let me dispose of you." True to her father's patriarchal order, Rich confused the map with the ground: "I saw the power and arrogance of the male as your true watermark; I did not see beneath it the suffering of the Jew, the alien stamp you bore, because you had deliberately arranged that it should be invisible to me." Addressing her father, thinking of her husband who "ended isolate," Rich sees the connection where before she had seen distance: "For so many years I had thought you and he were in opposition. I needed your unlikeness then; now, it's your likeness that stares me in the face." Their likeness, after years of necessary avoidance, blends with her own.

Zion, the city on the hill, the lesbian *civitas*—after all that has led to "Sources" and as prelude to what will follow—stands revealed as the place Rich's husband never found, the place she envisions when she addresses him directly in section 22:

> That's why I want to speak to you now. To say: no person, trying to take responsibility for her or his identity, should have to be so alone. There must be those among whom we can sit down and weep, and still be counted as warriors. (I make up this strange angry packet for you, threaded with love.) I think you thought there was no such place for you, and perhaps there was none then, and perhaps there is none now; but we will have to make it, we who want an end to suffering, who want to change the laws of history, if we are not to *give ourselves away*.

Whitman could not have imagined a more democratic vista.

The price of the vision, for Rich, was her process and her pain. She now knows that extension—whether directed toward the sufferings of her father and husband or those of the Nicaraguans or Eritreans—requires integrity. Seeing her father for the first time, she writes: "It is only now, under a powerful womanly lens, that I can decipher your suffering and deny no part of my own." She knows the price must still and always be paid. The city on the hill is no abstraction, the common language no anodyne: "I have wished I could rest among the beautiful and common weeds I can name, both here and in other tracts of the globe. But there is no finite knowing, no such rest." The process continues, in every detail: "Innocent birds, deserts, morning-glories, point to choices, leading away from the familiar." Rededicating herself, she speaks, as her process begins again, of "an end to suffering." Zion, the city on the hill, like the lesbian *civitas* or YERUSHALAYIM, must be realized, must be real:

> When I speak of an end to suffering I don't mean anesthesia. I mean knowing the world, and my place in it, not in order to stare with bitterness or detachment, but as a powerful and womanly series of choices: and here I write the words, in their fullness: powerful: womanly.

Bibliography

Works by Adrienne Rich

POETRY *(in order of publication)*

A Change of World. New Haven: Yale Univ. Pr., 1951
The Diamond Cutters and Other Poems. New York: Harper, 1955.
Snapshots of a Daughter-in-Law. New York: Harper, 1963. Revised edition, New York: Norton, 1967.
Necessities of Life. New York: Norton, 1966.
Leaflets. New York: Norton, 1969.
The Will to Change. New York: Norton, 1971.
Diving into the Wreck. New York: Norton, 1973.
Poems: Selected and New, 1950-1974. New York: Norton, 1975.
The Dream of a Common Language. New York: Norton, 1978.
A Wild Patience Has Taken Me This Far. New York: Norton, 1981.
The Fact of a Doorframe: Poems Selected and New, 1950-1984. New York: Norton, 1984.
Your Native Land, Your Life. New York: Norton, 1986.

PROSE BOOKS *(in order of publication)*

Of Woman Born. New York: Norton, 1976. Tenth Anniversary Edition, New York: Norton, 1986.
On Lies, Secrets, and Silence. New York: Norton, 1979.
Blood, Bread, and Poetry. New York: Norton, 1986.

UNCOLLECTED PROSE

"Living with Henry: Review of *His Toy, His Dream, His Rest* by John Berryman," *Harvard Advocate* 103 (Spring 1969), 10-11.
"'Wholeness Is No Trifling Matter': Some Fiction by Black Women," *New Women's Times Feminist Review* (Dec. 1980/ Jan. 1981), 10-13; (Feb.-Mar. 1981), 12.
"An Interview with Audre Lorde," *Signs* (Summer 1981), 713-36.
"Comment on Friedman's 'I Go Where I Love': An Intertextual Study of H.D. and Adrienne Rich," *Signs* (Summer 1984), 733-38.
"Across the Great Divide," *The Village Voice* (May 28, 1985), 57, 60.

Additional Selected Materials

Addelson, Kathryn Pyne.   "Words and Lives: On 'Compulsory Heterosexuality and Lesbian Existence," *Signs* (Autumn 1981), 197-99.
Ahmad, Aijaz, ed. *Ghazals of Ghalib*. New York: Columbia Univ. Pr., 1971.
Allen, Donald, ed. *The New American Poetry 1945-1960*. New York: Grove, 1960.
Altieri, Charles. *Self and Sensibility in Contemporary American Poetry*. New York: Cambridge Univ. Pr., 1984.
Ardener, Shirley, ed. *Perceiving Women*. London: J. M. Dent and Sons, 1975.
Ashbery, John. "Tradition and Talent," *New York Herald Tribune Book Week* (Sept. 4, 1966), 2.
Atlas, James. "New Voices in American Poetry," *New York Times Magazine* (Feb. 3, 1980), 6, 9-11, 17.
√ Atwood, Margaret. "Review of *Diving into the Wreck*," *New York Times Book Review* (Dec. 30, 1973), 1-2.
Auden, W. H.   "Foreword" in *A Change of World* by Adrienne Rich. New Haven: Yale Univ. Pr., 1951.
Baldwin, James. *No Name in the Street*. New York: Dial, 1972.
Bennett, Paula. *My Life a Loaded Gun: Female Creativity and Feminist Poetics*. Boston: Beacon, 1986.
Benstock, Shari. *Women of the Left Bank: Paris, 1900-1940*. Austin: Univ. of Texas Pr., 1986.
Berg, Stephen and Robert Mezey, eds. *The New Naked Poetry*. Indianapolis: Bobbs-Merrill, 1976.
Booth, Philip. "Rethinking the World," *Christian Science Monitor* (Jan. 3, 1963), 15.

Boyers, Robert. "On Adrienne Rich: Intelligence and Will," *Salmagundi* (Spring-Summer 1973), 132-48.

Breslin, James. *From Modern to Contemporary: American Poetry 1945-1965.* Chicago: Univ. of Chicago Pr., 1984.

Brownmiller, Susan. *Against Our Will: Men, Women, and Rape.* New York: Simon and Schuster, 1975.

Bulkin, Elly. "An Interview with Adrienne Rich," *Conditions One* (April 1977), 58-60.

Capra, Fritzjof. *The Turning Point.* New York: Simon and Schuster, 1982.

Carruthers, Mary. "The Re-Vision of the Muse: Adrienne Rich, Audre Lorde, Judy Grahn, Olga Broumas," *Hudson Review* (Summer 1983), 293-322.

/ Christ, Carol. *Diving Deep and Surfacing: Women Writers on Spiritual Quest.* Boston: Beacon, 1980.

/ Cooper, Jane Roberta, ed. *Reading Adrienne Rich.* Ann Arbor: Univ. of Michigan Pr., 1984.

Culler, Jonathan. *On Deconstruction: Theory and Criticism after Structuralism.* Ithaca, N.Y.: Cornell Univ. Pr., 1982.

Daly, Mary. *Beyond God the Father: Toward a Philosophy of Women's Liberation.* Boston: Beacon, 1973.

Daly, Mary. *Pure Lust: Elemental Feminist Philosophy.* Boston: Beacon, 1984.

de Beauvoir, Simone. *The Second Sex*, translated by H. M. Parshley. New York: Knopf, 1952.

Diehl, Joanne Feit. "'Cartographies of Silence'; Rich's Common Language and the Woman Poet," *Feminist Studies* (Fall 1980), 530-46.

Donoghue, Denis. "Oasis Poetry," *New York Review of Books* (May 7, 1970), 35-38.

Donovan, Josephine. *Feminist Theory: The Intellectual Traditions of American Feminism.* New York: Ungar, 1985.

DuBois, W. E. B. *The Souls of Black Folk*, 1903.

DuPlessis, Rachel Blau. *Writing Beyond the Ending: Narrative Strategies of Twentieth-Century Women Writers.* Bloomington: Indiana Univ. Pr., 1985.

Eagleton, Terry. *Literary Theory: An Introduction.* Minneapolis: Univ. of Minnesota Pr., 1983.

Eisenstein, Hester. *Contemporary Feminist Thought.* Boston: G. K. Hall, 1983.

Ferguson, Ann. "Patriarchy, Sexual Identity, and the Sexual Revolution: On 'Compulsory Heterosexuality and Lesbian Existence' —Defining the Issues," *Signs* (Autumn 1981), 158-72.

Fiedler, Leslie. *Love and Death in the American Novel.* New York: Stein & Day, 1966.

Foucault, Michel. *Power/Knowledge: Selected Interviews and Other Writings, 1972-1977,* edited and translated by Colin Gordon. New York: Pantheon, 1980.

Friedman, Susan Stanford. "'I Go Where I Love': An Intertextual Study of H.D. and Adrienne Rich," *Signs* (Winter 1983), 228-45.

Gelpi, Albert. "Adrienne Rich: The Poetics of Change" in *American Poetry Since 1960,* edited by Robert Shaw, pp. 123-43. Cheadle, Cheshire: Carcanet Pr., 1973.

Gelpi, Barbara Charlesworth and Albert Gelpi, eds. *Adrienne Rich's Poetry: A Norton Critical Edition.* New York: Norton, 1975.

Gilbert, Sandra M. and Susan Gubar. *The Madwoman in the Attic: The Woman Writer and the Nineteenth-Century Literary Imagination.* New Haven: Yale Univ. Pr., 1979.

Grahn, Judy. *The Highest Apple: Sappho and The Lesbian Poetic Tradition.* San Francisco: Spinsters Ink, 1985.

Griffin, Susan. *Woman and Nature: The Roaring Inside Her.* New York: Harper & Row, 1978.

Hall, Donald. "A Diet of Dissatisfaction," *Poetry* (Feb. 1956), 299-302.

Hall, Donald, Robert Pack and Lewis Simpson, eds. *New Poets of England and America.* New York: Meridian, 1957.

Homans, Margaret. "'Oh, Vision of Language!' Dickinson's Poems of Love and Death" in *Feminist Critics Read Emily Dickinson,* edited by Suzanne Juhasz. Bloomington: Indiana Univ. Pr., 1983.

Homans, Margaret. *Women Writers and Poetic Identity.* Princeton: Princeton Univ. Pr., 1980.

Howard, Richard. *Alone with America: Essays on the Art of Poetry in the United States Since 1950.* New York: Atheneum, 1980.

Iraguray, Lucie. *Speculum of the Other Woman,* translated by Gillian C. Gill. Ithaca, N.Y.: Cornell Univ. Pr., 1985.

Jameson, Fredric. *The Political Unconscious.* Ithaca, N.Y.: Cornell Univ. Pr., 1981.

Jarrell, Randall. "New Books in Review," *Yale Review* (Sept. 1956), 100-03.

Jong, Erica. "Visionary Anger," *Ms.* (July 1973), 31-33.

Juhasz, Suzanne, ed. *Feminist Critics Read Emily Dickinson.* Bloomington: Indiana Univ. Pr., 1983.

Juhasz, Suzanne. *Naked and Fiery Forms: Modern American Poetry by Women.* New York: Harper & Row, 1976.

Karl, Frederick. *Modern and Modernism: The Sovereignty of the Artist 1885-1925.* New York: Atheneum, 1985.

Keller, Karl. *The Only Kangaroo Among the Beauty: Emily Dickinson and America*. Baltimore: Johns Hopkins Univ. Pr., 1979.

Kenner, Hugh. *The Pound Era*. Berkeley and Los Angeles: Univ. of California Pr., 1971.

Keyes, Claire. *The Aesthetics of Power: The Poetry of Adrienne Rich*. Athens, Ga.: Univ. of Georgia Pr., 1986.

Kolodny, Annette. *The Lay of the Land: Metaphor and History in American Life and Letters*. Chapel Hill: Univ. of North Carolina Pr., 1975.

Lasch, Christopher. *The Culture of Narcissism*. New York: Norton, 1978.

Lawrence, D. H. *Studies in Classic American Literature*. New York: Viking, 1964.

Lerner, Gerda. *The Creation of Patriarchy*. New York: Oxford Univ. Pr., 1986.

Lieberman, Laurence. *Unassigned Frequencies*. Urbana: Univ. of Illinois Pr., 1977.

Lorde, Audre. *Sister Outsider*. Trumansburg, N.Y.: Crossing Pr., 1977.

Lowell, Robert. "Modesty Without Mumbling," *New York Times Book Review* (July 17, 1966), 5.

MacCabe, Colin. *Godard: Images, Sounds, Politics*. Bloomington: Indiana Univ. Pr., 1980.

Majors, Bruce Powell. "The Comparable Worth Muddle," *Journal of Contemporary Studies* (Summer 1984), 53.

Martin, Wendy. "Adrienne Rich" in *American Writers: A Collection of Literary Biographies*, supplement I, part 2, edited by Leonard Ungar, pp. 550-78. New York: Scribner's, 1979.

Martin, Wendy. *An American Triptych: Anne Bradstreet, Emily Dickinson, Adrienne Rich*. Chapel Hill: Univ. of North Carolina Pr., 1984.

Martin, Wendy. "From Patriarchy to the Female Principle: A Chronological Reading of Adrienne Rich's Poems" in *Adrienne Rich's Poetry: A Norton Critical Edition*, edited by Barbara Charlesworth Gelpi and Albert Gelpi, pp. 175-89. New York: Norton, 1975.

Milford, Nancy. "This Woman's Movement" in *Adrienne Rich's Poetry: A Norton Critical Edition*, edited by Barbara Charlesworth Gelpi and Albert Gelpi, pp. 189-202. New York: Norton, 1975.

Molesworth, Charles. *The Fierce Embrace: A Study of Contemporary American Poetry*. Columbia: Univ. of Missouri Pr., 1979.

Morgan, Robin. "Adrienne Rich and Robin Morgan Talk About Poetry and Women's Culture" in *New Women's Survival Sourcebook*, edited by Kirsten Grimstad and Susan Rennie, pp. 106-11. New York: Knopf, 1975.

Nelson, Cary. *Our Last First Poets: Vision and History in Contemporary American Poetry*. Urbana: Univ. of Illinois Pr., 1981.

Newman, Anne. "Adrienne Rich" in *Dictionary of Literary Biography:*

American Poets Since World War II, part 2, edited by Donald J. Greiner, pp. 184-96. Detroit: Bruccoli Clark, 1980.

Newman, Charles. *The Post-Modern Aura: The Act of Fiction in an Age of Inflation*. Evanston: Northwestern Univ. Pr., 1985.

Oberg, Arthur. *The Modern American Lyric*. New Brunswick, N.J.: Rutgers Univ. Pr., 1978.

Oktenberg, Adrian. "'Disloyal to Civlization: The *Twenty-One Love Poems* of Adrienne Rich" in *Reading Adrienne Rich*, edited by Jane Roberta Cooper, pp. 72-90. Ann Arbor: Univ. of Michigan Pr., 1984.

Ostriker, Alicia. *Stealing the Language: The Emergence of Women's Poetry in America*. Boston: Beacon, 1986.

Ostriker, Alicia. *Writing Like a Woman*. Ann Arbor: Univ. of Michigan Pr., 1983.

Perloff, Marjorie. "Private Lives/Public Images," *Michigan Quarterly Review* (Jan. 1983), 130-43.

Peters, Robert. *The Great American Poetry Bake-Off*, second series. Metuchen, N.J.: Scarecrow, 1982.

Piercy, Marge. *Parti-Colored Blocks for a Quilt*. Ann Arbor: Univ. of Michigan Pr., 1982.

Pope, Deborah. *A Separate Vision: Isolation in Contemporary Women's Poetry*. Baton Rouge: Louisiana State Univ. Pr., 1984.

Poulin, A., ed. *Contemporary American Poetry*, third edition. Boston: Houghton Mifflin, 1980.

Ratner, Rochelle. *Trying to Understand What It Means to Be a Feminist*. New York: Contact II Publications, 1984.

Reiss, Timothy J. *The Discourse of Modernism*. Ithaca, N.Y.: Cornell Univ. Pr., 1982.

Rigney, Barbara Hill. *Lilith's Daughters: Women and Religion in Contemporary Fiction*. Madison: Univ. of Wisconsin Pr., 1982.

Romanow, Peter. "Adrienne Rich" in *Critical Survey of Poetry: English Language Series*, edited by Frank Magill, pp. 2363-71. Englewood Cliffs, N.J.: Salem Press, 1982.

Rosenberg, Liz. "The Power of Victims," *New York Times Book Review* (July 20, 1986), 21-22.

Rosenthal, M. L. and Sally M. Gall. *The Modern Poetic Sequence: The Genius of Modern Poetry*. New York: Oxford Univ. Pr., 1983.

Rowbotham, Sheila. *Woman's Consciousness, Man's World*. New York: Penguin Books, 1973.

Showalter, Elaine. "Feminist Criticism in the Wilderness" in *The New Feminist Criticism*, edited by Elaine Showalter, pp. 243-70. New York: Pantheon, 1981.

Slowik, Mary. "The Friction of the Mind: The Early Poetry of Adrienne Rich," *The Massachusetts Review* (Spring 1984), 142-60.

Smith, Barbara. *Toward a Black Feminist Criticism*. Trumansburg, N.Y.: Crossing Pr., 1977.

Spender, Dale. *Women of Ideas and What Men Have Done to Them: From Aphra Behn to Adrienne Rich*. Boston: Ark, 1983.

Stepto, Robert. *From Behind the Veil: A Study of Afro-American Narrative*. Urbana: Univ. of Illinois Pr., 1979.

Stimpson, Catharine. "Adrienne Rich and Lesbian/Feminist Poetry," *Parnassus* (Spring/Summer/Fall/Winter 1985), 249-68.

Tonks, Rosemary. "Cutting the Marble," *New York Review of Books* (Oct. 4, 1973), 8-10.

Van Duyn, Mona. "Seven Women," *Poetry* (Mar. 1970), 430-39.

Vanderbosch, Jane. "Beginning Again" in *Reading Adrienne Rich*, edited by Jane Roberta Cooper, pp. 111-39. Ann Arbor: Univ. of Michigan Pr., 1984.

Vendler, Helen. *Part of Nature, Part of Us*. Cambridge: Harvard Univ. Pr., 1980.

Von Hallberg, Robert. *American Poetry and Culture, 1945-1980*. Cambridge: Harvard Univ. Pr., 1985.

Whelchel, Marianne. "Mining the 'Earth-Deposits': Women's History in Adrienne Rich's Poetry" in *Reading Adrienne Rich*, edited by Jane Roberta Cooper, pp. 51-71. Ann Arbor: Univ. of Michigan Pr., 1984.

Zita, Jacquelyn N. "Historical Amnesia and the Lesbian Continuum: On 'Compulsory Heterosexuality and Lesbian Existence'—Defining the Issues," *Signs* (Autumn 1981), 172-87.

Index

Prepared by Pamela Hori

Names, books, and essays listed only in the References at the conclusion of each chapter are not included in the Index.

Craig Werner is associate professor of Afro-American Studies at the University of Wisconsin at Madison and holds a doctorate in American literature from the University of Illinois. He is the author of numerous essays and critical reviews and the book *Paradoxical Resolutions: American Fiction since James Joyce* (University of Illinois Press, 1982).

Series designed by Vladimir Reichl

Composed by Stuart Whitwell from disk
    in Palatino, output to a PS Jet
    laser printer

Printed on 50-pound Glatfelter,
    a pH neutral stock, and bound
    in 12-point Kivar 314 Cambric
    stock by Malloy Lithographing, Inc.

∞